# Contents

# Acknowledgments

Chapter 8 contains a summary of the guidelines in the *Publication Manual of the American Psychological Association* (Sixth Edition). We gratefully acknowledge the *APA Publication Manual*'s contribution to this chapter.

# Preface

*The Psychologist's Companion* has been comprehensively updated, revised, and extended for this fifth edition. It is intended for students as well as young professionals and writers at all stages of their careers seeking inspiration and definitive guidelines for better scientific writing. The book is a tremendous resource not only for psychologists but for researchers in other fields as well:

- The fifth edition includes the latest style guidelines of the *Publication Manual of the American Psychological Association*, Sixth Edition.
- A new chapter has been added on literature research.
- A new chapter has been added on generating, evaluating, and selling ideas.
- A new chapter has been added on ethics in research and writing.
- Many new examples have been added to increase clarity.
- Existing examples have been updated where appropriate.
- Checklists have been added to many of the chapters.
- Advance organizers have been added to provide an overview of the guidelines in a given chapter.
- The revised *Psychologist's Companion* is now aimed not only at students but also at junior faculty and even seasoned professionals seeking guidance.
- All chapters contain enumerated headers for easier use of the book.
- The list of psychology journals has been totally updated and now includes for each journal its impact factor, immediacy index, and number of articles published per year.
- The book is printed in a more reader-friendly format.

Further covered, with vital updates, are topics such as misconceptions about psychology papers; rules for writing literature reviews and experimental papers; how best to make use of the Internet in research; content, language, and style guidelines; commonly misused words; guidelines for data presentation; standards for evaluating papers; guidelines for submitting papers to journals and winning acceptance; how to write grant and contract proposals; how to find book publishers; and how to write lectures and articles. The book contains a sample psychology paper and is written in a lively and witty style that will make it easy reading for even the busiest student or professional.

Robert J. Sternberg
Karin Sternberg
June 2010

# Introduction

Most students and even faculty in psychology receive little or no formal training in how to write psychology papers. Nor do they necessarily learn how to write grant and contract proposals, book proposals, or talks and lectures. Many people believe that writers receive sufficient training in writing through informal channels and thus will acquire the necessary skills on their own. Do students learn the writing techniques for psychology on their own? Our experience reading psychology papers suggests that often they do not. Moreover, this experience is shared by other psychology professors and by professors in other disciplines, as well.

The purpose of this book is to provide the basic information that students and professionals alike need to write and write well in psychology. This information is contained in 17 chapters. Although the intent is that you read the chapters in the order in which they are presented, they are for the most part self-contained and hence can be read in almost any sequence.

Chapter 1 presents and discusses eight common misconceptions that students hold about psychology papers. We have found that many of these misconceptions are reinforced rather than extinguished by conventional academic training. Most students come to believe, for example, that journal articles are and should be autobiographical – that the logical development of ideas in a psychology paper reflects their historical development in the psychologist's head. Accepting this notion as a presupposition, students often believe that authors of journal articles can plan their research and predict their findings well in advance, often down to the last detail. Readers will know better after finishing Chapter 1.

One can write good papers only when one has good ideas that constitute the basis for the papers. Chapter 2 suggests alternative ways to generate ideas for papers. Because not all ideas are good ideas, the latter part of the chapter provides guidelines to decide which ideas are good ones that should be pursued. Finally, the chapter also gives tips on how to sell one's ideas to others.

Chapter 3 describes ways to conduct literature research in the best manner possible. We describe diverse reference materials, introduce literature research methods and useful databases, and explain how to use the Internet for scientific research and to evaluate the information found online.

Chapters 4 and 5 present the sequence of steps that psychologists follow in writing papers. Chapter 4 deals with literature reviews, and Chapter 5 with experimental research papers. The sequence of steps begins with the decision regarding a topic and ends with the publication of a finished paper. Many writers have only a fuzzy idea of the sequence of steps and of how to present this sequence to readers of psychology papers.

Consider two examples. First, would the procedure by which participants are assigned to treatment groups be described more appropriately in the "Procedure" section or in the "Design" section of a psychology paper? Second, do journal editors encourage or discourage extensive use of tables and figures in articles to clarify the presentation of experimental data? The answer to the first question is "Design"; the answer to the second question is "discourage."

Chapter 6 presents guidelines for writing psychology papers. They are divided into three different subsections, dealing with content, language, and style. The guidelines are ones that many students and even professionals fail to follow. One of the reasons they fail to follow these rules is that they forget what the rules are. The chances are good that you remember learning something about avoiding dangling constructions but that either you don't look for dangling constructions in your writing or you don't even remember exactly what a dangling construction is. Chapter 6 will remind you about dangling constructions and other pitfalls in writing papers.

Chapter 7 contains a list of commonly misused words and describes the proper use of each of these words. The meanings of these words, like the rules of writing, are quickly learned but quickly forgotten early in one's career as a student. For example, probably fewer than 10% of the papers [that/which] are published in psychological journals consistently use the relative pronouns *that* and *which* correctly. [While/Although] these papers are certainly publishable, their readability would be enhanced by the proper use of English. Which word belongs in each place where two choices are given within parentheses? In the first sentence, the proper word is *that*; in the second sentence, the proper word is *Although*.

Chapter 8 summarizes the American Psychological Association's (2009) guidelines for writing psychology papers. Regardless of how well you write, you must learn a number of different rules that are specific to the writing of psychology papers. Different disciplines follow different guidelines for writing, and one is expected to learn to write according to the guidelines of the appropriate discipline. Common mistakes occur when writers follow Modern Language Association (MLA) guidelines, which are the ones most students learn in high school. Although these guidelines are appropriate for much writing in the humanities, they typically are not appropriate for writing in psychology. Test yourself. Does one abbreviate *centimeters* as *cm* or as *cm.*? Does one abbreviate *feet* as *ft* or as *ft.*? Does one test 10 subjects or ten subjects? Does one test 8 subjects or eight subjects? The rules of the American Psychological Association lead to answers of "cm," "ft," "10," and "eight." The rules of the Modern Language Association lead to answers of "cm.," "ft.," "ten," and "eight." Learning to write a psychology paper involves learning certain rules that are unique to writing psychology papers.

Chapter 9 provides guidelines for data presentation. It gives rules for presenting data in the form of tables or graphs, as well as guidance on the advantages and drawbacks of different types of presentations. Following these guidelines will aid both your understanding of your data and your ability to communicate them effectively to others.

Chapter 10 deals with the criteria psychologists use to evaluate a particular paper's contribution to knowledge. What characteristics distinguish truly exceptional psychology papers from good ones and good ones from poor ones? Why do some papers continue to have an impact on the field long after other papers have been forgotten? Chapter 10 addresses these questions.

Ethics are of great importance when conducting research and writing scientific papers. Chapter 11 discusses several issues and pitfalls that psychologists may face during their careers and gives advice on to how to avoid them.

Chapter 12 contains practical suggestions for submitting a psychology paper to a professional journal. What considerations enter into the choice of a journal? What happens to a paper once it is submitted? What are the possible courses of action a journal editor can take? You will find out when you read Chapter 12.

You are not done with your paper just because you have finished your first draft. If you intend to write a good paper, what follows are proofreading and revisions. After submission to a journal and even after acceptance of your article, you may have to revise and edit your work. Chapter 13 gives you some tips how to make this process as successful as possible.

Chapters 14–16 are oriented more toward professional and soon-to-be-professional users of this book than toward student users. Chapter 14 contains techniques people can use to increase the chances of their getting funding through a grant or contract. Ultimately, the most important determinant of funding is the set of ideas in the proposal. But many proposals are rejected on grounds that have little or nothing to do with ideas. Competition for grants and contracts is extremely stiff. Therefore, every edge can help. This chapter helps grant writers maximize their chances of winning funding, giving them the edge that may make a difference to the outcome.

Chapter 15 describes the steps a person takes in seeking a book publisher. How do you write a book proposal, and what do you do with the proposal once you are done? Despite the importance to scholars of writing books as well as articles, people tend to know even less about how to find a publisher for a book than they do about how to get an article published. This chapter describes from beginning to end the process of finding a book publisher.

Chapter 16 discusses the writing of effective lectures. Many psychologists end up, sooner or later, teaching. For some, it may be in the form of courses for undergraduate and graduate students. For others, it may be in the form of public lectures. And for still others, it may be in the form of occasional seminars. All of us who have gone through school know how important good lectures are to learning. This chapter will help the reader write and deliver such lectures.

Chapter 17 is a primer on effective writing of articles for psychological journals. It contains tips both on what you should do and what you should not do.

The Appendix contains a sample paper typed according to APA guidelines. The paper is presented as it was typed rather than as it would appear in a journal. The paper illustrates many of the principles described in Chapter 8.

As you progress through this book, you will discover that writing for an audience of psychologists requires a unique set of skills. For most students and professionals alike, merely reading and writing psychology papers is an insufficient way to acquire these skills. This book is intended for and dedicated to all of you who want to improve your writing.

# 1 | Eight Common Misconceptions About Psychology Papers

Students and inexperienced writers often have misconceptions about the writing process and characteristics of good papers that effectively prevent them from writing as good a paper as they possibly could. Here are eight common misconceptions you should be aware of before you even begin writing:

1. Writing the psychology paper is the most routine, least creative aspect of the scientific enterprise, requiring much time but little imagination.
2. The important thing is what you say, not how you say it.
3. Longer papers are better papers, and more papers are better yet.
4. The main purpose of a psychology paper is the presentation of facts, whether newly established (as in reports of experiments) or well established (as in literature reviews).
5. The distinction between scientific writing, on the one hand, and advertising or propaganda, on the other hand, is that the purpose of scientific writing is to inform, whereas the purpose of advertising or propaganda is to persuade.
6. A good way to gain acceptance of your theory is by refuting someone else's theory.
7. Negative results that fail to support the researcher's hypothesis are every bit as valuable as positive results that do support the researcher's hypothesis.
8. The logical development of ideas in a psychology paper reflects the historical development of ideas in the psychologist's head.

**Misconception 1.** Writing the psychology paper is the most routine, least creative aspect of the scientific enterprise, requiring much time but little imagination.

Many students lose interest in their research projects as soon as the time comes to write about them. Their interest is in planning for and making new discoveries, not in communicating their discoveries to others. A widely believed fallacy underlies their attitudes. The fallacy is that the discovery process ends when the communication process begins. Although the major purpose of writing a paper is to communicate your thoughts to others, another important purpose is to help you form and organize your thoughts.

Reporting your findings in writing requires you to commit yourself to those findings and to your interpretation of them, and it opens you to criticism (as well as praise) from others. It is perhaps for this reason as much as any other that many students are reluctant to report their research. But the finality of a written report also serves as a powerful incentive to do your best thinking and to continue thinking as you write your paper. It requires you to tie up loose ends that you might otherwise have left untied. As a result, reporting your findings presents just as much of a challenge as planning the research and analyses that led to those findings.

We have often thought we knew what we wanted to say, only to find that when the time came to say it, we were unable to. The reason for this, we believe, is that in thinking about a topic, we often allow ourselves conceptual gaps that we hardly know exist. When we attempt to communicate our thoughts, however, these gaps become obvious. Organizing and then writing down our thoughts enables us to discover what gaps have yet to be filled.

**Misconception 2.** The important thing is what you say, not how you say it.

As a college student, the lead author was mystified to find that students who wrote well consistently received better grades on their compositions than did students who wrote poorly. Even in his own compositions, he found that the grades he received seemed less to reflect what he had to say than how he said it. At the time, he was unable to decide whether this pattern in grading resulted from the professors' warped value systems or from their inability to penetrate the facade of written prose. Whereas their criteria for grading papers might be appropriate for an English course, these criteria seemed inappropriate for courses in subjects like psychology.

As a college professor, the lead author has at last discovered the secret of the mysterious grading practices. The discovery came about in two stages, each one part of the initiation rites that new college teachers must go through. The first stage occurred when he found himself with a large number of students' papers to read and very little time in which to read them. He was then sincerely grateful to students who wrote well because he could read their papers quickly and understand what they were saying. He did not have the time to puzzle through every cryptic remark in the poorly written papers, however, and he resented the authors' presenting their ideas in a way that did not enable him to understand or evaluate them properly. He also found himself with no desire to reward the authors for this state of affairs. If their ideas were good, they should have taken the time to explain them clearly.

The second stage of discovery occurred when he found himself with just a few seminar papers to read and plenty of time in which to read them. Now, he thought, he could be fair both to students who write well and to those who do not. He was quickly disabused of this notion. He discovered that whereas it is usually easy to distinguish well-presented good ideas from well-presented bad ideas, it is often impossible to distinguish poorly presented good ideas from poorly presented bad ideas. The problem is that the professor's comprehension of what the student says occurs solely through the student's way of saying it. Professors can't read minds better than anyone else. If an idea is presented in a sloppy, disorganized fashion, how is one to know whether this fashion of presentation reflects the quality of the idea or merely the quality of its presentation?

The question is not easily answered. In one case, the lead author had talked to a student beforehand about what that student was going to say, and he expected an outstanding paper on the basis of these conversations. During those conversations, certain details had not been clarified, but the professor expected these details to be clarified in the paper. Instead, the same ideas that had been inadequately explained in the conversations were inadequately explained in the paper, as well. Either the student was unable to clarify these ideas for himself, or he was unable to clarify them for others.

The outcome for the reader is the same: confusion and disappointment.

A comparable situation exists for researchers. One quickly notices that the best and most well-known psychologists are also among the best writers. Although there are exceptions, they are infrequent: Poorer writers have fewer readers. One reason for this fact is that poorly written articles are usually rejected by journal editors. Although journal editors are willing to make minor editorial changes in the articles they receive, they are usually unwilling to publish or rewrite poorly written articles. Even if a poorly written article is accepted and published, however, psychologists who receive a journal with 5–20 articles in it do not want to spend their limited time reading such an article. It is therefore important that you learn now how to present your ideas in a readable fashion.

### Misconception 3. Longer papers are better papers, and more papers are better yet.

Until his first year of teaching, the lead author believed that longer papers were better papers. Teachers had for years told him and his classmates that they didn't evaluate papers on the basis of length, but he viewed their remarks as a benign ruse designed to discourage length for its own sake. He changed his viewpoint when he started reading students' papers. Evaluating papers on both quality and quantity of ideas, he found little relation between either of these two criteria and the length of students' papers. Sometimes students wrote longer papers because they had more to say; other times they wrote longer papers because it took them several pages to say what could have been said in several sentences. There is nothing wrong with length per se, so long as length is not used as a substitute for tight organization and clear writing.

Rather than writing longer papers, some people have taken the other route of writing more papers. Why say in one paper what can be said in two for twice the credit? This kind of mentality meets the needs of people who count publications but not of those who read publications. An integrated series of related experiments will have more impact if published as a single, tightly knit package than if published as a string of hastily written articles, none of them of much interest in itself.

**Misconception 4.** The main purpose of a psychology paper is the presentation of facts, whether newly established (as in reports of experiments) or well established (as in literature reviews).

A common misconception among the general public is that the goal of science is the accumulation of facts. This misconception is fostered by popular scientific writing that emphasizes scientific findings, which may be easy to describe, at the expense of explanations of those findings, which may be both diverse and difficult to describe. Diverse explanations, however, are the hallmark of science.

Students in introductory psychology courses are prone to this misconception, and it carries over into their writing. We could cite numerous examples of this carryover, but one in particular comes to mind. We received some years ago a beautifully written paper reviewing the literature on the testing of infant intelligence. This was one case, however, in which flowing prose was insufficient to obtain a high grade. The paper was flawed in two respects. First, the author made no effort to interrelate the various attempts to measure infant intelligence. Each attempt was described as though it had been made in isolation, even though the various attempts to measure infant intelligence have drawn on each other. Second, the evaluative part of the paper consisted of a single sentence in which the author stated that it is still too early to draw final conclusions regarding the relative success of the various infant intelligence tests. This sentence is literally true: It was too early to draw final conclusions. But it will be too early to draw final conclusions as long as new data about the tests continue to be collected. Because data will continue to be collected for the foreseeable future, and because the tests date back to the early part of the 20th century, it now seems appropriate to draw at least tentative conclusions. In writing a psychology paper, you must commit yourself to a point of view, even if you may change your mind later on. If the evidence on an issue is scanty, by all means say so. But draw at least tentative conclusions so that the reader knows how you evaluate what evidence is available.

Your paper should be guided by your ideas and your point of view. Facts are presented in service of ideas: to help elucidate, support, or rewrite these ideas. They provide a test against which the validity of ideas can be measured. You should therefore select the facts that help clarify or test your point of view and omit facts that are irrelevant. In being selective, however, you must not select only those facts that support your position. Scientists demand that scientific reporting be scrupulously honest. Without such honesty, scientific communication would collapse. Cite the relevant facts, therefore, regardless of whose point of view they support.

**Misconception 5.** The distinction between scientific writing, on the one hand, and advertising or propaganda, on the other hand, is that the purpose of scientific writing is to inform, whereas the purpose of advertising or propaganda is to persuade.

Successful advertising or propaganda need only persuade. Successful scientific writing must both inform and persuade. Writers often believe that a successful piece of scientific writing need only inform the reader of the scientists' data and their interpretation of the data. The reader is then left to decide whether the theory provides a plausible account of those (and possibly other) data. This conception of scientific writing is incorrect.

When scientists write a paper, they have a product to sell. The product is their set of ideas about why certain phenomena exist. Occasionally, it is the only product on the market, and they need only convince the consumer to buy any product at all. Whether or not scientists are successful will depend in part on how persuasive they are and in part on how much the product is needed. No advertising campaign is likely to sell flowers that are guaranteed not to germinate or an explanation of why people don't normally stand on their heads rather than their feet. In most cases, however, there is an already established demand for the product. Because competing salespersons are trying to corner the market, scientists must persuade the consumer not just to buy any product but to buy their product.

One of the most common mistakes writers make is to sell the wrong product: They misjudge the contribution of their work. We recently received a paper that was full of good, original ideas. The presentation of these ideas, and of other people's as well, was unusually lucid. The only major problem with the paper was that the discussion of the original ideas was condensed into one paragraph buried inconspicuously in the middle of the paper, whereas the discussion of the other people's ideas spanned about 10 pages, starting on page 1. The contribution of this paper should have been in its new perspective on an old problem. But the author had deemphasized this potentially significant contribution in favor of a relatively unimportant one: providing a well-written but unexciting review of other people's perspectives. The hurried reader will usually take the author's emphasis at face value. In this case, the reader might conclude that the paper did not have much of an original contribution to make.

At the opposite extreme, it is possible to dwell so heavily on the contribution of your paper that the contribution is actually muted. The lead author learned this lesson the hard way. A colleague and he wrote a paper intended to compare different measures of a psychological construct called subjective organization and to demonstrate that one of these measures is superior to all the rest (Sternberg & Tulving, 1977). They compared the measures on a number of different criteria. One measure proved to be superior to the rest on every one of these criteria. Despite his colleague's warnings, he explicitly called attention to this fact several times in the paper. Leaving nothing to chance, he pointed out the inescapable conclusion that one measure is better than all the rest and therefore should be the measure of choice.

They submitted the paper for publication, and several months later received two scathing reviews. They were attacked for making what both reviewers believed to be exorbitant claims. According to the reviewers, they had by no means developed an open-and-shut case in favor of the measure they claimed was best. The lead author thought that the arguments made by the reviewers were weak and in some cases plainly incorrect. He was so annoyed with the whole affair that he let the paper sit on his shelf for about a year. Rereading the paper and the reviews a year later, he still believed the reviewers were on the wrong track. His colleague and he decided to tone down their claims for the preferred measure, however, while retaining the same basic line of argument. They resubmitted the paper, and this time received a very favorable review. They achieved much more effective results by understating their case than they had by overstating it, an outcome the colleague had anticipated from the start. Our subsequent experiences have confirmed repeatedly that, in psychology papers, a soft-selling technique is more successful than a hard-selling technique. By using the latter, you invite a reaction against you as salesperson that is likely to hurt the sale of your product. We can recall numerous occasions on which we refused to buy a product because we detested a pushy salesperson. In writing the first draft of the paper on measures of subjective organization, the lead author unwittingly occupied the role of the pushy salesperson, and he received what should have been a predictable response.

**Misconception 6.** A good way to gain acceptance of your theory is by refuting someone else's theory.

A surprisingly common ploy in scientific papers, even some published in prestigious journals, is to resort to explanation by default. Whereas students may not know better, professionals should. Investigators describe two (or more) theories of the well-known XYZ phenomenon. They then present devastating evidence against all theories except one. They conclude on the basis of this evidence that this one theory is correct.

This indirect method of proof is compelling only when the two (or more) alternatives are (a) mutually exclusive and (b) exhaustive. Mutually exclusive alternatives are ones in which one outcome precludes the other(s). If a coin lands heads, for example, it cannot at the same time land tails. Exhaustive alternatives are ones that include all possible outcomes. A flip of a coin can result in heads or tails, but nothing else.

The ploy described above has been used in some (but by no means all) research studying sources of differences between groups in intelligence test scores. A study would be presented in which obtained differences in test scores could not be attributable to environmental factors. The author would conclude on that basis that the differences must be due to hereditary factors. These alternatives, however, are neither mutually exclusive nor exhaustive. First, it is possible – indeed, probable – that both heredity and environment influence intelligence test scores. Second, a further source of influence on intelligence test scores is the interaction between heredity and environment – the effect produced by their nonadditive influence. As an example, certain genes for intelligence may manifest themselves only under favorable environmental conditions.

One other disadvantage of the indirect method of proof bears mention. Criticism of other people's theories often gains one more opponents than it does converts to one's own theory. This was another lesson the lead author learned the hard way. He once wrote a paper that had two major goals: (a) to show that his theory of a phenomenon was correct and (b) to show that someone else's theory of the phenomenon was incorrect. He presented what he believed was strong evidence in favor of his theory and in opposition to the other person's theory. He submitted the paper to a journal, and it was rejected. The main reviewer of the paper, predictably enough, was the other theorist. It is a common practice to send papers attacking theory X to theorist X, with editors then using their judgment as to whether the review is a fair one. The reviewer criticized not the positive aspect of the paper, but its negative aspect. He argued that the theories actually dealt with somewhat different aspects of the phenomenon under investigation, so that there was no need to attack the reviewer's theory in the process of supporting the lead author's own.

In retrospect, the reviewer probably had some valid points, but we believe he overreacted. In papers we've reviewed that attack our work, we've probably overreacted as well. Scientists have a reputation among the general public for being objective seekers and impartial evaluators of the truth. We think this reputation is generally deserved, but only when it comes to each other's work. When it comes to their own work, scientists lose their objectivity. When scientists are attacked, they behave in much the same manner as anyone else under attack. When someone lunges at you with a fist flying toward your face, you don't stop to reflect on the various considerations that may have led your opponent to attack you. You counterattack. Because scientists are personally so involved in their work, they often treat an attack on their work as a personal attack, even if there is no rational basis for treating it as such. The result can be a personal confrontation in which scientific issues are placed on the back burner.

In conclusion, it is wise to stress the positive contribution of your paper. This does not mean that you should forgo criticizing other theories. Such criticism may be essential to your point. If it is, keep in mind our earlier admonition that understatement is a more effective means of persuasion than is overstatement. Avoid statements that can be interpreted as contentious but lacking in substance. And if you publish your paper, don't expect investigators you criticize to congratulate you on your cogent refutation of their work.

**Misconception 7.** Negative results that fail to support the researcher's hypothesis are every bit as valuable as positive results that do support the researcher's hypothesis.

Because science is a fair game, the scientist wins some and loses some. Novices often believe that the only honest course of action is for scientists to report their losses as well as their wins. To do otherwise would seem to present a false picture of both the scientist and the state of nature.

After reading a diverse sampling of journal articles, the reader is bound to arrive at one of two conclusions – either scientists have uncannily sound intuitions about the way experiments will turn out, or they maintain closets full of unsuccessful and unreported experiments. Although scientists usually have at least fairly sound intuitions about how experiments will turn out, the state of the journals is more a reflection of well-stocked closets than of unerring intuitions.

Scientists' failures to report failures are attributable not to their dishonesty but to the frequent uninterpretability of negative results. Suppose, for example, that investigators predict that giving children rewards after learning will increase their learning. The investigators conduct an experiment with two groups. In one group, children receive rewards after learning; in the other group, they do not receive rewards. The investigators find no difference in learning between groups. What can they conclude? Unfortunately, not much. Whereas a significant difference between groups could have provided good evidence that rewards can facilitate learning, absence of a significant difference could be explained in a number of ways, most of them uninteresting. Consider three such uninteresting explanations:

1. **Weak rewards:** The reward used in the study did not prove a powerful enough incentive. If the reward, for example, was a peanut, then children's cravings for a single peanut might not have been strong enough to increase their efforts to learn.
2. **Sample size too small:** The sample of children might not have been large enough. It is a well-known rule of statistics that, if any treatment effect exists at all, then it can be discovered if one's sample is large enough. A small effect may be detectable only with a relatively large sample. If there were only three children in each group, then the investigators might have failed to detect the effect of the reward.
3. **Inadequate measures:** The measure of learning might have been inadequate. Suppose, for example, that the task was to learn the set of multiplication facts for one-digit numbers and that the measure of learning was a single multiplication fact. This measure probably would have been inadequate to detect learning in either group and hence a difference in learning between groups.

Under two sets of circumstances, negative results can be of interest: when an investigator fails to replicate someone else's results, and when the results change due to some other factors. Let us first consider the failure to replicate results. Suppose someone reports that subjects who stand on their heads for 30 seconds prior to taking a test of visual-motor coordination perform better on the test than do control subjects who do not stand on their heads. Another investigator, suspicious of this result, tries to replicate it with two groups of subjects and fails. Realizing that the failure to replicate the result may be due to sampling fluctuations, the investigator tests two more groups of subjects and again finds no significant difference between groups. At this point, the investigator feels ready to report the result. Whereas one failure to replicate a result is not informative, repeated failures to replicate can be informative. The number of failures needed depends in large part on the strength of prior evidence in support of the result in question. Two failures are probably more than adequate for the "headstand hypothesis," whereas a great many failures would be needed to overthrow a better-established result, such as that under normal circumstances learning increases with practice.

Negative results are also of interest if a significant result vanishes when a methodological weakness is corrected. Suppose that the experimenter who wrote the headstand paper knew which subjects had stood on their heads and which had not. This aspect of the methodology suggests a possible bias in the experimenter's scoring of the coordination test (especially if the experimenter is public relations director of the American Association for the Advancement of Acrobatics). A worthwhile methodological refinement would be to conduct the experiment under circumstances in which the experimenter does not know which subjects stood on their heads and which did not. A negative result would be of interest in this case, because it would suggest that the significant difference between groups in the first experiment was due to experimenter bias.

**Misconception 8.** The logical development of ideas in a psychology paper reflects the historical development of ideas in the psychologist's head.

If one were to take journal articles at face value, one would conclude that scientific results come in neat, attractively wrapped packages. Writers often believe that one needs only to go through a uniform series of well-defined steps to ensure delivery of such packages. These steps are outlined in the "Myth" column of Table 1.1. However, we doubt that even as many as 1% of the papers published in scientific journals developed in a way even remotely resembling the outline given in the "Myth" column. In fact, they develop according to the sequence described in the "Reality" column of Table 1.1. Yet the large majority of published papers are written as though they had developed in the former way, or in some way closely resembling it. Let us compare the series of steps.

Why does the picture of research presented by journal articles correspond so poorly to the actual state of affairs? There are at least three reasons:

1. **Space limitations:** Journals operate under severe space limitations. A large percentage of articles submitted to journals must be rejected for lack of space. In some journals, more than 90% of submitted articles are rejected. Those articles that are accepted must be as concise as possible. An "autobiographical" form of presentation, describing all one's false starts and initial misjudgments, consumes a great deal of space. That space is more profitably devoted to other articles.

2. **Efficacy of presentation:** An autobiographical account of an experiment tends to be of more interest to oneself than to one's colleagues. An associate recounted to us the way in which he learned this lesson. He submitted a 20-page theoretical article to one of the most prestigious psychological journals. He spent the first 19 pages of the article describing how he had come to his conclusions after a lengthy series of false starts; he presented his final conclusions on the 20th page. The article was rejected, not because the final conclusions were wrong, but because the editor believed that there was only one publishable page in the article – the last one. The editor was interested in the psychologist's conclusions but not in the lengthy soul searching the psychologist had done to arrive at them.

3. **Focus on the phenomenon:** The object of description in a scientific report is a phenomenon and its explanation, not the reporter of the phenomenon and explanation. The focus of the report must reflect this fact. A graduate student and the lead author once completed an experiment investigating the development of reasoning skills in children at the second-, fourth-, and sixth-grade levels. Children were presented with reasoning problems, which

**Table 1.1. The steps of writing a paper: myth versus reality**

| Myth | Reality |
|---|---|
| 1. Scientists start with ideas about a phenomenon, which they explain in the introduction to the paper. These ideas are formulated before the scientist has collected any data; the data serve to confirm (or in rare cases disconfirm) their validity. | 1. Before carrying out an experiment, one usually has only a vague and tentative idea of what the outcome will be, if only because there are so many possible outcomes. One's ideas develop along with the experiment. |
| 2. Scientists test these ideas by carefully choosing variables that can be manipulated in a controlled experiment. The scientists' understanding of the phenomenon under observation and of scientific method enables them to choose the correct variables and experimental manipulation on their very first attempt, which they describe in the "Method" section of the paper. | 2. One sometimes performs the right experimental manipulation on the wrong variables or the wrong experimental manipulation on the right variables. To avoid wasting resources, scientists frequently conduct small-scale pilot experiments that test the feasibility of the experiment. Adjustments may then be made for the full-scale experiment, or the experiment may be scrapped altogether. |
| 3. Scientists perform the experiment, presenting in the "Results" section of their paper the outcomes of data analyses scrupulously planned in advance. | 3. Major data analyses are usually planned in advance, planning that is necessary to ensure that the design of the experiment permits one to analyze the data in the most advantageous way. Minor data analyses are frequently decided on after data collection. Often the results of a planned data analysis will suggest a subsequent unplanned one. A given set of data can be analyzed in an infinite number of ways, some of them more revealing than others. The scientist must select a small number of ways that are likely to yield maximum payoff. |
| 4. Scientists finally reflect on the broader implications of the results, presenting their reflections in the "Discussion" section of the paper. | 4. Ideas for the *Discussion* section of a paper usually start forming at the same time the experiment does, not only after its completion. The reason for this is that unless the experiment has some potentially broad and interesting implications, or unless it can lead to some sensible next step in research, it is probably not worth doing. |

they were then asked to solve. Because the experiment involved a considerable investment in time and money, they decided to pretest their reasoning problems on some colleagues' children. The original plan had been to use number of problems correctly solved as the dependent measure. They discovered, however, that even the youngest children made almost no errors on the problems once they fully understood the task. They therefore changed their dependent measure when they did the full-scale experiment, using response time to solve problems correctly instead of numbers of problems correctly solved. Had someone else planned this experiment, that person might have realized immediately that the problems were too easy to use number correct as the dependent measure or might have stumbled longer than the authors did until they discovered that the problems were too easy. A description of this trial-and-error process is slightly informative about the development of the investigator's intuitions, but it is uninformative about the object of the investigation, in this case, the development of reasoning in children. The scientifically informative statement is that the problems were of a level of difficulty that made response time an appropriate dependent measure.

There is often a fine line between the omission of autobiographical information and the omission of critical details. If a hypothesis is post hoc, then one is obliged to indicate this fact.

In sum, the steps one follows in planning and carrying out research do not neatly correspond to the successive sections of the psychology paper. In the next two chapters, we will consider the steps in carrying out literature and experimental research and how to describe them in the psychology paper.

# 2 How to Generate, Evaluate, and Sell Your Ideas for Research and Papers

There is no one foolproof way of getting ideas for papers. You have to find the ways that work for you. In the first part of this chapter, we present you with different ways in which you can develop ideas for your research projects. Of course, it is not enough to have ideas. To be a successful researcher, you also need the ability to evaluate your ideas and find out whether they are good ones. You do not want to waste your time on bad ideas. The second part of this chapter deals with the evaluation of your ideas. And once you have come to the conclusion that yours is a wonderful idea, it will be important for you to sell your idea. How do you convince others that your planned study is one that is worthwhile to conduct, and how do you convince an editor of a journal and reviewers that your paper is worth publishing? Especially creative ideas are often hard to sell. Therefore, the third part of this chapter shows you some ways to sell your ideas.

## 2.1 GENERATING IDEAS

### 2.1.1 Generating Ideas by Consulting with Others

In many colleges and universities, the faculty is among the most underutilized of resources. In the senior author's first semester of teaching at Yale, he set aside three hours each week for office hours. He encouraged – sometimes he practically begged – students to come see him during those hours for advice on papers, projects, and the like. He left his door wide open to encourage students to enter. For the most part, though, he sat staring at the walls or at the people scurrying by (but not in) the door. He also encouraged students to make individual appointments if they were unable to see him during his prearranged hours, but for the most part, students also failed to take him up on this offer. Later, business picked up, although much more so among graduate than among undergraduate students.

Once, the psychology department faculty at Yale spent the better part of an hour trying to figure out why students are so timid in approaching faculty. Sometimes students try once, are unsuccessful in reaching the faculty member, and give up. Sometimes they don't try at all. Faculty members (as well as postdoctoral students and graduate students) can be a most helpful first avenue of approach in writing a paper for students as well as for postdocs and junior faculty. You should be assertive in seeking their advice.

## 2.1.2 Generating Ideas by Reading

### 2.1.2.1 What to Read

Ideas often come out of one's reading. Some kinds of reading are more likely to lead to good ideas than are others:

1. **Pursue a small number of topics in depth:** Most undergraduate psychology courses, and many graduate ones, are not well suited to the stimulation of creative ideas for experiments. This unsuitability is because they cover a large amount of material superficially rather than a small amount in depth. To come up with a good idea for an experiment, it helps to have a deep understanding of the issues involved in some relatively small area of psychological research. Find some topic that interests you. Pursue the references that the papers you are interested in cite, and pursue the references most frequently cited in those references. By digging into the literature on a topic, you will acquire a deeper understanding of the issues that are the focus of psychological research.

2. **Acquaint yourself with research at the frontiers of knowledge:** As an undergraduate, the senior author once followed the advice of the preceding paragraph, only to find himself acquiring a deep understanding of an issue that had ceased to interest psychologists twenty years before. In pursuing a topic, consider whether it is of current interest. Because of the long time lag between the

writing and the publication of a book, most textbooks are some-what out of date by the time they are published. Within five to ten years, they usually become hopelessly out of date. As a result, students relying on such textbooks may find themselves gener-ating ideas that someone else thought of several years before. To become acquainted with literature on the frontiers of knowl-edge, scan recent journal articles and make use of the references described in Chapter 3 of this book.

3. **Start with general readings and proceed to more specific ones:** Because of space limitations, authors of journal articles are often unable to present in detail the previous research that motivated their particular experiments. If you are unacquainted with that previous research, you may find yourself unable to understand the rationale of the experiments. It is therefore wise to start your reading with a review of the relevant literature, if you can find one, or with a theoretical article that compares the major the-oretical positions. Reports of individual experiments will make more sense to you if you are first acquainted with the research context in which they were done.

## 2.1.2.2 How to Read

How you read is as important as what you read. Suppose, for example, that you read an article testing the theory that repeated exposure to persuasive communications results in attitude change toward the viewpoint advocated by those communications, regardless of one's initial attitudes. You might pursue further research taking you in any one of four directions:

1. **Extend the theory:** After reading the article, you may be per-suaded that the theory is sound and could be extended. You might want to show that repeated exposure to communications advo-cating a viewpoint, but in a nonpersuasive manner, also results in attitude change toward the position taken by the communi-cations.

2. **Generate an analogous theory:** If you find the theory and data compelling, you may want to think up an analogous theory. Per-haps repeated exposure to a particular kind of music increases liking for that music. Or perhaps repeated exposure to any kind of communication increases positive affect toward that kind of communication.

3. **Limit the theory:** Perhaps you believe that the conclusion derived from the data is too broad. If the subjects in the experiment were all children, for example, you may wish to show that the theory is applicable only to children. Or if the communications used in the experiment were all health-related ones, you may want to show that the theory is applicable only to arguments related to bodily care.

4. **Challenge the evidence testing the theory:** In reading the article, you may spot a methodological, statistical, or logical flaw in the author's argument. In this case, you may want to test the theory in a way that corrects the flaw. For example, suppose that the author of the paper tested the hypothesis merely by showing that after two hours of listening to a set of three persuasive communications, most subjects agreed with the viewpoint advocated by those communications. If the author has not shown, however, that at least some of the subjects disagreed with the viewpoints of the communications prior to the test, then the conclusion does not follow from the data.

## 2.1.3 Other Ways to Generate Ideas

The following list provides 10 ways to generate ideas that work at least for some people. We will illustrate each of the ideas with examples from our own research. We use our own research because we know how we got our ideas, but we have no sure way of knowing how other researchers got their ideas! For an additional view on getting ideas, upon which this chapter partially draws, see McGuire (1997):

1. Observe behavior in other people that arouses your curiosity.

2. Observe behavior in yourself that arouses your curiosity.

3. Question researchers' interpretations of their work.

4. Look for anomalies in patterns of behavior, whether your own or others'.

5. Look for patterns of behavior that are themselves puzzling.

6. Think the opposite of what others think.

7. Synthesize disparate existing ideas.

8. Ask yourself what the next question is.

9. Revisit discarded ideas.

10. Look for ideas in everyday models and metaphors.

**1.** Observe behavior in other people that arouses your curiosity.

Why, sometimes, when you try to help people, do they get angry at you instead of feeling grateful? Why is it that some people, when they shake hands, feel like they are trying to crush your hand, and others give you what feels like a dead-fish grip? Why do some people almost literally drink themselves to death? Why do some people almost always seem to get lost and others almost always to find their way? Why do people like to go on frightening amusement-park rides, and why do they like scary movies? One way to get ideas is to observe the behavior of others and to try to understand why they do what they do.

Some years ago, the senior author of this book did a series of papers on conflict resolution (Sternberg & Dobson, 1987; Sternberg & Soriano, 1984). The goal of the studies was to understand consistent individual differences in ways people approach conflicts. The research grew out of the author's observation of some past chairs of his psychology department. In particular, one was excellent at defusing conflicts and seemed to be able to take a conflict and reach some kind of compromise that, more or less, satisfied the participants in the conflict. The other chair seemed to be almost the opposite: He had a real talent for making existing conflicts even worse than they were. It seemed unlikely he was trying to fan the flames, but he nevertheless succeeded in doing so. But what was most notable was the consistency in each of the chair's styles. They seemed always, in the one case, to mitigate conflict, and in the other case, to exacerbate it. The ensuing research ended up finding seven consistent styles of conflict resolution: physical action, economic action, wait and see, accept the situation, step down, third party, and undermine esteem. One of the chairs used a step-down strategy of trying to ease the conflict; the other was personally insecure, it seemed, and ended up undermining the self-esteem of both parties, which made them feel worse and made their conflict worse.

The junior author was blissfully working in Key Largo, Florida, when the September 11, 2001, attacks took place. She observed drastic behavior changes in people afterward: They were much more cohesive, made appointments to go to church together even though before the incident nobody had ever even mentioned the church, and stuck to themselves and isolated themselves from other groups they did not see as relevant to them. Some of them became suspicious of certain types of out-groups. The amazement about the effects of the terrorist attacks eventually led to the junior author's dissertation on hate and to her interest in prejudice and terrorism.

The research would not have been done had the author not been curious about the behavior of the people around her. So when you observe other people's behavior, look at it as a set of puzzles that psychologists can understand. You can get some of your best ideas right from those observations.

**2.** Observe behavior in yourself that arouses your curiosity.

Why do you always fall in love with Mr. or Ms. Wrong? Why do you blush when people praise you? Why do you feel afraid when you watch a scary movie, even though you know it is all fiction? Why do you fail to remember information that you just learned a few seconds ago? Why do you sometimes start studying for tests at the last minute, knowing that you are hurting yourself in doing so? You can get many of your research ideas by observing your own behavior and then doing research to try to understand it.

When the senior author was young, he did poorly on IQ tests. His problems in IQ testing seriously affected his life. His teachers thought he was stupid; he thought he was stupid; he did stupid work; and the teachers were happy that their predictions about his stupidity were correct; he in turn was happy that they were happy. And so continued a vicious circle that did not end until he had a teacher in fourth grade who saw more in him than his being a poor test taker. As a result of this experience, the author acquired a lifelong interest in intelligence. To this day, he is still trying to understand why he did poorly on the IQ tests!

The author ended up forming a theory of intelligence according to which there are three aspects to intelligence: creative, analytical, and practical (Sternberg, 1997a, 2005). A person needs creative intelligence to formulate new ideas, analytical intelligence to ascertain whether they are good ideas, and practical intelligence to implement the ideas and convince others of their value. In his case, he probably suffered from test anxiety, but the author also lacked the practical skills to control the anxiety. Fortunately, intelligence is malleable, and he acquired more practical skills later on.

The research ended up being typical of much psychological research in one key way. It set out to answer one question and ended addressing a different question instead. The author still does not know for sure why he did poorly on the tests when he was younger. But in the process of trying to find out, he learned a lot of other things about human intelligence.

The junior author once had a friend who was intellectually absolutely brilliant. He worked at a bank, where he advised people on their investment options for their money. The friend seemed to know all there was to know about the stock market, was able to come up with the fanciest calculations to indicate the best investments, and even developed ideas for new investment instruments. And still, he had a lot of trouble at his job and was finally fired for underperformance. When talking to the friend and trying to find out what had gone wrong, the junior author discovered that he had always had trouble connecting to his clients and was no more popular with his employers than with the clients. Ultimately, he had failed to make his quota because customers came to him only once but rarely returned or invested money with him. This experience led the junior author to think about the importance of social and emotional intelligence in people's lives, and she developed a test of emotional intelligence for her diploma thesis at her university.

When you do research, be open to the possibility that your research may end up addressing questions in addition to or even instead of those you initially posed. Often, the greatest findings in psychology are wholly serendipitous.

**3.** Question researchers' interpretations of their work.

Do people really do better on successive exposures to information because repeated exposures strengthen memory traces? When people act in ways that are contrary to their beliefs, do they really experience some kind of cognitive dissonance? Do children have autism because of parents who have acted in ambiguous ways that alternately encourage the children to come closer and then to distance themselves? Much of the best research in psychology has come out of ambiguities in the interpretation of past research findings. Very few findings lend themselves to unambiguous interpretation, even if they initially seem to be unambiguous.

The senior author's first research project in graduate school arose out of his questioning an empirical finding in the research literature (Sternberg & Bower, 1974). Unfortunately, the finding was by his own undergraduate adviser (Tulving, 1966)! (He does not recommend picking holes in your own adviser's work!) In this case, suppose you give people a list of words to learn, A. Then, after they have learned the A list fairly well, you give them one of two other lists to learn, either AB or BC. Half the words on AB are the complete set of words from list A, whereas BC has no words at all from A. Curiously, after the first few learning trials, students actually do better in learning the all-new list (BC) than the part-new list (AB) that partially overlaps with the original list (A). This is odd, because one would expect it to be easier to learn a list that is already half-learned than one that has not been learned at all. Tulving proposed that the difficulty of those learning the AB list was a matter of the way participants organized the words in memory. We proposed instead that the difficulty was in discriminating which words were carried over from the A list to the AB list. Well, you might say, all the words were carried over. Right! But participants had not been informed of that. When they were, the negative transfer between A and AB disappeared. So the problem did indeed appear to be one of list discrimination.

When reading a paper or listening to a talk, you should think carefully about whether the researcher's interpretation of the data matches your own interpretation. If not, could you design a study to test whether your interpretation or the other researcher's is correct? Many of the best studies in psychology have come from people questioning others' interpretations of their data.

**4.** Look for anomalies in patterns of behavior, whether your own or others'.

Why do people who lose weight for long periods of time – perhaps even many months – all of a sudden break their pattern and start to gain weight again? Why do people who seem in their day-to-day life to be quiet and quite unobtrusive sometimes explode and go on rampages? Why do people who have been top students throughout their school careers sometimes go to college and suddenly become mediocre students? You can get ideas for research by looking for patterns in human behavior that are suddenly broken. What caused the break and why?

The senior author of this book became interested in this problem of broken patterns as it pertains to intimate relationships. Why is it that some relationships that seem to be going very well and peacefully unexpectedly – at least to outsiders – end in a breakup, possibly an acrimonious one, whereas other relationships that seem rife with conflict endure? How can a relationship that seems so harmonious break this pattern and end up in bitterness and acrimony? The author developed a theory of relationships that he came to refer to as the theory of love as a story (Sternberg, 1998b; Sternberg, Hojjat, & Barnes, 2001). According to the theory, almost from the time people are born, they confront many different stories of love. They observe the love stories of their parents, friends of their parents, couples in movies, and couples on television. They read about couples in books. Over time, as the result of an interaction between their experiences and their personality, they start to develop stories of what they believe love should be. These stories then guide their thinking about the kinds of relationships they should or should not be in. Examples of stories are the fairy-tale story, in which one partner seeks a prince and the other a princess; the business story, in which partners each seek a business partner; the war story, in which partners appear to be at war with each other; and the travel story, in which partners seek a traveling companion through life or a part of it.

The research was helpful in suggesting how couples that seem to be doing well can split and couples that seem to be doing poorly can stay together. If two partners both have a war story, for example, then frequent fights may be an integral part of their relationship and even part of what they mean by love. But if one partner has a war story and the other does not, the relationship may not go so well at all. A relationship may seem to be going well but actually be failing. For example, suppose that two partners are happy with each other, in general. They like the way each other looks; they have similar interests; they have similar ethical and religious values; they share political and other beliefs. But one has a fairy-tale story of love and the other a business story. In other words, one is looking for a prince and the other for a business partner. The relationship may initially seem successful because the couple has so much in common, but it may eventually fail because, at a deeper level, each member of the couple is looking for a different thing. So a relationship that can appear to be going well can fail because of conflicting stories, or one that appears to be going poorly can succeed because of comparable stories (such as the war story).

So look for broken patterns in behavior. Often they provide the best ideas you can get for new and exciting research!

**5.** Look for patterns of behavior that are themselves puzzling.

Why are people repeatedly so optimistic when a new political party comes into power, only soon to be disappointed after the party has a chance to perform? Why do some people repeatedly look for romantic partners who bring out the worst in them? Why do people often remember clearly people they met and things they did when they were young, but then forget people they met and things they did just a few years (or even months) ago? Why do some people almost always seem to learn from their mistakes, whereas others seem immune to learning from experience and destined to repeat their mistakes? Sometimes, it is not the break in a pattern but the pattern itself that can be puzzling and worthy of investigation. So look for patterns of behavior that are puzzling. Often people will not investigate such patterns because they get so used to them.

The senior author became interested in anomalous patterns of leadership during a time when corporate scandals seemed to blossom, one right after the other. Scandals at Enron, WorldCom, Global Crossing, Arthur Andersen, Tyco, and other firms all became known at roughly the same time. History repeated itself in 2008 when several major financial institutions, such as Lehman Brothers, Merrill Lynch, and Washington Mutual, all failed around the same time. There was a clear pattern leading to these failures, but what was it, and why had it been hidden until it was too late?

The conclusion the senior author came to is that it is possible to be smart and foolish at the same time (Sternberg, 2002a, 2004). In particular, smart, well-educated people may be not only susceptible to cognitive fallacies but even especially susceptible because they think they are not susceptible. In other words, the weird pattern is that smart people may act more stupidly than stupid people because they think they are not susceptible to acting stupidly. The author identified six cognitive fallacies that seemed to characterize people who had spectacular failures (Sternberg, 2005a). The cognitive fallacies include the following: (a) Unrealistic optimism, in which they believe they are so smart that whatever they do will work out just fine, regardless of whether it really makes sense; (b) egocentrism, in which they start to view decisions only in terms of how the decisions benefit them; (c) omniscience, in which they think they are all-knowing but don't know what they don't know; (d) omnipotence, in which they think they can do whatever they want; (e) invulnerability, in which they think they are so smart they can get away with anything they do; and (f) ethical disengagement, in which they believe that ethical behavior is important for others but not for themselves.

## 6. Think the opposite of what others think.

Is the world flat? Will heavier objects fall more quickly than lighter ones? Is it possible that much of what people think is unconscious rather than conscious? Many of the greatest scientists of all time have made their reputations by defying conventions – by questioning assumptions that others routinely make or by asking questions that others do not ask. The senior author's undergraduate adviser, Endel Tulving, was a master of this technique (e.g., Tulving, 1966). He repeatedly has published groundbreaking articles that shock readers because they turn on their head assumptions people have held throughout their careers. Daniel Kahneman and his collaborator, the late Amos Tversky, researchers on human decision making, also proved themselves to be masters of turning conventional wisdom on its head in their research on decision-making heuristics (e.g., Kahneman & Tversky, 1971, 1979).

Todd Lubart and the senior author proposed a theory of creativity, the investment theory, according to which highly creative people are those who routinely turn things around – who see things in ways others do not see them (e.g., Sternberg & Lubart, 1995). Such people, according to the theory, buy low and sell high in the world of ideas. They defy the crowd, often thinking the opposite of what most others think. Our tests of the theory suggested that, indeed, more creative people are more likely to think in ways that defy convention (Lubart & Sternberg, 1995).

We came up with this idea not because it defied conventions about creativity but in part because it defied conventions about how to test students in college and other admissions situations. Conventional tests of admissions such as the SAT and the ACT test memory and analytical skills, but they do not test creative thinking skills. Our hope was that by testing creative-thinking skills, colleges might see students in a whole new light. More than a decade later, our research found that, indeed, including creative tests in an admissions battery could improve the prediction of freshman grade-point average and decrease average ethnic-group differences (Sternberg & Rainbow Project Collaborators, 2006). The inclusion of creative tests, contrary to conventional beliefs, did improve prediction of college performance.

**7.** Synthesize disparate existing ideas.

Is it possible that love and hate are not opposites or really even wholly opposed to each other but more complexly related? Is it possible that people are not merely intrinsically or extrinsically motivated but some combination of those? Is it possible that people do not use either direct perception or intelligent perception but some combination of those? Are people neither serial nor parallel processors of information but simultaneously serial and parallel processors? Sometimes ideas or concepts are proposed that initially seem incongruent with each other. People assume that the constructs are related to each other in an either-or way. But it may turn out instead that the concepts can be synthesized in a way that is not mutually exclusive.

The two authors of this book have jointly done work on hate that suggests that hate and love are not opposites nor even wholly incompatible with each other; rather, they are more complexly related (Sternberg, 2003; Sternberg & Sternberg, 2008). According to this duplex theory, hate and love have in common that they comprise the three components of intimacy, passion, and commitment. Whereas in love, people feel intimacy toward each other, in hate, they feel negation of intimacy. So intimacy is an opposite. But passion is different. Passion is an intense motivational drive, and the same passion can be labeled in different ways depending on one's beliefs about one's relationship. So the same intense passion can be labeled as "love" or "hate" depending on how one perceives the relationship. It is for this reason that someone who intensely loves someone else and discovers a betrayal may instantaneously go from loving to hating the person. The passion still exists but is not converted and relabeled. Both love and hate also involve commitments but of different kinds. Commitment in love is to tighten bonds, and in hate it is to harm and possibly destroy the hated person or group. So the duplex theory views love and hate as complexly related and synthesizes in a somewhat novel way what had seemed to some to be two opposing constructs.

**8.** Ask yourself what the next question is.

So if love and hate are complexly related, where do liking and disliking fit in? If there are consistent styles of conflict resolution across people, from where did the styles come – if from experiences, then from what kinds of experiences? If people have stories of love, do they also have stories of hate? A useful way to think of ideas for research is to ask yourself what the next question is likely to be, given the answer to the last question you asked: What is the next thing to know?

This is actually what the senior author did when he proposed his balance theory of wisdom (Sternberg, 1998a, 2001), according to which wisdom is the use of one's abilities and knowledge to achieve a common good by balancing one's own, others', and higher order interests over the long and short terms through the infusion of positive ethical values. He had previously proposed a theory of intelligence (discussed previously) that had three parts: creative, analytical, and practical. But he would go out and give talks and particular questions would come up: What about Hitler or Stalin or similar monsters? Were they not creatively, analytically, and practically intelligent? Would they score at the top on what the author was calling "successful intelligence"? So the next question seemed to be, Is there something wrong with or at least missing in a theory that would seemingly put wretched dictators at the top of the heap? This anomaly led the investigator to study wisdom and eventually to propose a theory of leadership, WICS (wisdom, intelligence, creativity, synthesized), which incorporates wisdom (Sternberg, 2007, 2008).

Note that, in this example, the idea came not from the author but from members of audiences to which the author spoke. It behooves you to share your ideas with others in a variety of forums and actively to solicit their feedback, because your idea about what the next question you should ask is may well come from others rather than from yourself!

There is one other important thing to remember. It is very rare that researchers in psychology reach a final answer to any question. It is rare that the next question is the last one. Only once in either of the careers of the authors has either of us come close to resolving a question in the literature. This opportunity arose for the senior author in the Sternberg and Bower (1974) paper on negative transfer cited earlier. The author was still in graduate school and was very proud that he and his adviser had, seemingly, actually resolved an issue: After that paper, few papers were published anymore on the topic, then called negative transfer in part-whole and whole-part free recall. But the author then made a dismaying discovery: When you actually answer a question, you lose the option to do further research on that question, because it is answered. You have to find yourself a new topic to investigate! Fortunately, then, perhaps, neither of us ever again reached anything even approaching a final resolution to a psychological problem!

**9.** Revisit discarded ideas.

Was Sigmund Freud really as off-base as many current clinical theorists think he was? How about Jean Piaget? Behaviorism is not in fashion in many circles, but is it possible that there were ideas there that would still be valuable today? As mentioned previously, very few issues in psychology reach a final resolution. More often, people just get tired of the issues or move on to the next ones. They may reject old paradigms because they find, inevitably, that the paradigms were flawed. But typically, they introduce new paradigms that themselves have flaws, just different ones from the old paradigms. So sometimes it is worthwhile to revisit old ideas and ask whether, when they were discarded, researchers metaphorically threw out the baby with the bathwater.

When the senior author was just starting out, he proposed a model of how people solve problems called linear syllogisms, such as "John is taller than Bill. Bill is taller than Mike. Who is shortest?" (Sternberg, 1980). The model combined linguistic and spatial reasoning processes. The author proposed this model to replace existing models, which were either linguistic (e.g., Clark, 1969) or spatial (e.g., Huttenlocher, 1968). His point was that the older models were out of date and that his model, which synthesized the older models (see the preceding Point 7), was superior to the older ones. But he was wrong. A subsequent study showed that there are individual differences in strategy: Some people use a verbal strategy, some use a spatial strategy, and some use a mixed strategy (Sternberg & Weil, 1980). So when one models the averaged data, the mixed strategy proved to be the best because it best captured what people do on average but not what each individual was doing. In other words, the author was too quick to throw out the past models. In fact, they had validity, and he realized that those models served as valuable sources of insight for follow-up research.

**10.** Look for ideas in everyday models and metaphors.

Which is it: Absence makes the heart grow fonder or out of sight, out of mind? Do people really function like hydraulic systems, as was suggested in Freudian psychoanalysis? Or do they think like computers, as was suggested by early information-processing psychologists like Herbert Simon? Everyday models and metaphors rarely provide precise characterizations of how people think or feel. But they may provide a starting point for understanding human behavior.

The senior author was once riding on a plane to a meeting in Virginia when, seemingly out of the blue, an idea came into his head: Maybe the way people govern or manage themselves is analogous to the way in which governments govern (Sternberg, 1988a, 1997). The idea was that some people are more legislative: They like to legislate – to come up with ideas. Other people are more executive. They like to execute – to be told what to do and then to do it. Still other people are more judicial – they like to judge things and people. Some people are more liberal – they like to do things in new ways. Others are more conservative – they prefer tried and tested ways of doing something. In the end, the theory contained 13 different styles based on the notion of mental self-government. Tests of the theory revealed that the styles provided useful characterizations of how people like to utilize their abilities (Sternberg, 1997a). But the original idea came from taking a model from everyday life – government – and applying it to styles of thinking.

In the first part of this chapter, we have proposed different ways in which you can get ideas for theories and research studies. We wish to emphasize that no one technique will work for everyone and that different people will find different techniques to be useful. Moreover, these are far from the only techniques. The McGuire (1997) paper, mentioned earlier, provides additional techniques. Moreover, books on creativity and innovation will contain other techniques as well. As you go through your career, you will learn what works for you. The important thing is to find ways of generating ideas and then to use them not only to produce ideas but also to enjoy yourself while doing so.

So far, we have concentrated on how you get new ideas. But the creative process actually includes two more steps: deciding whether a new idea is a good idea and then persuading others of the value of the idea. We discuss these two issues next.

## 2.2 EVALUATING YOUR IDEAS

Coming up with an idea is hard. Knowing whether it is a good idea is harder. Worse, there is no failsafe way of knowing whether an idea is good. Here are 12 techniques you can try. Not every idea necessarily has to pass all of the following criteria. But if it doesn't pass most of them, you may wish to reconsider:

| |
|---|
| 1. Is the idea internally consistent? |
| 2. Is the idea empirically testable? |
| 3. Do you have the means to test the idea? |
| 4. Does the idea go beyond what is known? |
| 5. Does the idea fit with what is known? |
| 6. Are you enthusiastic about the idea? |
| 7. Would you be able to persuade other people of the value of the idea? |
| 8. Have you answered what you anticipate to be possible objections to your idea? |
| 9. Is the idea the "right size"? |
| 10. Are others besides yourself likely to find the idea interesting? |
| 11. What do others whose opinions you value actually say about your idea? |
| 12. Could you explain your idea to your grandmother? |

## 1. Is the idea internally consistent?

Make sure that the idea coheres internally – that it does not contradict itself. This point is obvious, but nevertheless, you want to check for coherence.

## 2. Is the idea empirically testable?

Psychology is a science, so its propositions have to be empirically testable. Make sure that there is some way to test the idea you are proposing. If there isn't, it's not science.

## 3. Do you have the means to test the idea?

An idea may be empirically testable, but testing it may require more resources than you either have or would be able to acquire. Make sure the idea is testable within the constraints of what is reasonably possible for you.

## 4. Does the idea go beyond what is known?

Be sure to research the literature reasonably thoroughly before you propose an idea so that you do not end up, metaphorically, reinventing the wheel.

### 5. Does the idea fit with what is known?

Make sure that existing empirical evidence does not contradict the idea, or if it does, be prepared to say why that evidence did not provide an adequate test of your hypothesis.

### 6. Are you enthusiastic about the idea?

Especially early in your career, there is a temptation to get started on research just so you can feel that you got started on research! Research projects generally take quite a bit of time. If you lack enthusiasm for an idea, you are unlikely to give it your best effort, and even small amounts of time will seem like a lot of time.

### 7. Would you be able to persuade other people of the value of the idea?

Remember that other people are often going to be more skeptical of your new ideas than you are. Will you be able to persuade others of the value of the idea so you can get their backing and support?

### 8. Have you answered what you anticipate to be possible objections to your idea?

Elaborating on Point 5, you should ask yourself specifically what kinds of objections others are likely to raise and how you would answer them.

### 9. Is the idea the right size?

Some ideas are very small. They may be reasonable ideas, but they are so narrow or small in scope that they just will not contribute much to knowledge. Some ideas are very large and perhaps complicated. Testing them might require quite a long series of studies. People differ in the size of idea they are comfortable with. Ask yourself whether the idea is too small or too large for your taste.

### 10. Are others besides yourself likely to find the idea interesting?

Science is public. You need to have an audience for your idea. So you have to ask yourself not only whether the idea interests you but also whether it is likely to interest others.

### 11. What do others whose opinions you value actually say about your idea?

It is always worth getting feedback from others. You should not view their feedback as definitive. In the end, you are the one who has to decide whether your idea is good. But at the very least, others may be able to help you improve on your idea.

### 12. Could you explain your idea to your grandmother?

Good ideas may be simple or complex. But if an idea is well formulated, it can be explained, even if in simplified form, to someone without a technical background. If you cannot give a clear and simple explanation of the idea, you need to ask yourself whether you really have a clear conception of what the idea is.

In the end, you are the one who has to decide whether an idea is good and worth pursuing. We hope these techniques are valuable in helping you to decide whether the idea is one that is worthy of your further attention.

## 2.3  SELLING YOUR IDEAS

The ways in which you persuade others of the value of an idea depend on the idea. However, there are some techniques that tend to be useful in a variety of circumstances. Here are 12 such techniques:

| |
|---|
| 1. Present your idea in a way that is crystal clear. |
| 2. Show that your idea is consistent with past research. |
| 3. Present your own research in support of the idea. |
| 4. Neither undersell nor oversell. |
| 5. Don't be dismissive of or insult disbelievers. |
| 6. Show your audience why the idea should be of interest to them. |
| 7. Where possible, tie in your idea with the background and interests of the audience. |
| 8. Be forthcoming about the weaknesses or limitations of your idea as well as about its strengths. |
| 9. If asked a question you cannot answer, admit you do not know and say that you will try to find out. |

10. Show enthusiasm for your idea.

11. Be super- well- organized in your presentation.

12. If at first you don't succeed, try, try again – don't be easily discouraged.

### 1. Present your idea in a way that is crystal clear.

Nothing hurts acceptance of an idea quite so much as a presentation of the idea that is vague, obscure, or confusing. Consider in advance how you can present the idea in a way that is so clear that anyone, or at least almost anyone, in your audience can understand it.

### 2. Show that your idea is consistent with past research.

No matter what your own research may find, people will be interested not just in what you have found but also in the full existing literature. The more you can show that your idea is consistent with past literature, the more likely you are to persuade people of your idea.

### 3. Present your own research in support of the idea.

It always helps if you have empirical data of some kind to support the idea. And make sure that others, and not just you, will see how the data support the idea.

### 4. Neither undersell nor oversell.

If you undersell an idea, people may wonder why they should believe in your idea if you seem hardly to believe in the idea yourself. But if you oversell the idea, people may become offended and question whether you are not being merely self-aggrandizing. In general, it is better to err on the side of more modest claims than on the side of inflated ones.

### 5. Don't be dismissive of or insult disbelievers.

Sometimes, you may find it incredible that others would question your idea. After all, you know it is a great idea – why wouldn't anyone else in his or her right mind see it the same way? But if you are dismissive of or insulting toward disbelievers, you will lose the audience you most want to persuade.

6. **Show your audience why the idea should be of interest to them.**

It may be obvious to you that an idea is interesting. It may not be obvious to your audience. You have to persuade them that it is interesting. That is your job, not theirs. And do not say that your idea or results are "interesting and important." Let your audience say that.

7. **Where possible, tie in your idea with the background and interests of the audience.**

A good presentation is targeted to the audience it attempts to reach. There is no one-size-fits-all paper or talk. You need to tailor your presentation to the audience so that it fits their interests and background knowledge.

8. **Be forthcoming about the weaknesses or limitations of your idea as well as its strengths.**

You will gain much respect from your audience if you show that you recognize the weaknesses of your idea, not just its strengths.

9. **If asked a question you cannot answer, admit you do not know and say that you will try to find out.**

When you present your idea, someone may ask you a question you cannot answer. Don't try to brazen your way through an answer, hoping that the interlocutor won't notice that you are faking it. If you don't know, say so, and if possible, find out the answer and get back to the interlocutor.

10. **Show enthusiasm for your idea.**

If you are not enthusiastic, why would you expect others to be?

11. **Be super well organized in your presentation.**

An idea is more persuasive if it is presented in an organized way, including the idea, past support for it, your new support for it, and so on. When presentations of ideas are disorganized, they tend to be much less convincing.

## 12.  If at first you don't succeed, try, try again – don't be easily discouraged.

We have found that the first time we present a new idea, it often does not fly with our audiences. Give it another try and maybe even a third try. At some point, you may decide that you are not ready to go forward with the idea. But the more creative an idea, the harder it is to persuade others of its value. Persistence makes all the difference.

# 3 | Literature Research

Whether you are writing a literature review or working on an experimental research paper, literature research is an important factor. Nowadays, you can get the information you need in several ways. First, you can consult journals and books that you can find in libraries and archives. Second, you can conveniently use the Internet from your own home or workplace to retrieve an enormous amount of information.

In this chapter, we first describe different kinds of reference materials. We also provide a list of reference materials that may be useful for your research. We then give you an introduction to literature research and some of the databases that you will likely use. Afterward, a section on Internet research gives you an overview of search engines, how best to search for keywords, types of information available on the Internet, and how to evaluate the information you find online. Last, we elaborate on the function of bibliographical software and its use for your research.

## 3.1 REFERENCE MATERIALS

Authors of psychology papers should be aware of the references available to them. There are many different kinds of resources you can consult. Here are some of them:

■ **Almanacs**
Almanacs are annual publications that contain information and statistics on a wide array of topics. *The World Factbook* is an almanac, for example. There are almanacs for many specialized fields, for example, for special education. The entries are sorted according to

general headings, so you may have to think about superordinate topics that belong to your interest to find the information you need.

### ■ Bibliographies

Bibliographies list the works of a certain writer or focus on certain
topics. If you are interested in a particular topic, like the concept of
time in psychology, for example, a bibliography can help you find
literature on this topic.

### ■ Dictionaries

Dictionaries show the correct spellings of words and may list synonyms or alternative words to look up. Similar to encyclopedias, they
often also contain short entries that explain the word. There are general dictionaries and dictionaries that specialize in one subject area,
for example, psychology. There are also specialized dictionaries, such
as of synonyms and antonyms.

### ■ Directories

Directories list resources and contact information for sources that are
of interest to you. For example, there are membership directories of
organizations or directories that help you get an overview of journals
in a field.

### ■ Encyclopedias

There are both general and specialized encyclopedias in which you
can look up keywords of interest. Furthermore, encyclopedias usually
have an index in the back that will refer you to related keywords as
well. When you look up the keyword "risk," for example, you may
find references to "risk assessment," "availability heuristic," "social
dilemmas," and more. The use of such encyclopedias can help you
expand your views on a topic. Citations to encyclopedias are generally
frowned on in professional articles, and often in papers written at the
university level as well. Encyclopedias are more useful for beginning
your research than for final citations.

### ■ Thesauri

A thesaurus lists words that are related to a term. This may be helpful,
for example, when you encounter words with which you are unfamiliar, or if you want to check whether there are related terms that you
have not considered in your research so far.

■ **Yearbooks**

A yearbook contains information that refers to a specific year. Yearbooks usually pertain to narrow fields. There are yearbooks on sport psychology, child psychology, and communication, for example.

Here is a list of general references that may be useful in all areas of psychology:

**APA College Dictionary of Psychology**
This book is a compact version of the *APA Dictionary of Psychology* and has more than 5,000 entries. Its first edition was published in 2009 by the American Psychological Association.

**APA Concise Dictionary of Psychology (abridged)**
This dictionary contains about 10,000 entries as well as a list of major historical figures in psychology. It first appeared in 2008 and was published by the American Psychological Association.

**APA Dictionary of Psychology**
This book defines and explains about 25,000 terms and phrases from psychology as well as other related areas like medicine, biology, and computer science. Its first edition was published in 2006 by the American Psychological Association.

**The Corsini Encyclopedia of Psychology and Behavioral Science, 3rd Edition**
This four-volume encyclopedia offers detailed discussion on 10 areas of psychology, for example, applied, clinical cognitive, developmental, educational, measurement, personality, physiological, social, and history/theory. The volumes, edited by W. Edward Craighead and Charles B. Nemeroff, were last revised in 2002. The publisher is John Wiley & Sons.

**Dictionary of Psychology**
The *Penguin Dictionary of Psychology*, third edition, by A. S. Reber, E. S. Reber, and R. Allen, resolves some of the problems raised by psychological terms. It focuses on what a given technical term means and shows how the term is actually employed, its connotations, and how it has been used and abused. The book appeared in its fourth edition in 2009, published by Penguin Books.

### Dissertations and Theses from Start to Finish: Psychology and Related Fields

*Dissertations and Theses from Start to Finish* discusses some of the nuts and bolts needed to put together a thesis and a dissertation. It was written by J. D. Cone and S. L. Foster; its second edition was published in 2006 by the American Psychological Association.

### Encyclopedia of Psychology

This encyclopedia includes more than 1,500 entries. Editor Alan Kazdin designed the encyclopedia to cover all approaches and all issues in psychology while keeping an eye on past history, current practice, and future development. A sampling of encyclopedia topics are research methods, study design and analysis, assessment, biological and cognitive processes, interactive systems, life-span development, cultural psychology, and clinical psychology. The relationship between psychology and other fields, including medicine, sociology, law, and philosophy, is described in detail. Also included are more than 400 biographies. The "Synoptic Outline of Contents" in the final volume provides a field guide to exploring specific topics using the encyclopedia, guiding the reader to principal entries, entries on related issues, and field surveys. The *Encyclopedia of Psychology* was published by the Oxford University Press in 2000 in collaboration with the American Psychological Association.

### Decoding the Ethics Code: A Practical Guide for Psychologists

*Decoding the Ethics Code* by Celia B. Fisher discusses and explains the ethics code of the American Psychological Association (APA). It delineates standards on different topics like confidentiality, record keeping, advertising, and therapy. The book was published by Sage; its second edition appeared in 2008. The most recent version of the APA ethics code was published in December 2002 and is available at http://www.apa.org/ethics/code2002.html.

### Ethics Desk Reference for Psychologists

The goal of the *Ethics Desk Reference for Psychologists* is to help psychologists recognize ethical dilemmas and circumvent them. It also contains a description of common dilemmas and conflicts. Written by Jeffrey E. Barnett and W. Brad Johnson, the book was published by the American Psychological Association in 2008.

### Ethics in Plain English: An Illustrative Casebook for Psychologists

*Ethics in Plain English* presents the APA ethics code in everyday language. Case studies illustrate how the code applies in practice. Edited by

Thomas Nagy, this book was published by the American Psychological Association and appeared in 2005 in its second edition.

### Graduate Study in Psychology

*Graduate Study in Psychology*, a standard reference that is updated every year, provides complete and current information on more than 600 graduate programs in both the United States and Canada. The book includes information regarding application procedures, admissions requirements, degree requirements, tuition, financial assistance, and considerations of special relevance to applicants from underrepresented groups. The book is published by the American Psychological Association.

### Information Sources in the Social Sciences

The textbook *Information Sources in the Social Sciences* is intended as a guide to references for library-science students and reference librarians. Edited by David Fisher et al., and published by K. G. Saur, the book was last revised in 2002.

### International Encyclopedia of the Social and Behavioral Sciences

The 26 volumes of *International Encyclopedia* represent an ambitious project to describe the state of the art in all the fields within the social and behavioral sciences. It includes more than 4,000 articles indexed by name and subject in 52 sections. The set is edited by N. J. Smelser and P. B. Baltes and was published by Pergamon Press in 2001. You may be able to access this encyclopedia online through your local or university library.

### Literature Research in Psychology: Finding It Easily

This pamphlet was created by the APA to help students and nonpsychologists find relevant research on psychological topics of interest. Topics range from newspaper articles on current topics to detailed articles found in scientific journals. The pamphlet provides a head start in finding where psychological research is published, how it is indexed, and where to go in the library to find different resources. It is available on the Web at http://www.apa.org/science/lib.html.

### Mastering APA Style: Instructor's Resource Guide

*Mastering APA Style: Instructor's Resource Guide*, by Harold Gelfand and Charles J. Walker, is designed to improve students' understanding and use of APA's points of style in their writing before they begin writing the research paper. The guide contains eight multiple-choice assessment surveys, correction keys, and answer sheets, along with informative instructions to incorporate this material into a teaching curriculum. The fourth edition of the guide was published in 2009 by the American Psychological Association.

### Mastering APA Style: Student's Workbook and Training Guide

Used in collaboration with the sixth edition of the *Publication Manual of the APA*, *Mastering APA Style* is a self-pacing, self-teaching workbook that can be used to learn APA style quickly and effectively. The volume contains groups of instructional exercises on various aspects and features of the manual, including references and citations, headings, serialization, statistical and mathematical copy, italics and capitalization, number style, and table format. Its sixth edition was published in 2009 by the American Psychological Association.

### Membership Directory of the American Psychological Association

The *Membership Directory of the American Psychological Association* lists for each member of the APA his or her name, address, telephone number, education, present major field, areas of specialization, certification as a psychologist, diplomate status, and membership status in each relevant division; the association's bylaws; a list of present and past officers of the association; ethical standards; and current data on laws governing the practice of psychology. The directory can be accessed at http://www.apa .org/pubs/databases/directory/index.aspx.

### Preparing for Graduate Study in Psychology: 101 Questions and Answers

Written by William Buskist and Caroline Burke, *Preparing for Graduate Study in Psychology* addresses questions for applicants to graduate psychology programs. Its second edition was published by Wiley-Blackwell in 2006.

### Psychology as a Major: Is It Right for Me and What Can I Do With My Degree?

Written by Donna E. Paladino Schultheiss, *Psychology as a Major* helps students determine whether psychology is the right major for them and what opportunities the field of psychology offers. It was published by the American Psychological Association in 2008.

### Publication Manual of the American Psychological Association, Sixth Edition

The *Publication Manual of the American Psychological Association*, sixth edition, is an indispensable guide to the writing of psychology papers for publication. In the remainder of this book, we will also refer to it as the *APA Manual*. The manual contains chapters on content and organization of a manuscript, writing style, APA editorial style, typing, mailing, proofreading, and the journals of the APA. It also includes a useful bibliography. The manual was revised and published by the American Psychological Association in 2009.

### Science Citation Index

The *Science Citation Index* is an index of who has cited whom in the natural science literature. It includes the fields of natural sciences, medicine, agriculture, technology, and the behavioral sciences. Because of its inclusion of the behavioral sciences, psychologists will find that it largely overlaps with the *Social Science Citation Index*, described herein. The index is published quarterly and is bound into an annual volume. It is published by the Institute for Scientific Information (ISI). The index is available on the Web at the ISI's Web of Science at http://thomsonreuters.com /products_services/science/science_products/scholarly_research_analysis /research_discovery/web_of_science.

### Social Science Citation Index (SSCI)

The *Social Science Citation Index* is an index of who has cited whom in the social science literature. It is organized both by author and by subject cited. Under each author or subject is a list of persons who have made the citation and the location of the citation. The index is updated annually and is published by the ISI. The index is available on the Web at the ISI's Web of Science at http://thomsonreuters.com/products _services/science/science_products/scholarly_research_analysis/research _discovery/web_of_science.

### Standards for Educational and Psychological Testing

*Standards for Educational and Psychological Testing* establishes guidelines for the development, use, and sale of standardized tests. The standards were revised in 1999 by the American Psychological Association.

### Social Science Reference Sources: A Practical Guide

This book gives an overview of references and research resources as well as bibliographies in the social sciences. It was written by Tze-chung Li and published by Greenwood Press. Its third edition appeared in 2000.

**Thesaurus of Psychological Index Terms, 11th Edition**
The *Thesaurus of Psychological Index Terms* contains a compilation of the vocabulary used in psychology and related fields. It is a useful source for those encountering technical terms with which they are unfamiliar. The eleventh edition of the book was published in 2007 by the American Psychological Association.

## 3.2 LITERATURE RESEARCH

Once you have narrowed down your topic, you are ready to search for resources and material at the library. You don't necessarily have to go there in person right away, because most libraries have their catalogs online. In fact, browsing the online catalogs will give you an overview of what is available in your area of interest, help you narrow down your search, and give you a preliminary set of references with which you can begin your research.

Libraries not only have catalogs of the books they own but also can grant you access to many online databases that contain magazines, journals, and newspapers. If you do not know where to start or how to find what you are looking for, you have several possibilities. First of all, you can ask a librarian for help. Today, many libraries also offer several electronic possibilities for you to get in touch with their librarians. You may be able to chat online with a librarian or to submit questions by text message or e-mail. Remember that the more detailed your question is, the more likely it is that the librarian will be able to direct you to the sources that are of help to you.

Generally, the different research tools that libraries offer are the following:

- A **library catalog** in which you can search for the different books, journals, newspapers, and magazines that are available.
- **Databases** in which you can search for keywords, authors, and so on, in databases that contain a large number of journals on one particular subject.
- Libraries often grant you free access to **online journals and newspapers** so you can choose the newspaper or journal of your choice and browse freely through the table of contents and other publications.

In addition, libraries may have **subject guides** and **online tutorials** that can help you with your research. A subject guide in psychology can direct you to databases that help you find books, journals, or assessment instruments, for example.

### 3.2.1 Databases for psychologists

There are a number of databases that are specifically designed for research in psychology and related fields. Here are a few of them:

| | |
|---|---|
| CINAHL | Contains more than 330 English-language journals of nursing and allied fields like social services in health care and health education. It also includes books. |
| ERIC | Education database that includes more than 1 million abstracts of publications in educational research and educational psychology. |
| ProjectMUSE | Database that contains more than 400 journals from more than 100 not-for-profit publishers in diverse fields such as education, gender studies, and cultural studies. |
| JSTOR | JSTOR comprises more than 1,000 journals and other sources focused on the social sciences but also the humanities and natural sciences. |
| PsycInfo | Includes more than 1,300 journals, books, book chapters, and dissertations in the fields of psychology, sociology, education, medicine, and others. The referenced publications are in more than 30 languages. |
| PubMed | This database mainly focuses on medicine and the life and health sciences. |

### 3.2.2 How to find psychological tests

If you are interested in finding a test that has been published, there are several resources you can use to find it:

| | |
|---|---|
| **Tests in Print (TIP),** 7th ed., 2006 Published by the Buros Institute for Mental Measurements, Lincoln, NE | Bibliographic encyclopedia that contains information on every published (and purchasable) assessment instrument in the field of psychology |
| **Mental Measurements Yearbook (MMY),** 17th ed., 2007 Published by the Buros Institute for Mental Measurements, Lincoln, NE | Lists all tests that have been revised or newly developed since the publication of the previous yearbook. Information on prices, authors, psychometric properties, and so on |
| **Tests**, 6th ed., 2008 Published by Pro-Ed, Austin, TX | Bibliographic encyclopedia that contains all tests available in English and describes them in detail |

**Test Critiques**, Vol. 11 2005
Published by Pro-Ed, Austin, TX

Includes additional information on tests such as psychometric properties as well as a critique of each test, contains the most frequently used tests, and is a supplement to *Tests*

Online resources you can use to find tests are the Web sites of the Clearinghouse on Assessment and Evaluation (http://ericae .net), the the Buros Institute of Mental Measurements (http://buros .unl.edu/buros/jsp/search.jsp), and the Educational Testing Service (http://www.ets.org/testcoll).

If you need some more information on how to locate tests (both published and unpublished ones), the American Psychological Association has a helpful Web site that spells out the details on test search. You can find it at http://apa.org/science/faq-findtests.html.

## 3.3 INTERNET RESEARCH

The Internet can be a powerful research tool. It allows easy and quick access to information about a wide range of psychological topics. This access can be very helpful in exploring potential research ideas as well as in gathering background information for writing papers.

There are also pitfalls in using the Internet for research that can mitigate its advantages. For example, although information may be accessed easily and quickly, much of it may be either irrelevant or invalid. Effective use of the Internet requires knowing how to search for information efficiently and how to evaluate the quality of the information that is found. Taking advantage of the Internet's potential as a research tool requires avoiding its pitfalls, as we will see in the following sections.

### 3.3.1 The Components of the Internet

When we speak of the Internet, we are referring to a collection of components that constitute different ways of accessing and sharing information across computers. In assessing the usefulness of the Internet for research purposes, it is important to know the characteristics of the major components:

■ **World Wide Web**
The World Wide Web is a network of computers that allow linking of documents by means of hypertext, links embedded in one document

(a Web page) that provide instant access to files located on different computers.

■ **Usenet/Netnews**

Usenet is a worldwide system of discussion groups, with comments passed among hundreds of thousands of machines. Usenet is completely decentralized and nearly uncensored, with more than 10,000 discussion areas, called newsgroups. Messages are discrete postings to the area; therefore, discussions may occur over weeks or months. Most Internet service providers include access to Usenet discussion groups. The list of current groups and messages can be viewed using major Web browsers, with instructions for subscribing to discussion groups contained in their help files.

■ **Mailing Lists**

Mailing lists, or LISTSERVs, are a system of exchanging e-mail messages among people who subscribe to the same topical forum. When e-mail is addressed to a LISTSERV mailing list, it is automatically broadcast to everyone who subscribes to the list. The result is similar to a Usenet newsgroup or forum, except that the messages are transmitted as e-mail and are therefore available only to individuals on the list. Many psychological organizations maintain LISTSERVs, which can be joined by accessing those organizations' Web sites. Other public LISTSERVs are cataloged at http://www.lsoft.com/catalist.html.

■ **Chat Groups and Instant Messaging**

Chat groups and instant messaging are systems that allow the nearly instantaneous exchange of messages among individuals located on computers that are widely dispersed geographically. Chat groups are usually topically oriented and can be joined by anyone. Chat groups on psychological topics can be located through professional organizations and societies, and they are an increasingly common component of online conferences. Instant messaging systems allow private and intimate online discussions among a small number of individuals. Current versions of major Web browsers have instant message systems as a built-in component.

### 3.3.2 Overview of Internet Searching and Search Engines

The information available on the Internet has been likened to all the pages in all the books in a library being torn out and thrown into a huge pile. The information would still be available, of course, but locating and organizing material on a particular topic would be extremely daunting. Fortunately, this view is overly cynical because effective strategies and tools for locating information exist that can make the task more manageable.

The primary tool for finding specific information on the Internet is the search engine, a software program that provides a list of links to documents and Web pages that contain the keywords specified by the user. The most popular search engines include Google, Yahoo!, AOL, Ask, and Bing. Each of these engines can be accessed using a Web browser and entering the Internet address in the format http://www.searchengine.com, where you replace "searchengine" with the name of the engine you wish to employ. Most users are familiar with one or more of these programs, but few people take full advantage of their features. Here are some tips for effective searching:

**1.** Carefully construct the search phrase.

The search phrase, or query, can greatly influence the relevance and quality of the results, and creating effective phrases requires careful thought and practice. For example, suppose the topic being investigated was spousal abuse in rural settings. What would be a good search phrase? The following are suggestions from an excellent online tutorial by the Bright Planet Software Company (http://www.brightplanet.com/deepcontent/tutorials/Search/):

- use nouns or objects rather than verbs (*abuse* versus *abusing*);
- indicate exact phrases by using quotes ("spouse abuse");
- include synonyms of key concepts, using Boolean operators if required by the specific search engine (spouse OR "intimate partner"; "domestic abuse" OR violence OR assault); and
- order concepts with the main subject first ("loving spouse" OR "intimate partner"). Note that the syntax for combining words in a search phrase may vary somewhat from engine to engine – consult the help section of the search engine for details.

**2.** Use more than one search engine.

Search engines differ in the breadth of their search, how they order the search results, how up to date the links are that are listed; and therefore, the same search phrase entered into two search engines may not return the same list of links. Also, consider using a meta–search engine, which automatically queries several search engines and eliminates duplicate links, such as Vivisimo or Dogpile. You can access any of these by using the same address method suggested previously for single-source search engines.

**3.** Limit your search to certain domains.

Most search engines allow the search to be restricted to certain domains (e.g., .org, .edu, .gov). This restriction can be useful for maximizing the relevance of links that are identified. For example, suppose the researcher wanted to locate government-sponsored reports on the subject of spousal abuse in rural settings. The search phrase could be entered with the restriction that only links with .gov be listed. Check the search engine's help page for the exact format of a restricted search.

**4.** Search for links to a specific document.

Imagine in the foregoing example that a restricted search of the .gov domain leads to a site that is particularly informative. Other sites that are linked to it might be informative as well, and most search engines allow a search for linked sites. This strategy is the Internet equivalent of using citation indices in searching for printed materials. A related approach involves taking an exact phrase from one document and using it as a search query. For example, a government report on intimate partner violence contained the sentence "Intimate partners committed fewer murders in each of the 3 years 2007, 2008, and 2009." Inserting this phrase as a search query will locate other Internet documents that used the same reference.

### 3.3.3 Excursion: Internet Search Using Boolean Logic

Many of the databases on the Internet can be searched most efficiently by using the principles of Boolean logic. Boolean logic was named after George Boole, who was a British mathematician and philosopher. It concerns the logical relationships among a number of search terms. There are three operators: AND, OR, and NOT. You can also combine them or use symbols to represent Boolean operators (implied logic). Here is a short explanation of how each of these concepts works:

1.  **AND**

    Assume that you are interested in finding out more about how noise impairs concentration. The keywords for your search are therefore "noise" and "concentration." You are not interested in articles that deal with noise alone or that are solely about concentration. In fact, you need search results that include both of your keywords. You can ensure that your results include both "noise" and "concentration" by connecting them with AND, so that you enter into the search engine "noise AND concentration."

2.  **OR**

    Imagine that you are interested in the general topic of headaches and migraines. You would like to retrieve any documents that contain either the word *headache* or the word *migraine*. Therefore you enter "headache OR migraine" into the search engine. Your retrieved results will be much broader than if you had entered "headache AND migraine" because in the latter case you would have retrieved only documents that contain both words, whereas a search with OR gets you all documents that contain the words *migraine, headache*, or both.

3.  **NOT**

    If you are interested in the general topic of headaches, but not migraines specifically, you can exclude documents in your search that contain the word *migraine*. To do that, enter the search term "headache NOT migraine." This way, no article about headaches that also contains the word *migraine* will be shown in your list of results.

4.  **Combined operators**

    You can also conduct more complicated searches by combining several operators. If you are interested in violence in connection with hate or prejudice, you could enter the search term "violence AND (hate OR prejudice)." This search will retrieve any document that contains the word *violence* as well as one or both of the words *hate* and *prejudice*. This search option may be available only on the advanced search page, depending on the search engine you use. If you want to conduct a more specific search, you are well advised to check out the advanced search page of your search engine. It may give you many more options, for example, to search only for Web pages with the extension .edu.

5. Implied logic

Today, search engines often use implied logic, meaning that when you enter more than one search term, they automatically default to either the AND operator or the OR operator. To which of the two the search engine defaults depends on which engine you are using; in most cases, the default will be AND. So, if you enter the search term *headache migraine* and the search engine defaults to AND, you will retrieve documents that contain both the words *headache* and *migraine*. If you would like to use the NOT logic, usually you can put a minus sign in front of the word that you want to exclude from your search. The search term "headache -migraine" will retrieve documents that contain the keyword "headache" but not the keyword "migraine.

### 3.3.4 Some Specific Types of Useful Online Research Information

There are several types of valuable online information that might not be located using a general search strategy of the sort described previously. Some of these are proprietary but are available through public computer systems at libraries and universities that have paid for access to the information source. Check with a librarian to see what resources may be available in your situation.

■ **Journal articles**
Full texts of articles published in major psychology journals can be searched and viewed online using PsycINFO and other databases. Many of these databases are purchased by universities and some public library systems.

■ **Magazine and newspaper articles**
Most major magazines and newspapers have Web sites that allow free searches of past articles. The search engines available on these sites function in much the same way as the major search engines, and the same tips for using them effectively apply.

■ **Government databases**

Many online databases are maintained by the U.S. government, including archives of the *Congressional Record*, Supreme Court decisions, crime statistics, and reports of various government agencies. A number of these databases can be accessed and searched through the U.S. government Web site FedWorld (http://www.fedworld.gov). The advanced search option allows searches of federal and specific state government databases.

■ **Home pages of specific researchers**

A useful source of information can be the individual home page of a researcher in your field of interest. Researchers usually list their own publications and presentations on the topic, and sometimes provide links to other relevant information. You can locate home pages by conducting a general Internet search using a researcher's name as the search phrase or by going to the Web site of the individual's academic institution and searching there. Alternatively, many directories of professional society memberships, such as the American Psychological Association and the Association for Psychological Science, provide Web site addresses for their members.

■ **Popular Internet sites for research resources**

There are a number of organizational Web sites that have useful information for researchers. For example, the American Psychological Association's Web site (http://www.apa.org) can be searched for short research articles on a variety of topics. The Association for Psychological Science's site (http://www.psychologicalscience.org) contains a compendium of links to university psychology departments, psychology organizations, and sites that provide tips and resources for conducting research and writing reports. The Social Psychology Network (http://www.socialpsychology.org) maintains links to individual home pages of psychologists, as well as links to research and teaching resources, including tips on writing in APA style, conducting data analysis, and so on.

### 3.3.5 Critical Evaluation of Internet-Based Information

Relying on information obtained from an Internet search without critically evaluating its quality can be very risky. Much of the information on the Internet has not been subject to the same publishing standards or filters as material found in major scientific journals, books, and newspapers.

Almost anyone can post information to the Internet without checks on its reliability and accuracy. The result is that a great deal of misinformation exists on the Internet – information that seems legitimate but is factually incorrect or incomplete. Misinformation is not necessarily intentionally misleading; it is more likely the result of the author's carelessness or ignorance. However, the ease and low cost of creating Web sites has also led to many sites where the intent is not so much to provide information as to persuade readers to hold a particular belief or point of view, and the lack of checks on objectivity may make it difficult to tell the difference. Information intended to persuade the audience is called propaganda. In some cases, attempts to be persuasive may include deliberate distortions or fabrications of information – often referred to as disinformation. For online examples and comparisons of misinformation, propaganda, and disinformation, see the Information and Its Counterfeits Web site maintained by Johns Hopkins Library at http://www.library.jhu .edu/researchhelp/general/evaluating/counterfeit.html.

The existence of misinformation, propaganda, and disinformation on the Internet means that researchers must carefully evaluate material that might be used in a particular project. There are several criteria for evaluating information that can be adapted to the Internet (see Alexander & Tate, 1999). The following is adapted from online material provided by librarians at Widener University (http://www.widener.edu/libraries/wolfgram/evaluate), New Mexico State University (http://lib.nmsu.edu/instruction/eval.html), and Johns Hopkins University (http://www.library.jhu.edu/researchhelp /general/evaluating/):

## ■ Accuracy
It is difficult to determine the accuracy of information when you are not an expert on the topic. However, certain indicators can help you assess the likelihood that Internet material is accurate. Does the author indicate the source of the information, and is the source public so that it can be accessed and verified? Are there fact checkers and editors who may have screened the document (probably so for an online journal article or newspaper article but probably not for a personal home page)?

### ■ Authority

Is the author and publishing body of the Internet document indicated? Are the credentials of the author given, or is there a way to locate and evaluate them? If the publishing body is indicated (e.g., an organization or educational institution), is it reputable? If the document is found on a university server (i.e., has an .edu domain), is the page sponsored by the institution itself, or is it the personal home page of the author? If the author is not someone you recognize as an authority on the topic, do others refer to the work in a positive way? Can you find links to the document from authors you do know and trust?

### ■ Objectivity

What is the point of view or bias of the document or the Web site? Is the author a person or organization with a stake in the issue you are researching? Does the document reside on the server of an organization that has a political or philosophical agenda? Is the author motivated to present information selectively or perhaps to distort it? Sometimes these questions are easy to answer, but often the motivation and bias in a document may not be clear. For example, do not assume that all documents residing on a university server or authored by doctorate holders are bias free. Academics may have strong points of view that influence their interpretation of information just as anyone else does. Perhaps the question is not whether a document is objective but to what degree the presentation of information is biased and in what ways.

### ■ Currency

How recent or up to date is the information that the site provides? In a fast-moving field of research, articles just a few years old may need to be supplemented by newer findings that change the conclusions about a topic. It can be important, then, to know the currency of the Internet information you are using. Is there a publication or last-modified date indicated on the document? Are there references in the document to the dates on which data were collected? If the author refers to published works, how recent are the dates?

### ■ Coverage

How thoroughly or deeply does the document deal with the topic? Does it provide background information and references that seem appropriately extensive? Has the author demonstrated the connection of his or her work to other research and theory? Assessing coverage allows you to determine the unique contribution and value of the author's document.

It is possible to practice applying these criteria to Web sites and Internet documents. Alexander and Tate at Widener University have collected examples of Internet documents and Web sites that illustrate variations on each of the criteria (http://www3.widener.edu /Academics/Libraries/Wolfgram_Memorial_Library/Evaluate_Web _Pages/Actual_Web_Pages_as_Examples/5722/). They also provide examples of special types of Web sites, such as those that blend advertising with information and those that subtly advocate political or philosophical causes. Another excellent source of examples is Susan Beck's Web site "The Good, the Bad, and the Ugly" (http://lib .nmsu.edu/instruction/eval.html). Beck provides examples of each criterion, as do Alexander and Tate, but she also presents sets of links to Internet material on four different topics (i.e., smoking and tobacco use, AIDS, immigration, and drugs). The links for each topic vary in quality, and the viewer must decide which criteria are most relevant – it is a very realistic exercise. Research by Dietz-Uhler (2002) has shown that students who work through Beck's examples are significantly more confident and critical evaluators of Internet information.

## 3.4 BIBLIOGRAPHY SOFTWARE

When you do literature research, it is important for you to keep an overview of all the different sources you have found. After all, when writing your paper, you will need to look up different facts again that you read about but may only roughly remember. You also have to give references in your paper so that interested readers can look up the sources you cited. One way to stay organized while doing literature research and writing your paper is to use bibliographical software. There are several different programs like EndNote, Reference Manager, and CiteULike. The former two are software available for purchase, and the latter one is a free online service to search and manage literature. You may be able to get bibliographical software for free or at a reduced price through your university. Generally, bibliographical software lets you perform a lot of different functions.

You may be able to search the Internet with your software and import the references that are of interest to you. You can insert references from the software into your paper, and the software automatically inserts a complete bibliography at the end of your paper, formatted in the style you choose (e.g., APA style). In many programs, you can also electronically store a copy of the article.

# 4 | Writing a Literature Review

Most undergraduate research papers, and many graduate and professional research papers as well, are based on literature reviews. The aims of a literature review are different from those of an empirical research paper, and hence the skills required differ somewhat as well. The goals of literature reviews are the following (American Psychological Association, 2009):

1. To define and clarify problems
2. To inform the reader about a subject by summarizing and evaluating studies
3. To identify inconsistencies, gaps, contradictions, and relationships in the literature
4. To suggest future steps and approaches to solve the issues identified

There are five kinds of literature reviews that can be distinguished on the basis of the aim of the review. Reviews can strive to (a) generate new knowledge, (b) test theories, (c) integrate theories, (d) develop a new theory, or (e) integrate existing knowledge.

If you plan to submit your literature review to a journal and have to decide where to submit it, you may want to read some literature reviews that have been published in the journals you are considering to find out whether your paper is a good fit to the journal. Generally, the probability of an article being accepted is highest when you develop new knowledge, a new theory, or integrate several theories (instead of just reviewing and summarizing the literature on a particular topic) (Eisenberg, 2000). In general, the best literature reviews do not merely summarize literature; they also create new knowledge by placing the literature into a new framework or at least seeing the literature in a new way.

The literature review can proceed smoothly if you follow a sequence of simple steps:

1. Decide on a topic for a paper.
2. Organize and search the literature.
3. Prepare an outline.
4. Write the paper.
5. Evaluate the paper yourself and seek others' feedback on it.

## 4.1 DECIDING ON A TOPIC FOR A PAPER

Your first task is to decide on a topic for a paper. This is, in a sense, the most important task because the paper can be no better than the topic. We have found five mistakes that repeatedly turn up in writers' choices of topics:

1. The topic doesn't interest the writer.
2. The topic is too easy or too safe for the writer.
3. The topic is too difficult for the writer.
4. There is inadequate literature on the topic.
5. The topic is too broad.

### 1. The topic doesn't interest the writer.

Many writers put off thinking about their choice of topic until the latest possible date. They then find themselves pressed to select a topic and hastily decide on something that is of only marginal interest to them. Procrastination in thinking about a topic is a mistake because interesting topics do not often pop into your head overnight. So allow yourself plenty of time to think of a topic. Then, if you are unhappy with the first few ideas that come to mind, you can try out others before you resign yourself to a topic that doesn't interest you. Unless you are at least somewhat interested in the topic you pick, you will find the exercise of doing literature research a deadly bore, and your paper will probably show it. We are convinced that a major determinant of quality is the degree of interest the writer sustains in the topic about which he or she writes.

## 2. The topic is too easy or too safe for the writer.

The purpose of literature reviews often is for the writer, and especially for student writers, to learn something about some topic. It is therefore to writers' advantage to select a topic with which they are relatively (although not necessarily totally) unfamiliar. Writers sometimes seek to optimize safety (or grades) rather than learning, however, thereby choosing a topic with which they are quite familiar.

The senior author saw an example of such a choice one year in his Theories of Intelligence course. A student showed in class that she was quite familiar with the literature on creativity in children, perhaps because she had previously written a paper on it. Her remarks in class also showed, however, that she had little background in other areas covered by the course. The senior author was therefore disappointed when she proposed to write a paper on creativity in children. Although she probably could learn something from writing such a paper, it was clear that she had more to gain by selecting a topic from one of the many areas in which she had little background.

## 3. The topic is too difficult for the writer.

The opposite problem from the previous one is the selection of a topic that is too difficult for the writer. In the Theories of Intelligence course, the senior author also had a student write a paper on the heritability of intelligence. The student was obviously interested in the topic and wanted to do a good job, but he found that most of the literature went over his head. Understanding the literature on inherited traits requires a knowledge of certain advanced statistical concepts that most undergraduates have not yet encountered. Consequently, it is not easy or perhaps even possible for most of them to write a really sophisticated paper on this topic, unless they are prepared to learn the necessary statistics. This task is both difficult and time consuming. In general, you should make certain that the topic you choose does not require an understanding of concepts that your background does not permit you to grasp.

## 4. There is inadequate literature on the topic.

For various reasons, some of the potentially most interesting topics in psychology have been little investigated. In some cases, people simply haven't thought much about the topics; in other cases, they have thought about the topics but have found that the topics did not lend themselves to experimental (or other types of) analysis. These topics are not suitable for literature reviews. Before committing yourself to a topic, make sure that there is adequate literature on it. As a student, the senior author was interested in how people understand proverbs. The topic seemed to deal with a psychologically important function (one that is tested in several intelligence tests) and seemed to have considerable real-world relevance. He found almost no relevant experimental literature, however. Although there was more literature on related topics, such as metaphor, it was obvious that his tentative choice of a paper topic would have to be changed because there was not sufficient relevant literature.

## 5. The topic is too broad.

Perhaps the most common mistake that writers make in selecting a topic is to select one that is too broad. This problem is understandable because, before writing the paper, writers often have only a vague idea of how much literature has been published on a given topic. Textbooks usually only scratch the surface. As a result, it is not until one delves into primary sources that one discovers the full extent of the relevant literature.

Once you tentatively decide on a topic, it is a good idea to start compiling a list of references and to scan some of these references quickly before you start taking notes in preparation for writing the paper. By following this procedure, you avoid the pitfall of too broad (or too narrow) a topic. By narrowing your topic before you start note taking, you save yourself the time wasted on taking notes that later will prove of no use in writing the paper.

If you have settled on a topic that proves to be too broad, you should consider ways you can narrow the topic without abandoning it altogether. Consider as an example the topic of problem solving. A search of the available references quickly reveals that this topic is too broad. This topic (and others) might be narrowed in any of several ways:

1. **Restriction by age.** The review is limited to problem solving in adults or children or infants.
2. **Restriction by species.** Only problem solving in humans or in rats is considered.

3. **Restriction by clinical type.** The review deals with problem solving by people who lack mental handicaps or by people with mental handicaps.

4. **Restriction by psychological perspective.** The review is of the behaviorist, information-processing, or psychometric approach to problem solving, or the review compares those perspectives and deals only with issues that are relevant to the comparison.

5. **Restriction by content.** The review deals only with the solution of verbal, mathematical, or spatial problems.

There are obviously many ways in which you can limit the scope of your topic. The best way will depend on the topic, the available literature on the topic, and your interests. Be sure to state in the opening paragraphs of your paper what restrictions you have imposed. A good title will also help the reader understand how you have limited your topic.

## 4.2  ORGANIZING AND SEARCHING THE LITERATURE

When you conduct a literature review, you obviously will end up with a large number of papers containing much information. You will need somehow to organize that information to write a meaningful review. We have found it useful to organize the collected information in two ways: with regard to authors and with regard to topics.

### 4.2.1  Author Notes

You can create virtual index cards on the computer that record all the information you will later need to compile the references for your paper. Alternatively, you can use software for the management of bibliographies, such as EndNote (see Chapter 3). The advantage of using such a program is that it contains fields for the necessary information so you cannot forget or lose track of any information about the reference that you might later need. Once you write the paper, the software can also format your references according to APA style (as well as many other styles). In any case, when doing your literature research, you should document each source. The form of documentation differs somewhat depending on the nature of the source.

1. Journal articles

   Your documentation for journal articles should include (a) the author's last name as well as first and middle initials (or whatever appears in the authorship of the article), (b) the year of publication, (c) the title of the article, (d) the name of the journal, (e) the volume number, and (f) the page numbers of the article. A sample author note would look like this:

   Barden, J., & Petty, R. E. (2008). The mere perception of elaboration creates attitude certainty: Exploring the thoughtfulness heuristic. *Journal of Personality and Social Psychology, 95*(3), 489–509.

2. Books

   Your documentation for books should include (a) the author's last name and first and middle initials, (b) the year of publication, (c) the title of the book, (d) the city in which the book was published, and (e) the name of the publisher. If the city of publication is not well known, include the state as well. Include the country if the city is not in the United States and is not well known. For publishers in Canada or Australia, include the name of the province (e.g., Saskatchewan) in which the work was published. For example:

   Zimbardo, P. G. (2007). *The Lucifer effect: Understanding how good people turn evil.* New York: Random House.

3. Edited Books

   Your documentation for articles in edited books should include (a) the author's or authors' last name and first and middle initials (or whatever is used by the author or authors), (b) the year of publication, (c) the title of the book chapter, (d) the editor of the book, (e) the title of the book, (f) the pages of the book in which the chapter appears, (g) the city in which the book was published, and (h) the name of the publisher. For example:

   Bandura, A. (2004). The role of selective moral disengagement in terrorism and counterterrorism. In F. M. Moghaddam & A. J. Marsella (Eds.), *Understanding terrorism: Psychosocial roots, consequences, and interventions (pp. 215-235).* Washington, DC: American Psychological Association.

Although this system of documentation may appear cumbersome when you do your research, it will have several advantages later on:

1. **You will have a complete set of references.** There is no possibility of forgetting any sources you need, because you recorded all your sources at the one time when you can't forget them – the time you used them.
2. **You will have complete documentation for each reference.** Researchers sometimes keep a complete list of references but fail to keep complete documentation on each reference. They must then relocate the references later on – if they can find them – to complete the documentation.
3. **The "References" section of the paper will be all but done.** When you are ready to complete this section, simply reorder the author list alphabetically and use the information from the list.

### 4.2.2 Topic Notes

You should record on each note card (a) the name of the topic at the top, (b) information about that topic, (c) the source of each item of information, and (d) comments.

Sort your notes according to the topic. Each time you encounter a new topic on which you want to take notes, start a new section of note cards. You will save time later on if you avoid multiple entries that express the same topic in different ways. For example, the topics *Rorschach test* and *inkblot test* can be combined (unless more than one inkblot test is used).

Your notes on each topic should be comprehensive enough so that you will not have to return to your sources later. Avoid extraneous words that convey no useful information. In taking notes on arguments, make sure you capture the gist of the arguments so that later you can reconstruct the author's point of view.

For each statement you compile, record the source by writing down the author's last name and the date of publication. If you make a direct quotation or paraphrase, be sure to indicate this fact in your notes and cite appropriate page numbers.

When you make comments on a source or the information supplied in it, indicate clearly in your notes that the comment is yours and not the author's. The best time to make comments on what you read is often when you read it, because at that time, the material and its context are freshest in your mind. These comments will be valuable to you later on, because you will be expected in your paper to evaluate information as well as to summarize it. In reading through psychological literature, you should be constantly evaluating five characteristics of the author's arguments:

## 1. Validity of arguments

On what basis does the author make each argument? Are the arguments properly substantiated? How? Almost any psychologist who has reviewed papers for a journal (or read student papers) becomes very sensitive to the question of proper validation. A surprisingly common ploy is for an author to present a theory, which may well be plausible; design an experiment or marshal evidence to test some other theory, which also may be plausible; and then conclude that the original theory is correct. In reading an article or book, therefore, assure yourself not only that a test of a theory is a strong one but also that it assesses the proper theory.

## 2. Internal consistency of arguments

Are the arguments consistent, or do they contradict each other? Are the arguments consistent with the author's general point of view? Whereas with validity you are concerned primarily with the relationship between arguments and facts, with internal consistency you are concerned primarily with the relationship between arguments and other arguments. Authors are often unaware of internal inconsistencies in their own data. As a result, readers sometimes spot contradictions that authors have lived with for many years, blithely unaware of their existence.

## 3. Presuppositions of arguments

What does the author presuppose in making each argument; especially, what presuppositions does the author make that he or she does not communicate to readers or may not even be aware of? Are the presuppositions realistic? Do the presuppositions strengthen or weaken the impact of the argument? Consider, for example, the statement: "The Bozo theory of cognitive development is incorrect because it is based on the assumption that cognitive development is continuous."

What presuppositions does the statement make? First, it presupposes that the Bozo theory assumes continuity in cognitive development. Second, it presupposes that the theory making this assumption is incorrect. Third, it presupposes (incorrectly, as it turns out) that there is such a theory as the Bozo theory of cognitive development.

### 4. Implications of arguments

What are the implications of each argument; especially, what implications does the author overlook? Do the implications strengthen or weaken the impact of the argument? Are these implications consistent with others reached from other arguments, both in the same paper and across the literature? Consider, for example, this statement: "I violently object to violent objections." What is the obvious implication of the statement?

### 5. Importance of arguments

Is a particular argument an important one, and therefore one you will want to describe in detail in your paper? Or is it unimportant, and hence not worthy of mention, or worthy of mention only in passing? A common flaw in papers is to emphasize all arguments equally, regardless of their importance. This flaw inevitably reduces the impact of the paper as a whole.

By keeping in mind these five criteria for evaluating the literature you read, and by writing down your evaluative comments immediately subsequent to the relevant argument, you will supply yourself with much of the substance you will later need to write your paper. Later on, of course, you can always expand on or change your evaluation. But you will have your evaluative notes from the topic cards to work with rather than having to start from scratch.

By compiling topic notes, you will gain several advantages: First, when you are ready to write your paper, you will have available to you all the information you need to write it. You won't have to do any more library work at the last minute when you may no longer have time to do it. Second, you will have available to you the source of each argument or piece of information. You won't have to try to remember who said what. Third, you will find it easier to organize your paper than you might have otherwise. The reason for this greater ease is that the topic cards form the input to the next step, preparing an outline.

## 4.3 PREPARING AN OUTLINE

### 4.3.1 Use of Topic Notes

After you have finished note taking, you are ready to prepare an outline. The topic notes form the basis of the outline, because they readily can be used as headings and subheadings. Write down all the topics on one or more pieces of paper. Then, cut out strips of paper, one for each topic. Or, if you are using a computer, you can use an outlining feature that is available in most word-processing programs. Your job now is to rearrange the topics to form a logical order of presentation. The various topics need not and should not be at the same level of specificity. Some of the topics form major headings, others form minor headings, and others are nested under these minor headings. You may have to add introductory and concluding sections to the outline, as well as any intermediate headings that are needed for smooth transitions. The lowest level of subordination for each heading should represent a single sentence of the final paper.

### 4.3.2 Types of Outlines

Once you have ordered the headings of your outline, you must decide on one of three ways in which you can complete the outline (Harris & Blake, 1976). We will discuss the three kinds of outlines with reference to a miniature example in which we will compare two personality tests, the Thematic Apperception Test (TAT) and the Minnesota Multiphasic Personality Inventory (MMPI).

#### 4.3.2.1 The Keyword Outline

In this kind of outline, you restrict yourself to keywords at each level of description. For example:

        I. Introduction
       II. Content
           A. TAT: pictorial
           B. MMPI: verbal
      III. Administration
           A. TAT: oral
           B. MMPI: written

IV. Scoring
   A. TAT: subjective
   B. MMPI: objective
V. Conclusion

### 4.3.2.2 The Topic Outline

In this kind of outline, you use phrases and clauses at each level of description. For example:

I. Comparison between the TAT and MMPI
II. Type of content
   A. TAT: pictures of people in various settings, some realistic and others not
   B. MMPI: statements describing behaviors or beliefs that subjects mark as true or false as descriptions of themselves
III. Mode of administration
   A. TAT: pictures sequentially presented by examiner to subject, who supplies a narrative of events leading to, during, and following from the pictured scene
   B. MMPI: booklet containing entire set of statements given to subjects, who proceed through the booklet at their own pace
IV. Method of scoring
   A. TAT: scored subjectively, often using Murray's taxonomy of needs and press
   B. MMPI: scored objectively by means of a separate key for each diagnostic scale
V. Differences: content, administration, scoring

### 4.3.2.3 The Sentence Outline

In this kind of outline, you use complete sentences at each level of description. For example:

I. This outline compares the TAT and MMPI with respect to content, administration, and scoring.
II. The tests differ in type of content.
   A. The TAT consists of a series of pictures of people in various settings, some realistic and others not.

    B. The MMPI, however, consists of a series of statements describing behaviors or beliefs that subjects mark as either true or false as descriptions of themselves.

III. The tests also differ in mode of administration.

    A. In the TAT, pictures are sequentially presented by the examiner to the subject, who supplies a narrative of events leading to, during, and following from the pictured scene.

    B. In the MMPI, a booklet containing the entire set of statements is given to subjects, who proceed through the booklet at their own pace.

IV. Finally, the tests are scored by different methods.

    A. The TAT is scored subjectively, often using Murray's taxonomy of needs and press.

    B. The MMPI is scored objectively by means of a separate key for each diagnostic scale.

V. In conclusion, the tests differ substantially in content, administration, and scoring.

### 4.3.3  Choosing a Type of Outline

You should use the type of outline that most facilitates your writing. People vary according to which type of outline they find most facilitates their writing. Some people find a keyword outline most helpful because it organizes their thoughts while leaving them maximum flexibility in actually writing the paper; others find a keyword outline too sparse in content to be of much use. Some people like a sentence outline because it essentially writes their paper for them; others find a sentence outline time consuming to write and of no greater use in organizing their thoughts than a topical outline. By experimenting with all types of outlines, you will learn from your own experience which is most suitable for you.

### 4.3.4  Organization of Outlines

Outlines can be organized in many ways, and many decisions regarding organization are unique to each particular situation. Generally, the organization of your paper should be logical and straightforward; you should lead your reader from one point you make to the next, and so on. Don't organize your paper around individual studies but around models or viewpoints. Five principles of organization are common to all outlines and the papers that evolve from them:

■ **The organization should include a beginning, a middle, and an end, in which you say what you're going to say, then say it, and then say what you've said.**

When readers begin a paper, they need some general statements that tell them what the paper is about and how it is organized; without this orientation, they may become lost almost as soon as they start the paper. When readers complete the main part of the paper, they need a summary of the main ideas as well as whatever final comments you want to supply; without this review, readers may not realize what you consider to be your main points.

Suppose that the keyword outline presented earlier consists only of a middle section:

    I. Content
        A. TAT: pictorial
        B. MMPI: verbal
    II. Administration
        A. TAT: oral
        B. MMPI: written
    III. Scoring
        A. TAT: subjective
        B. MMPI: objective

The reader of a paper based on this outline would encounter immediately a comparison between the content of the TAT and the MMPI, without any idea of what the paper intends to accomplish or how it intends to accomplish it. The reader would finish the paper without any idea of what the author believed to be the main points or of what conclusions the author wanted to draw. Although the main body of the paper is well organized, the reader is left with no sense of direction or purpose in the paper.

■ **Once you decide on a principle of organization, stick with it.**

Beginning writers often change their way of organizing papers midstream, usually without first informing the reader that the change is about to take place. The change confuses the reader. If you must change your organization principle, be sure to let the reader know. But avoid the change if possible. Consider the plight of the reader faced with a paper based on the keyword outline at the left here. The original keyword outline is reproduced at the right:

| | |
|---|---|
| I. Introduction | I. Introduction |
| II. Content | II. Content |
|    A. TAT: pictorial |    A. TAT: pictorial |
|    B. MMPI: verbal |    B. MMPI: verbal |
| III. TAT | III. Administration |
|    A. Administration: oral |    A. TAT: oral |
|    B. Scoring: subjective |    B. MMPI: written |
| IV. MMPI | IV. Scoring |
|    A. Administration: written |    A. TAT: subjective |
|    B. Scoring: objective |    B. MMPI: objective |
| V. Conclusion | V. Conclusion |

Notice that the outline at the left switches its principles of organization, beginning with topic III. Topic II is organized by theme, whereas topics III and IV are organized by test. The outline at the left makes obvious what the careless writer hopes will remain hidden – that the paper is confusing and the author is confused.

■ **Organize your writing thematically.**

Thematic organization enhances the clarity of a paper. The keyword outline as originally presented was organized thematically. The three themes were content, administration, and scoring. The reader would complete a paper based on this outline with a clear idea of how the TAT and MMPI differ in these three respects. Compare this original outline, presented at the right, to the new outline presented at the left. This new outline is organized by test:

| | |
|---|---|
| I. Introduction | I. Introduction |
| II. TAT | II. Content |
|    A. Content: pictorial |    A. TAT: pictorial |
|    B. Administration: oral |    B. MMPI: verbal |
|    C. Scoring: subjective | III. Administration |
| III. MMPI |    A. TAT: oral |
|    A. Content: verbal |    B. MMPI: written |
|    B. Administration: written | IV. Scoring |
|    C. Scoring: objective |    A. TAT: subjective |
| IV. Conclusion |    B. MMPI: objective |
| | V. Conclusion |

The organization by test in the outline at the left is not confusing, but it is inferior to the thematic organization at the right. In the thematic organization, readers can compare the two tests on each theme as they read through the main part of the paper, gradually developing a perspective on how the tests differ. In the organization by test, readers are unable to begin comparing the tests until they are halfway through the main part of the paper. By this time, readers may have forgotten the characteristics of the first test, because they had no motivation to remember them. In reading the section of the paper on the MMPI, readers probably will have to refer back to the section on the TAT to draw a comparison. If readers are unwilling to spend the time or effort doing what the writer should have done, they may never understand the comparison.

The same principle would apply if, say, one wished to compare the viewpoints of Sigmund Freud and Konrad Lorenz on aggression toward oneself, aggression toward others, and aggression toward objects. The preferred way to organize the paper would be by the successive themes of aggression toward self, others, and objects, not by the successive authors, Freud and Lorenz.

There are two exceptions to this principle. The first arises when there are no well-developed themes in the literature you plan to review. Each theorist, for example, may deal with a different set of issues. The second exception arises when your focus is genuinely on the objects of comparison rather than on the themes along which they are compared. In a book presenting theories of personality, for example, the author's emphasis might be on the individual perspective of each theorist rather than on the themes dealt with in each theory.

■ **Organize your outline hierarchically.**

Beginning writers tend to overuse coordination of ideas and to underuse subordination of ideas. If a paper contains a large number of main ideas, the reader will have some difficulty understanding the ideas and more difficulty remembering them. When you find yourself with a large number of main ideas, try to subordinate some of them. You will then communicate the same number of ideas at the same time that you increase the effectiveness with which you communicate them.

Suppose that the keyword outline for the tests had taken this form:

    I. Introduction
    II. TAT content: pictorial
    III. MMPI content: verbal

    IV. TAT administration: oral

    V. MMPI administration: written

    VI. TAT scoring: subjective

    VII. MMPI scoring: objective

    VIII. Conclusion

Notice that this outline is much harder to follow than the original keyword outline because all ideas are presented at the same level, with no subordination. The outline therefore is much less effective in comparing the two personality tests.

■ **Organize for your audience.**

In arranging your outline, it is essential that you keep your audience in mind. The level of description for each topic in the outline should be appropriate for the target audience; level of description that is adequate for one audience may be inadequate for another. Consider, for example, the original keyword outline presented earlier. The introductory heading has no subheadings subordinated under it. Because the lowest level of subordination under each heading represents one sentence, the introduction will be just one sentence in length. A brief introduction of this kind may be adequate for a professional seeking a one-paragraph description of salient differences between the TAT and the MMPI, but it probably is inadequate for someone unfamiliar with personality tests. Such a person requires more orientation to the topic of the exposition. An expanded introduction is therefore appropriate:

    I. Introduction: personality tests

      A. Purpose

      B. General characteristics

      C. Divergences

        1. Personality tests in general

        2. TAT and MMPI in particular

The general reader will now be able to follow the remainder of the exposition.

### 4.3.5 Advantages of Outlines

Students often wonder whether outlines are worth the time and trouble. Using outlines has three advantages that more than offset the extra work they require:

**1. Outlines help you organize your writing.**

In writing the actual paper, organization will be just one of many concerns you have. Because there are so many different things to keep track of in writing the paper, and because your ability to keep track of many things at once is limited, organization will receive only limited attention. Because the organization of a paper is so important, however, it pays to insert a step prior to writing the paper in which you can devote your full attention to organizing the paper.

**2. Outlines prevent omission of relevant topics.**

In doing your research or in compiling your topic notes, you may have inadvertently omitted a topic that you intended or should have thought to include in your paper. Omissions are much easier for the author to spot in an outline than in a paper. They are also much easier to correct before writing of the paper has begun.

**3. Outlines prevent inclusion of irrelevant topics.**

Authors sometimes find that a topic that had seemed relevant to the paper in the early stages of research no longer seems relevant when the research is being organized. Irrelevant material shows itself in an obvious way during preparation of an outline, because the material seems to have no place in the outline. By discovering irrelevancies during preparation of the outline, authors can discard the irrelevancies so that later they do not distract the authors in writing the paper.

## 4.4 WRITING THE PAPER

In writing your literature review, you should keep several points in mind (see also Eisenberg, 2000):

**1. The message.**

Authors of literature reviews are at particular risk of writing long and elaborate papers in which they lose their readers. You have reviewed a large amount of literature that can be confusing at times, so it is all the more important that you provide your readers with a thread throughout your paper and a clear message they can take away from reading your work.

**2. Breadth of review.**

How many publications you include in your review depends on your topic and the goal you want to achieve with writing your paper. Generally, you should discuss a good part of the empirical literature and make sure that different methodological approaches are being considered. You don't have to discuss every study in detail, however. Just make sure that the literature that you do include is in fact relevant to your endeavor.

### 3. Accuracy.

Always pay attention that you do not misrepresent the results of studies you include in your literature review. It is OK to disagree with the author's interpretation of results, however.

### 4. Critique.

It is important to include in your literature review a critique of methods, conclusions, and strengths and weaknesses of the works you reviewed. You should do so not study by study, however, but rather by evaluating entire bodies of work. Remember to be fair and not merely to derogate other people's work.

### 5. The end.

The ending of your literature review should not only summarize findings but also draw new conclusions, point out new explanations, or suggest further steps for the exploration of the problem.

## 4.5 EVALUATING THE PAPER YOURSELF AND SEEKING OTHERS' FEEDBACK ON IT

Once you are finished writing your review, think back to the five criteria for evaluating authors' arguments that were described earlier. Readers of your paper will evaluate your paper by the same (or similar) criteria to those you used to evaluate the papers and books you read.

### 1. Validity

Are your arguments consistent with the literature you reviewed? Have you explained inconsistencies? Have you properly substantiated each of your arguments?

### 2. Internal consistency

Are your arguments consistent with each other? Are they consistent with your general point of view?

### 3. Presuppositions

Have you made clear to the reader what you presuppose? Are your presuppositions reasonable ones that the reader is likely to accept?

Have you discussed the impact of your presuppositions on your conclusions?

### 4. Implications
Have you discussed the implications of your arguments? Are these implications realistic? Do these implications strengthen or weaken your arguments?

### 5. Importance
Have you emphasized your important arguments and conclusions and subordinated the less important ones? Have you explained why you view certain arguments and conclusions as important and others as less so?

By using these five criteria to evaluate your literature review, you will improve its quality. Later, we will consider in more detail some criteria for evaluating the quality of all psychology papers.

## CHECKLIST FOR LITERATURE REVIEWS

- ☐ Does your paper have a clear message?
- ☐ Did you discuss the relevant literature (and no more or less)?
- ☐ Have you checked that you did not misinterpret the results of the studies you included?
- ☐ Have you fairly evaluated the bodies of work included in your review?
- ☐ Does your ending include new conclusions, explanations, or further steps for research?
- ☐ Are your arguments consistent with the literature?
- ☐ Were you able to explain inconsistencies?
- ☐ Are your arguments substantiated?
- ☐ Are your arguments consistent with each other and with your overall message?
- ☐ Have you clarified your presuppositions in the beginning, and are they ones that your readers will likely accept?
- ☐ Have you stated the implications of your arguments, and are they realistic?
- ☐ Have you organized your arguments and conclusions into more and less important ones, and have you explained why they differ in their importance?

# 5 | Planning and Writing the Experimental Research Paper

When research psychologists talk about writing a paper, they are talking about a lengthy and complicated chain of events that includes a great deal more than just reporting research results. In this chapter, we outline these events from start to finish:

1. Planning your experimental research project
   - Getting an idea
   - Selecting independent variables
   - Selecting dependent variables
   - Deciding on between-subjects and within-subjects variables
   - Deciding how data will be analyzed
   - Selecting participants
   - Choosing experimental materials
   - Choosing a means of presenting experimental materials
   - Writing directions
   - Deciding on a means of scoring data
   - Writing a consent form
   - Writing a debriefing sheet
   - Getting approval from the institutional review board
   - Conducting a pilot study
2. Executing the experimental research
3. Data analysis
4. Reporting the experimental research
   - Title
   - Author's name and institutional affiliation
   - Abstract
   - Introduction
   - Method

- Results
- Discussion
- References
- Appendix
- Order of sections

## 5.1 PLANNING EXPERIMENTAL RESEARCH

### 5.1.1 Getting an Idea

The basis of any good research is a viable idea that results in a study that contributes to the current state of knowledge. However, getting ideas, and especially getting good ideas, often turns out to be one of the hardest parts of research. If you need help forming ideas for your research, please read Chapter 2.

### 5.1.2 Selecting Independent Variables

After you have come up with an idea, you need a way to test it. To test the idea, you need one or more independent variables. Independent variables are those variables that are manipulated by the experimenter. In an experiment to test people's susceptibility to persuasive communications, for example, possible independent variables include (a) amount of exposure to persuasive communications, (b) content of persuasive communications, and (c) level of agreement between participants' initial attitudes and the position advocated by the persuasive communications. Once you have chosen your independent variable(s), you must decide how many and what level of them to use. For example, you might include in a persuasibility experiment three levels of exposure to the persuasive communications (no exposure, 10 minutes of exposure, and 1 hour of exposure) and two communications (one message dealing with capital punishment and one message dealing with compulsory use of seat belts in cars).

In most experiments, there are a large number of potentially interesting independent variables, but it is possible to choose only a small fraction of them. In many experimental designs (in particular, ones that are "crossed"), each time you add an independent variable to your experiment, you increase the size of your experiment multiplicatively. You must therefore choose your independent variables with care. In a persuasibility experiment, the type of font in which the persuasive communications are presented is not likely to affect the outcome of the experiment, and hence it would be a poor choice of an independent variable. The medium of communication – oral or written – might affect the outcome of the experiment, and hence would be a possible choice. The amount of exposure to the persuasive communications is almost certain to affect the outcome of the experiment, and hence is a very good choice.

In selecting independent variables, there is usually a trade-off between experimental control and ecological validity. Experimental control refers to the ease with which the experimenter can manipulate and later monitor the effects of the independent variables. Ecological validity refers to the generalizability of the obtained results to real-world situations. Total loss of experimental control can lead to uninterpretable results. Disregard of ecological validity can lead to trivial results. Researchers differ widely in the importance they assign to each of these items: Everyone must strike some sort of balance between the two.

### 5.1.3 Selecting Dependent Variables

In addition to choosing one or more independent variables, you must select one or more dependent variables. The dependent variable is the variable affected by (dependent on) the independent variables. It serves as the outcome to be measured. Whereas it is common to choose more than one independent variable in a single experiment, it is relatively less common to choose more than one dependent variable. When multiple dependent variables are used, they are usually studied separately, without much attempt to interrelate the outcomes. The major reason for psychologists' reluctance to deal with multiple outcomes is the greater difficulty involved in statistical analysis, not the inability of multiple outcomes to provide more meaningful data than single outcomes. However, multivariate methods do make it possible to test hypotheses regarding multiple dependent variables.

In most experiments, there are at least several possible dependent variables of interest to choose from, so the choice must be made carefully. In the persuasibility experiment, two possible dependent variables are (a) response to an opinion questionnaire administered at the end of the experimental session and (b) willingness one month later to join a citizens' lobbying group devoted to the cause advocated by the communication. Note that the first dependent variable measures immediate, overt opinion changes within the context of the experiment, whereas the latter dependent variable measures delayed covert opinion change outside the context of the experiment. Ideally, an experiment will include both kinds of measures. If only one is to be chosen, the experimenter must evaluate an important trade-off that psychological researchers frequently confront. The first measured outcome is much more likely than the second to be influenced by the experimental manipulation, but it is also of much less practical importance. Even if the opinion questionnaire administered at the end of the experiment shows a significant effect of the experimental treatment, one has no assurance that the effect will last for any long period of time, or even for any time beyond the conclusion of the experimental session. The second measured outcome is of considerable practical interest, but in relying on it, the experimenter may be throwing away any chance of an observable experimental effect. The experimenter must therefore decide on a dependent variable that gives a reasonable chance of obtaining an outcome that is both statistically and practically significant.

## 5.1.4 Deciding on Between-Subjects and Within-Subjects Variables

Each independent variable can be studied either between subjects or within subjects. A between-subjects independent variable is one in which a given participant receives only one level of the experimental treatment. A within-subjects independent variable is one in which a given participant receives all levels of the experimental treatment.

Return again to the persuasibility experiment. If both independent variables were between-subjects variables, then each participant would receive (a) no exposure, 10 minutes of exposure, or 1 hour of exposure to (b) either the communication on capital punishment or to that on the compulsory use of seat belts. Because there are three levels of the first independent variable and two levels of the second, there are 3 × 2 levels in all, or six different experimental groups, each composed of different participants. If both independent variables were within subjects, all participants would receive both persuasive communications and would be tested before receiving the communications, 10 minutes after receiving the communications, and 1 hour after receiving the communications for their current opinions on each.

In some cases, it is easy to decide whether to test a particular variable between subjects or within subjects. In other cases, however, the decision is a difficult one for the experimenter to make, and a potentially consequential one. The experimenter must evaluate a delicate trade-off. On the one hand, earlier within-subjects treatments may spoil the participant for later treatments. In other words, the participants receiving one experimental treatment may have unforeseen consequences for their responses to subsequent treatments. On the other hand, within-subjects designs guarantee the matching of participants across treatment conditions, because the participants are the same. This matching can be particularly important when there are relatively small numbers of participants.

Consider again the design of the persuasibility experiment. Suppose we administer the three opinion questionnaires – before treatment, 10 minutes after treatment, and 1 hour after treatment – to the same participants. We run the risk that the mere answering of an earlier questionnaire will influence participants' responses to later questionnaires. This influence can contaminate the results and render equivocal any interpretation of them. Suppose that instead we administer the three opinion questionnaires to three different groups of participants. We then have no way of knowing that our groups are matched in important ways. They may differ in initial level of agreement with the persuasive communication; they may differ in persuasibility (so that some are more susceptible by nature than others to persuasion attempts); or they may differ in the speed at which they assimilate new information, and hence in the speed at which their attitudes are affected by new information. The list can go on ad infinitum. Although random sampling of participants provides some protection against poor matching of groups, the adequacy of this protection depends on the size of the sample. Unless groups are quite large, protection may be inadequate. With six different groups in the full design of the persuasibility experiment, it is unlikely that very large groups can be obtained in a reasonably economical way.

A compromise can be worked out whereby all participants receive the opinion survey before treatment, but only some receive it after 10 minutes of treatment, whereas others receive it after 1 hour. This compromise, however, does not solve the basic dilemma, because the participants' receipt of the pretest can still affect their performance on the subsequent test. In deciding whether to test a particular variable between subjects or within subjects, experimenters must decide which kind of risk they are more willing to take.

### 5.1.5 Deciding How Data Will Be Analyzed

Major decisions about data analysis should be made prior to the collection of data. There are two reasons these decisions should be made in advance. First, statistical tests must be interpreted more cautiously if decided on post hoc. As it is sometimes said, everyone has 20/20 hindsight. Second, if major decisions about data analysis are not made in advance, experimenters run the risk of finding later that the experimental design does not permit them to analyze the data the way they want to or to analyze the data at all. Decisions about specific kinds of data analysis require a statistical background that is beyond the scope of this book.

### 5.1.6 Selecting Participants

Three major decisions must be made in selecting participants. First, from what population will participants be selected? Second, how will participants be selected from this population? Third, how many participants will be selected?

The population from which participants are selected is the population to which the experimental results will be generalizable. Hence, if one is interested in making generalizations to the general population of the United States or another country, then one must select a sample that is representative of the general population of the United States or the other country. If one is interested in a population of gifted children, then one must select a sample representative of gifted children. The question of generalizability of results is often quietly placed in the background of an experimental report, if it is discussed at all, because most experiments are conducted on samples that are not representative of the population of interest. Many of the experiments conducted today use college students as participants, although the experimenters' intent is to generalize the result to the population of adult Americans (or even to adults all over the world).

One faces a trade-off in deciding on a population from which to draw participants. On the one hand, researchers usually want to generalize their results to as broad a population as possible. On the other hand, participants are much easier to obtain from some populations than from others. College and university students are often readily available, whereas other groups of adults are much harder to corral into the laboratory.

Participants can be selected in any number of ways from the population. The two most common models of selection are the random sample and the stratified sample. In a random sampling procedure, the experimenter selects individuals from the population at random. In a stratified sampling procedure, the experimenter selects individuals in a way that ensures that major subdivisions of the population are represented in some proportion, usually the population proportion. For example, if 30% of the general population are Caucasian, then the sample will have about 30% Caucasians as well. In practice, it is almost never possible to obtain a purely random or stratified sample, because the entire population is not available to the experimenter. The participants who are available usually form a biased sample of the population from which they are drawn. Even if one's population is college students, for example, the sample of college students at any one university will inevitably be biased.

Decisions about numbers of participants are usually made on the basis of two considerations. First, how many participants can be tested feasibly, given the constraints of time, money, and participant availability? Second, how many participants are needed to show statistical significance for an effect of a certain magnitude? This latter consideration involves statistical concepts beyond the scope of this book. The basic idea, though, is that for a small treatment effect to be statistically significant, a large sample is needed. The greater the magnitude of the treatment effect, the smaller the sample size that is needed to show statistical significance.

## 5.1.7 Choosing Experimental Materials

Four considerations must be taken into account in choosing materials for an experiment:

1. Do the materials represent a reasonable sample of the universe of materials to which one wants to generalize?
2. Are there enough materials to obtain generalizable measurements?
3. Are the materials suitable for the participants to whom they will be administered?
4. Are the materials suitable for testing the hypothesis?

Researchers tend to pay too little attention to the generalizability of experimental materials. General conclusions about a broad universe of materials are often drawn on the basis of an experiment or several experiments using just one kind of material. Suppose, for example, that an investigator is interested in how people solve syllogisms. A participant is presented with two premises, called the major premise and the minor premise, and a conclusion. The participant's task is to say whether the conclusion follows logically from the premises. A simple syllogism would take the form:

1. All B are C.   (Major premise)
   All A are B.   (Minor premise)
   All A are C.   (Conclusion)

As an investigator, you might vary structural properties of the syllogism. For example, you might substitute for the major premise statements like "Some B are C," "No B are C," or "Some B are not C."

Your theory of how people solve syllogisms, however, could not be complete unless you took into account content as well as structure. Suppose, for example, that we leave the structure of the syllogism unchanged, varying only its content. Compare the difficulty of the following two syllogisms with each other and with the foregoing syllogism:

2. All birds are animals.
   All canaries are birds.
   All canaries are animals.

3. All birds are canaries.
   All animals are birds.
   All animals are canaries.

You will probably find, as others have found before you, that the content of the syllogism greatly affects its difficulty. Most people find syllogisms like (2) easier to comprehend than syllogisms like (3) because the premises of the former syllogism conform to real-world experience, whereas the premises of the latter syllogism violate it. A complete theory of syllogistic reasoning would have to take into account these effects of content, something no theory yet does. The general point, of course, is that no theory can be accepted with confidence unless it has been shown to explain data for a wide variety of experimental materials.

It is important to have not only a relatively broad sampling of materials but a relatively large sampling as well. The syllogism experiment would be unimpressive if it had three different kinds of content but only one syllogism of each kind. To obtain reliable measurements, it is usually necessary to have at least several replications of each kind of item.

Investigators must take care that their experimental materials are suitable for the target participant population. Syllogisms such as the preceding ones would be suitable for an adult population, but not for a population of 6-year-old children. If the children failed to solve syllogisms like the foregoing ones, investigators would be unable to determine whether the failure was due to inability to reason syllogistically or to an inability to comprehend the materials. The investigators might use concrete play materials instead of verbal ones. For example, they might show the children plastic replicas of animals and then demonstrate to them that all the elephants are gray and that all the animals with trunks are elephants. The children would then have to indicate whether all the animals with trunks are gray. Special care would have to be taken to ensure that the children understood the nature of the task.

The materials one uses must be appropriate to the hypothesis under investigation. Suppose, for example, that an investigator wants to test the hypothesis that syllogisms with counterfactual conclusions are more difficult to solve than syllogisms with factual conclusions. The following two sets of syllogisms would provide poor tests of this hypothesis:

| Factual Conclusions | Counterfactual Conclusions |
|---|---|
| 1.  All integers are rational. <br> All natural numbers are integers. <br> All natural numbers are rational. | 1.  All rational numbers are natural numbers. <br> All integers are rational numbers. <br> All integers are natural numbers. |
| 2.  All sunny days are enjoyable days. <br> All bright days are sunny days. <br> All bright days are enjoyable days. | 2.  All sunny days are unenjoyable days. <br> All cloudy days are sunny days. <br> All cloudy days are unenjoyable days. |

The first syllogism is inappropriate because most participants (except, perhaps, in a population of mathematicians) would not realize which syllogism has a factual conclusion and which has a counterfactual conclusion. The second syllogism is inappropriate because the conclusions (as well as the premises) are matters of opinion; although some people might agree with the first conclusion and disagree with the second conclusion, these agreements and disagreements are not over matters of fact.

## 5.1.8 Choosing a Means of Presenting Experimental Materials

Experimental materials usually can be presented in many forms. The form of presentation generally is determined largely by convenience, because little is known about the effects of the form of presentation on performance. Investigators usually assume that the effects of form of presentation on performance are trivial. Suppose, for example, that an investigator is interested in the effect of concreteness on free recall of a list of words. The hypothesis is that more concrete words, like *banana*, will be better recalled than more abstract words, like *freedom*. To test this hypothesis, the investigator compares recall of two lists of words, one concrete and the other abstract.

The list of words might be presented either visually or auditorily. If the words are presented visually, they might be presented via flash cards, slides, or a computer terminal. If the words are presented auditorily, they might be presented by a person speaking who is physically present, tape or CD player, or a computer. Modality of presentation (visual or auditory) and vehicle of presentation (e.g., computer, CD player) within modality might affect level of recall, but it is assumed that this effect will be constant across treatment conditions. Thus, if on average two fewer concrete words are recalled with an auditory presentation rather than a visual one, it is assumed that, on average, two fewer abstract words will be recalled as well. The investigator is not likely to use both auditory and visual presentations to show generality of the hypothesis to both modalities. In some experiments – for example, experiments on vision or audition – modality of presentation will be a critical variable. In most experiments, however, it is considered relatively unimportant. Investigators turn their attention to variables that are more likely to influence their results. In preparing experimental materials, you may not reproduce copyrighted material, such as tests or reading passages, without permission. Doing so subjects you to the possibility of legal action against you.

## 5.1.9 Writing Directions

Once you have decided on the experimental task and materials, you have to write directions telling participants what is expected of them.

It is essential that the directions be clear and complete, because unclear or incomplete instructions can result in participants doing a task different from the one you intend. The directions may be presented auditorily or visually. We usually have the experimenter present the directions aloud while the participant reads them silently. Participants thereby are exposed to the directions in two modalities.

In the free-recall experiment, the following directions might be used:

**DIRECTIONS FOR FREE-RECALL TASK**

In this task, the experimenter will read aloud a list of words. You should listen carefully to these words. After the experimenter has completed reading the list, he will pause, and then say the word *recall*. At that point, you should recall as many words as you can from the list in any order you wish. Write your answers on the sheet in front of you. If you are not sure of an item, then guess. Your recall will be scored for the number of words correctly recalled.

If you have any questions, please ask them now.

### 5.1.10 Deciding on a Means of Scoring Data

Because scoring can be time-consuming, the layout of participants' response sheets or booklets should be planned carefully in advance. An easy-to-score layout can save many hours of work later on. If the participants' responses are simple – letters, numbers, words – their answers usually can be recorded in successive columns of each page. An easily readable format will facilitate scoring, possibly enabling you to devise a stencil key that can be placed either next to or over each column. If responses are made by computer, be sure they are easy for subjects to make.

If the data will be entered for subsequent computer analysis, it is wise to show your answer-sheet layout to the data-entry person. If the layout is easily readable, that person (or you may do it yourself) may be able to enter the data directly from the answer sheets, bypassing the time-consuming step of coding the data.

### 5.1.11 Writing a Consent Form

Some years ago, government and other funding agencies started requiring experimenters supported by their funds to have all participants sign statements of informed consent before participating in experiments. Universities require such statements as well. In the case of child participants, parents are required to sign. Researchers are also required to have their experiments approved by a human subjects committee/institutional review board at their college or university before they conduct the experiments (see below). In view of the widespread concern today with the protection of participants, it is probably wise to use consent forms even for informal class projects. A sample consent form (in this case, for an experiment on decision making in groups) is shown in Figure 5.1.

The consent form must be modified to meet the needs of each particular experiment. The forms must always include, however, (a) a statement of informed consent, (b) sufficient information about the experiment so that the participant's consent is truly informed, and (c) the participant's signature and date.

The consent form here first informs participants about the purpose and procedure of the experiment. If your experiment involves deception, you should still be as truthful as possible in the explanation. Experiments involving deception will be reviewed with special attention by the institutional review board (IRB) to ensure that no harm will be done to the participants. It is then even more important to debrief participants after the experiment.

Next, the form describes the risks and benefits of participation in the experiment, as well as economic considerations and whether the collected data will be treated in a confidential way. This information gives your participants the opportunity to consider the overall risks and benefits to help them make an informed decision as to whether they want to participate in your study.

You should also tell participants that their participation is voluntary and that they can drop out of the study at any given time. It is nice to give participants an e-mail address or phone number of one of the investigators in case they have any further questions later.

Emphasis on the technical details of obtaining informed consent can obscure the reason for obtaining it. The important question the experimenter must face is whether the experiment places the participant at risk. If so, then the experimenter must examine the risk-benefit ratio: Do the benefits of the research outweigh its risks? Students should consult faculty advisers for additional perspectives on whether participants' rights are being protected, particularly their rights to personal privacy and confidentiality. Often, the research will have to be reviewed further by a departmental or university committee to ensure that participants receive adequate personal protection (see the section on Institutional Review Boards).

## DECLARATION OF INFORMED CONSENT

### 1. *Invitation to Participate*

You are invited to participate in this study concerning the perception of other groups. An overview of the procedure is given below.

### 2. *Purpose*

We are conducting this survey to assess people's attitudes toward various groups.

### 3. *Description of Procedures*

The survey consists of several questions assessing how you feel toward two groups. It also comprises some personality measures.

### 4. *Risks and Inconveniences*

The physical, psychological, social, or economic risks associated with participation in this experiment are minimal. The only known inconvenience is the time you spend here today (approximately 30 minutes).

### 5. *Benefits*

The benefit of participating in this study is purely educational. After you have completed the measures, the experimenter will discuss the procedures and purposes with you further. You will have an opportunity to ask questions about any part of the survey.

### 6. *Economic Considerations*

You will not be charged for any part of this experiment, nor will you receive financial compensation for your participation. You will receive 1 experimental credit for participation.

### 7. *Confidentiality*

Your responses are confidential and completely anonymous. You will not be asked to provide any identifying information that will enable your responses to be linked to you. We are not interested in responses from any individual; responses from all participants will be aggregated for analyses. Because all of your responses are anonymous, please feel free to answer all of the questions openly and honestly.

The questionnaires will be locked in a secure area to which only the researchers will have access.

You should also know that the University Institutional Review Board (IRB) and the Office of Research Compliance may inspect study records as part of its auditing program, but these reviews will only focus on the researchers and not on your responses or involvement. The IRB is a group of people that reviews research studies to make sure they are safe for participants.

**8.** *Voluntary Participation*

You do not have to be in this study if you do not want to. If you agree to be in the study but later change your mind, you may drop out at any time but will still receive credit. There are no penalties or consequences of any kind if you decide that you do not want to participate. You are free not to answer questions.

**9.** *Do You Have Any Questions?*

Take as long as you like before you make a decision. We will be happy to answer any question you have about this study. If you have further questions about this project or if you have a research-related problem, you may contact the investigator at 999-9999 (John Doe).

If you have any questions concerning your rights as a research subject, you may contact the University Institutional Review Board (IRB) at 888-888-8888.

**Authorization:**

I have read this form and decided that _____ will
                                                    *(name of subject)*
participate in the project described above. Its general purposes, the particulars of involvement and possible hazards and inconveniences have been explained to my satisfaction. My signature also indicates that I have received a copy of this consent form.

Signature: _____

Date: _____

_____     _____

Signature of Primary Investigator                        Phone

*or*

_____     _____

Signature of Person Obtaining Consent                    Phone

**Figure 5.1.** *An informed consent form is required for almost all research that involves human participants.*

## 5.1.12 Writing a Debriefing Sheet

After the experiment is over, participants often want to know the purpose of the experiment and the various experimental procedures.

Experimenters have a moral obligation, and in some universities, a legal obligation, to debrief participants about the experiment. The debriefing should be informative and nontechnical. It should inform the participants of what the experiment is supposed to test, how the experiment tests it, and what the anticipated outcomes are. Debriefing may be oral or written, although we prefer written debriefing because participants and experimenters then have a record of having participated in the experiment. Figure 5.2 shows a sample debriefing, in this case for an experiment on decision making in groups.

Before debriefing your participants, it is wise to have your participants debrief you. After the experiment is over, ask your participants to tell you (preferably in writing) how they went about doing the experimental task. Participants' comments can provide you with insights that you otherwise would not have obtained.

## EXPERIMENTAL DEBRIEFING

### Decision Making in Groups

The purpose of this experiment was to further our understanding of decision making in groups. The hypothesis tested by the experiment was that groups will make faster decisions if they are explicitly warned in advance that interpersonal frictions, rivalries, and animosities can impede the group decision-making process and that, therefore, group members should take special care not to let these impediments hinder them at the decision-making task.

Four groups participated in the experiment. In two groups, participants were asked to decide whether the United States should sell nuclear material for "peaceful purposes" to countries that have the ability to manufacture atomic bombs. In two other groups, participants were asked to decide in a rational way which two group members would receive a $10 bonus at the end of the experiment. They were informed that the other members would receive no bonus and that the decision could not be made using a random selection procedure (such as drawing lots). In one "nuclear material" group and in one "$10 bonus" group, participants were warned in advance not to let interpersonal frictions, rivalries, and animosities impede their decision-making process. The other two groups received no warning of any kind.

We expected that the forewarned group would reach a decision more quickly than the unwarned groups, regardless of whether they were making a decision about "nuclear material" or about the "$10 bonus." The purpose of using two different kinds of decisions was to show the generality of the instructional effect. The experiment will be repeated four times with different groups of participants to show that the instructional effect is a reliable one. The four repetitions of the experiment will be combined for data analysis.

If you have any questions, please feel free to ask them of the experimenter. If you would like a summary of the results when the research is completed, please leave your name and address with the experimenter.

Thank you for participating.

_____

(Experimenter's Signature)

**Figure 5.2.** *Debriefings explain the purpose and procedures of the experiment to the participants after they have completed all measures.*

### 5.1.13 Getting Approval from the Institutional Review Board

When you plan your study, you should allow enough time for your local IRB to approve it. The IRB is a committee of experts from different subjects who discuss every research proposal and decide whether the research can be conducted as proposed or whether amendments must be made to protect the participants. Such boards usually meet at least once a month, and if you have to make changes and need to get them approved, it can easily take you a few weeks, if not longer. Many IRBs offer expedited reviews for low-risk studies. Check with your local IRB if you meet those requirements; the low-risk route may also mean that you have to submit fewer documents than you would for a full review.

To a certain extent, IRBs differ from one place to another in what they consider important when approving research, in the phrases they like to be included in consent forms, and so on. For example, one IRB may want you to include a sentence in the "Risks and Inconveniences" section of an informed consent form that identifies the time the participant spends with the study as an inconvenience. An IRB at another university may not consider such a sentence important. Ask other students or professors about their experiences with your IRB and whether they have any tips or even templates so you can get a feel for the formulations used with respect to communications with the IRB. In general, IRB approval for a study is valid only for a certain amount of time (e.g., one year). If you have not completed your study by that time, you may have to resubmit for renewed approval to the IRB.

Often, the IRB requests detailed information about your study. Generally, IRBs ask for information about the following:

1. the purpose of your study;
2. the theoretical background of your study;
3. the design of your study;
4. the instruments you will use (you may need to submit all of your questionnaires and materials);
5. the number of participants and from which population they are drawn (e.g., male students of your university);
6. how you justify the sample size (e.g., if you only need 50 participants to complete your study but plan to have 300 people participate, this sampling design may not be approved);
7. how you recruit your participants (e.g., ads in a newspaper or flyers, and you may have to submit such materials for review);
8. inclusion and/or exclusion criteria (e.g., Do you discriminate against potential participants and exclude them from participation for no apparent reason? Why is your group of participants circumscribed as it is?);
9. risks and inconveniences, benefits, and a risk/benefit analysis;
10. economic considerations (e.g., will your participants earn money when they participate?);
11. data safety and monitoring (e.g., Are your data locked and inaccessible to others? How do you ensure security of the data? Are the participants anonymous?);
12. informed consent, including your informed consent forms.

When writing, keep in mind that some of the reviewers may not be psychologists, so make sure that reviewers unfamiliar with your field of study will be able to comprehend your documents.

## 5.1.14 Conducting a Pilot Study

Before starting final data collection, you should consider testing pilot participants. Pilot testing enables you to spot flaws in the experiment before you actually conduct it. You may find that your directions are unclear, that you have not allowed enough time for your participants to complete the task, or that the task is too difficult for your participants. The list of possible flaws is endless. Pilot testing is like an insurance policy. By making a small investment in advance, you can potentially save yourself much greater costs later. The more careful the pilot testing (the larger the insurance premium), the less likely it is that you will end up with disastrous results (i.e., the greater the insurance coverage). We have found that there is almost always some potential problem uncovered during pilot testing.

## 5.2  EXECUTING EXPERIMENTAL RESEARCH

If you have planned your experiment carefully, then its execution should be straightforward. You should make sure, as much as you possibly can, that extraneous variables are kept constant from session to session. Thus, things like lighting, ventilation, and seating arrangement should not be varied. Outside noise should be minimized. If the experiment involves a number of separate parts, you may want to keep a list so that you do not forget any of them. Experimenters, like participants, sometimes get distracted; and once data are lost, they are difficult or impossible to replace.

Use the experimental sessions as an informal opportunity to gain insights into how participants perform the experimental tasks. Participants occasionally make comments about what they are doing or how they are doing it. Also be on the lookout for nonroutine problems – participants who stayed up the night before writing a paper and can barely keep their eyes open, participants who are not paying attention to the experimental task, a flickering lightbulb, an erratic stopwatch. You should write down notes on any unusual problems, and try to correct them. Participants who stayed up all night should be rescheduled, participants who are not paying attention should be told politely to pay attention, the lightbulb should be replaced, and the stopwatch should be fixed or replaced. You will collect much better data if you are aware of problems and correct them immediately.

In theory, the experimenter should be blind to the assignment of participants to treatments so that any prior expectations about treatment effects will be unable to influence the experimental results. In practice, the experimenter often knows which participants have been assigned to which treatments. In reading the word lists for the free-recall experiment, for example, the experimenter will probably recognize whether the words are abstract or concrete. If experimenters observe the groups in the decision-making experiment, they will

know whether they have previously warned the groups about impediments to group decision making. A voluminous literature exists on
experimenters' effects on research results, and there is no question
that experimenters can influence the outcomes in subtle ways. An
experimenter might read the list of abstract words just a little more
quickly or less clearly than the list of concrete words or differentially
reinforce the decision-making groups with facial expressions. You
have a responsibility as experimenter to give your hypotheses the
fairest possible test. Subtle and not-so-subtle experimenter effects
undermine the interpretability and credibility of your results. It is
therefore essential that you take care not to influence the outcome
of your experiment through incidental and (presumably) unintended
actions.

## 5.3 EXCURSION: USING THE INTERNET TO CONDUCT ARCHIVAL RESEARCH AND DATA COLLECTION

Clearly, the Internet can be a valuable resource when seeking out
ideas for a research project. But even when you have settled on an
idea for a study and are confident that enough resources exist to successfully answer your research question, you still need to discover
a way to collect data that will allow you to answer your research
question. The Internet also can be a valuable tool during the data-
collection phase of the research process. In this section, we explore
how to use the Internet as a source of data and as a data-collection
tool. Specifically, we discuss how to use the Internet to conduct
archival research or to collect original data. We also discuss some
of the advantages and disadvantages of using the Internet to collect
data.

### 5.3.1 Archival Research

Archival research refers to a method of data collection involving the
use of records or previously existing information. For example, suppose you wanted to construct a personality profile of a U.S. president,
perhaps to examine whether a president's personality is related to his
performance in office. Although this is an excellent research idea, you
are likely to have two problems collecting data. First, the president
whose personality profile you want to construct might not be living
anymore. Second, even if the president is living, it is unlikely that you

will be able to interview him or get him to complete a personality survey for you. It turns out that personality profiles of U.S. presidents can be created without ever talking with a president or having him complete a personality questionnaire. Instead, the personality traits of a president can be inferred from such pieces of information as speeches, notes, and papers; conversations with other political leaders; interviews; and press conferences. The advantage for a researcher is that all of this material is archived and made available for public consumption. For example, any research that involves the use of previously existing material, whether public records (e.g., crime statistics, census information) or public documents (e.g., Supreme Court decisions, presidential speeches), is referred to as archival research. Archival research is a particularly useful research strategy for answering research questions that are difficult or impossible to answer via traditional data-collection methods.

The Internet is an especially valuable tool for researchers interested in archival research. As already discussed, the Internet and the World Wide Web contain an abundance of information, much of which can be used to conduct research. Following are some ideas for and examples of using the Internet to conduct archival research:

### ■ Newsgroups

The Internet is full of discussion boards, or newsgroups, on every imaginable topic. Newsgroups allow people from all over the world to engage in asynchronous conversations about a variety of topics. An Internet search of newsgroups yields thousands of virtual discussions (e.g., on a football team's performance, a support group for people who have chronic pain, the best restaurants on Maui). Most newsgroups are accessible to anyone as a participant or as an observer. For the purposes of archival research, newsgroups are typically archived, so that a researcher can access the transcripts of the discussions (although permission of the moderator is often required and always advisable). These transcripts can be a valuable source of data to researchers attempting to answer specific research questions. For example, if researchers wanted to learn whether fans of winning football teams express more pride in their team than do fans of losing football teams, they could analyze the transcripts of a newsgroup of a winning team and the newsgroup of a losing team. Or suppose researchers were interested in examining the extent of depressive symptoms displayed by chronic pain sufferers. They could analyze the discussion board of chronic pain sufferers for evidence of depressive symptoms.

■ **Public records**

Public records can be an excellent source of data. The Internet allows one to access most public records with incredible ease. The consequence for researchers is that they can answer innumerable research questions with the use of such data. For example, the government's Web site FedWorld (http://www.fedworld.gov) includes access to a variety of information, such as the complete transcripts of Supreme Court decisions, transportation fatality statistics, and a list of currently endangered species. Similarly, every state in the United States has a Web page, and each can be accessed by using the format http://www.state.SA.us, where "SA" stands for the state abbreviation (e.g., http://www.state.oh.us is Ohio's Web page). A state's Web page makes available information such as statewide incidence of cancer by type, year, and county; results of family health surveys; and the number of live births by county and year.

■ **Web sites**

The format of and information contained on a Web site can also be a source of data for researchers. Suppose a researcher was interested in examining whether females are more likely than males to disclose personal information about themselves. One method of answering this question is to analyze the Web sites of males and females, paying attention to the amount and type of personal information included on the sites. Or imagine that researchers want to investigate the correlation between the success (in net profit) of small businesses and the appearance of those businesses' Web sites. They could analyze the appearance of small business Web sites and then determine whether it is related to the success of the business.

## 5.3.2 Data Collection via the Internet

The Internet can also be a valuable tool for the collection of original data, because it allows researchers to collect survey data or conduct experiments. There are several methods available to researchers who wish to collect data using the Internet. First, a researcher can construct a Web page that permits respondents to answer a survey or participate in an experiment. Of course, this technique requires that a researcher have some knowledge of constructing Web pages and surveys on the Web and have access to a server. Second, a researcher can send a questionnaire or survey to potential respondents via e-mail. Third, a researcher can make use of a LISTSERV to send potential respondents a survey or questionnaire.

Conducting research via the Internet has a number of important advantages and disadvantages (Reips, 2000). Some of the advantages include the following:

1. **Population access.** The number of people using the Internet is increasing every day. Use of the Internet allows researchers to access many more people than would be possible using more traditional methods. Further, the Internet allows access to more diverse populations.
2. **Volunteer bias.** One criticism of most research conducted in universities is that participants may not be invested in the research in which they are participating. On the Internet, people who participate in a study do so because they want to. But they are then a biased sample.
3. **Statistical power.** The large sample size that use of the Internet permits also increases the statistical power of a study.
4. **Experimenter effects.** Face-to-face experiments typically require the presence of an experimenter, but that can sometimes (unintentionally) influence the outcome of a study. The Internet does not require the physical presence of an experimenter, which eliminates any experimenter effects.
5. **Costs.** The costs of conducting a study on the Internet are much less than carrying one out in a lab. Internet studies do not require the use of lab space, equipment, experimenters, or paper. The amount of time needed to complete a study on the Internet is also greatly reduced because Internet studies can be conducted 24 hours per day, 7 days per week.
6. **Ethical issues.** Participation in Internet studies is completely voluntary. Respondents can drop out of the study at any time without penalty.

Of course, there are also some disadvantages of using the Internet to conduct research. These include the following:

1. **Control issues.** In non-Internet studies, researchers can exercise a great deal of control over many of the practical issues of

research, such as who the participants are, when the study is conducted, and where the study takes place. On the Internet, researchers give up this control. Among the control issues that plague Internet research are the fact that people can participate in the study multiple times and that the researcher lacks control over the experimental situation. It is wise to ask participants not to participate more than once or to ask for personal information that can be verified independently.

2. **Self-selection.** Another issue with Internet studies is that all of the participants are self-selected, rather than randomly assigned. The results, therefore, may not be as generalizable as a randomly selected sample. One solution is to advertise the study widely so that Internet users from a variety of entry points have access to the study.

3. **Dropout.** Whenever research is completely voluntary, as is the case in Internet research, there tends to be a high dropout rate. Participants may decide, in the middle of the study, that they do not have the time to complete it. Or participants might decide, after having started a survey, that they are really not interested in the topic. Potential solutions to this problem include offering an incentive for participation, making the Web site as attractive as possible, and providing participants with estimates of the amount of time needed to complete the study.

4. **Technical variance.** Researchers try very hard to reduce the amount of error variance in their studies. Studies conducted on the Internet can pose some unique challenges to the control of error variance. For example, participants in a study are likely to have different Web browsers, different monitor sizes, and different Internet connections, all of which can inflate error variance. However, these sources of variance are likely to be random and may not affect the study in a systematic manner.

5. **Interaction with participants.** If participants in an Internet study have a question, they are unable to ask an experimenter. It is a good idea, therefore, always to include an e-mail address or other means of contacting the experimenter if the participant needs clarification of procedures.

Clearly, the Internet offers a variety of unique ways of conducting research. The Internet can be a valuable source of data to an investigator interested in conducting archival research. Many research questions can be answered via access to public records, public documents, and countless Web sites. The Internet can also be used as a way to collect original research. Minimal knowledge of Web page construction is really all that is needed to collect data via the Internet. And currently there are several Web sites, such as SurveyMonkey (http://www.surveymonkey.com) that essentially build your survey or experiment for you. You can find these Web sites by searching for keywords such as "online survey software." Finally, a review of the research (Krantz & Dalal, 2000) suggests that the results of Web experiments often are comparable to non-Web experiments, which makes the conduct of research via the Internet even more attractive.

## 5.4 ANALYZING DATA FROM EXPERIMENTAL RESEARCH

After the experiment is completed, you are ready to analyze your data. Techniques for analyzing data are beyond the scope of this book, although some simple exploratory techniques are presented in Chapter 9. Two especially lucid textbooks covering elementary statistical techniques are those by Gravetter and Wallnau (2008), and Aron, Aron, and Coups (2007). For description and explanation of multivariate statistical techniques, we recommend the works of Tabachnik and Fidell (2006), and Hair, Black, Babin, and Anderson (2009).

## 5.5 REPORTING EXPERIMENTAL RESEARCH

Once you have analyzed your data and thought about your results, you are ready to report them. In the following sections, we describe all the parts of a manuscript. If you are interested in a more detailed overview, we recommend *Guide to Publishing in Psychology Journals* (Sternberg, 2000). We suggest that you write an outline prior to writing the paper, just as you would if you were writing a literature research paper. A standard format for the outline looks like this:

> Title
> Author's name and institutional affiliation
> Author notes
> Abstract
> I. Introduction
> II. Method
>  A. Materials

B. Apparatus
C. Participants
D. Design
E. Procedure
III. Results
IV. Discussion
References
Footnotes
Tables
Figures
Appendix

## 5.5.1 Title

The title should inform the reader simply and concisely what the paper is about. It is important that the title be self-explanatory. Readers will come across the title in other papers that refer to your paper and in PsycINFO, and they may have to decide on the basis of the title alone whether they want to read your paper. Therefore, you want to catch the attention of your potential readers with the title. It should include, for example, keywords, the theoretical issue that the paper addresses, the dependent variable(s), and the independent variable(s). Keywords are important because the title will be stored in information-retrieval networks that rely on such words to determine the relevance of your study to someone else's research interests. For the same reason, it is important to avoid irrelevant and misleading words, because such words may spuriously lead an investigator uninterested in your topic to your paper. Try not to use abbreviations. The title should not exceed 12 to 15 words in length.

When submitting a paper to a journal, you will also be asked to provide a running title. The running title will be displayed at the top of each page. When readers open a journal in the middle of an article, they will still be able to determine what article they are looking at by means of the running title. As for the regular title, focus on keywords when you formulate your running title.

## 5.5.2 Author's Name and Institutional Affiliation

Write your name as you wish it to be recognized professionally; for example, John Jones might choose John Jones, John J. Jones, John James Jones, J. Jones, J. J. Jones, or J. James Jones. A first name, middle initial, and last name is the most commonly used form of presentation. Omit titles such as B.A., M.A., Ph.D., Lover of Mankind, and so on. Underneath your name, write your institutional affiliation: Podunk College, Frink University. If you have changed your affiliation since you did the research, list the old affiliation under your name and the new affiliation in a footnote. A dual affiliation is listed under your name only if both institutions contributed financially to the study. If you are unaffiliated with any institution, list your city and state. If there is more than one author, you may wish to discuss the order of appearance of names as soon as possible with your collaborators. You can find more information on this topic in Chapter 11.

### 5.5.3 Abstract

The abstract summarizes your paper. Its length depends on your target journal, but it generally ranges between 150 and 200 words. The abstract, like the title, should be self-explanatory and self-contained, because it is also used for indexing by information-retrieval networks. The abstract should include (a) the major hypotheses; (b) a summary of the method, including a description of the materials, apparatus, participants, design, and procedure; (c) a synopsis of the main results; and (d) the conclusions drawn from the results. Do not include in the abstract any information that is not included in the body of the paper. Because you will not know until you are done with the outline what information you will include, you are well advised to defer writing the abstract until after you have otherwise completed the outline, or even the paper itself.

Remember that most people will read your abstract only if your title interests them, and they will read your article only if your abstract interests them. It is therefore essential that the abstract interest your reader. You can interest the reader by showing that the problem is an important one, that your hypotheses about the problem are insightful ones, and that you will test the hypotheses in a convincing way. The *APA Manual* (2009) states that abstracts should be (a) accurate, (b) self-contained, (c) concise and specific, (d) nonevaluative, and (e) coherent and readable.

### 5.5.4 Introduction

The introduction orients the reader to the research. In the paper, it does not receive a heading, because its function is obvious. The task of your opening paragraph is to appeal to readers and to animate them to read on. There are several ways to achieve this goal (Kendall, Silk, & Chu, 2000):

- Ask a **rhetorical question** that inspires readers to consider what they think about a certain issue.
- Mention an **everyday experience** that readers can relate to and that makes the relevance of your topic apparent.
- Use an **analogy** or metaphor to address general principles.
- Mention an **interesting fact** that captures the interest of readers.
- Give some **historical facts** to place the problem in context.
- Point out the **lack of previous research** to highlight the importance of your work.

After the opening paragraph, in which you elicit readers' interest, your introduction should answer four basic questions:

1. What previous research led up to your research?
2. What does your research add to this previous research?
3. Why is the addition made by your research important or interesting?
4. How is the addition made?

The introduction usually contains a brief review of the literature most pertinent to your research. A lengthy literature review is inappropriate, except, sometimes, for theses and course assignments. Focus on integrating the literature rather than on summarizing many single studies. If a voluminous literature exists on the topic, cite a literature review to which the reader can refer for further information if they want it. Assume in your review, however, that readers are familiar with the general area of research. Readers' main interest is in what you have to contribute. They are interested in the previous literature only as it relates directly to your contribution.

Once you have told the reader what is already known, you must relate what still needs to be known, that is, what you intend to find out. Tell the reader not only what you intend to contribute but also what the nature of the contribution is. Does your research resolve an issue that has been unresolved in the past? Does it deal with an issue that others have not thought about? Does it attempt to correct an artifact in previous investigations? This information will give readers a good idea of what you view as the purpose of your study.

Next, you should show readers that the contribution is a potentially interesting or important one. Why have people paid attention to this particular issue? Or why is a new issue one to which people should pay attention? Or does an artifact in previous experimental research really undermine conclusions that previous investigators have drawn? Remember that a major purpose of the introduction is to interest readers in your paper and that your explanation of why your study is potentially important can motivate readers either to continue the article or to toss it aside.

Finally, you should tell readers how you intend to make your contribution. Sketch your experimental design, but leave a detailed description for the "Design" section later in the paper. Show how your design relates to the theoretical issues you address. It is important to convince your readers at this point that your experiment actually does test the hypothesis you want to investigate.

Many APA journals limit the length of the introduction to 5 to 9 manuscript pages. As a rule of thumb, the longer your "Results" section is, the longer your "Introduction" section can be (Kendall, Silk, & Chu, 2000).

### 5.5.5 Method

The "Method" section tells readers how the experiment was conducted. You should include just enough information so that readers can replicate your study. If you include less information, other investigators will be unable to verify your results. If you include more information, you risk boring and possibly losing readers in needless detail. When you are uncertain as to whether a piece of information is essential, it is better to err on the side of including too much rather than too little.

The "Method" section is usually divided into a number of subsections. Although use of subsections is optional, it usually simplifies and clarifies the presentation for readers. The subsections most often used are "Materials," "Apparatus," "Participants," "Design," and "Procedure," although not necessarily in that order. If there is no apparatus, you do not need the section. Use the order of subheadings that best conveys the methods used in your particular experiment.

### 5.5.5.1 Materials

In the "Materials" subsection, you should describe the stimulus material used in the experiment. Sufficient detail should be given so that the reader could generate the same or equivalent stimuli. If the stimuli are unconventional, you might reproduce examples in a table or figure.

### 5.5.5.2 Apparatus

The apparatus used in the experiment should be described in the "Apparatus" subsection. Present a general description of the apparatus, including any details that might affect the outcome of the experiment. If the apparatus is a standard piece of manufactured equipment, the name and model number will substitute for most details, because readers can then learn the details from the manufacturer. If the apparatus is unusual, you might want to photograph it and present it as a figure. This entire subsection can be omitted if no special apparatus is used. If you merely use a standard computer for stimulus presentation, you do not need a section describing the computer.

### 5.5.5.3 Participants

You should describe in the "Participants" subsection (a) the total number of participants, (b) the number of participants receiving each treatment, (c) the population from which the participants were drawn, (d) how participants were selected, and (e) the circumstances under which the participants participated (e.g., for pay, for course credit, as a favor to the experimenter). In describing the participating population, include any details that might affect the outcome of the experiment, such as sex, ethnic or socially defined racial groups, age, education, and so on. The nature of the experiment will determine what other attributes of participants might be relevant. The term *subject* can be used for nonhuman organisms or when referring to people in the abstract. For example, you can use the term when describing designs, as for a between-subjects design.

### 5.5.5.4 Design

This subsection should include a description of the following:

1. **The type of design.** Did you use an experimental, quasi-experimental, or correlational design? You should also give information on the number of factors and their levels, and on whether a between-subjects, within-subjects, or mixed design was used.

In between-subject designs, every participant is assigned to just one condition, whereas in within-subject designs, each person participates in more than one condition. Mixed designs have at least one between-subject and one within-subject variable. If you employ a within-subject design, the order in which participants are subjected to the conditions can influence the results; therefore, you need to mention if you took action, and if so, the actions you took to counterbalance the order effect (see also Reis, 2000).

2. **The independent variable(s).** Which independent variables were used and what were their values?
3. **The dependent variable(s).** On which variables did you measure the effect of the independent variable(s)?
4. **The way in which participants were assigned to groups.**

The "Design" section is sometimes omitted and the relevant information divided among the other sections. We prefer to include the "Design" section, because it provides readers with a compact overview of how the experiment was put together. If you are interested in a more detailed treatise on how to write the "Design" section, we suggest you consult Harry Reis's chapter "Writing Effectively about Design" in Sternberg (2000).

### 5.5.5.5 Procedure

The "Procedure" subsection should describe what happened to the participants in the experimental sessions from the time they walked in to the time they walked out. A chronological account is usually best. In the paper, paraphrase directions to participants, unless they were unconventional, in which case you might want to present them verbatim. Because you assume that your readers have a general knowledge of the relevant literature, you can also assume that they are familiar with standard testing procedures. Therefore, describe such procedures more generally, always being sure to include any details that plausibly might affect the outcome of the experiment.

## 5.5.6 Results

The order in which results are reported is of critical importance. Authors often report first those results that are of most interest or relevance to the hypotheses being tested. Less interesting or relevant results are reported later. You may wish to report first a general conclusion or interpretation, followed by some descriptive statistics that support your assertion, followed only at the end by the inferential statistics that buttress the conclusion. This style of presentation often makes for more interesting reading than does a mélange of facts and statistics followed by an obscurely placed conclusion that bored readers may never even reach if they have given up on your article pages before. Also keep in mind that results should not be reported in the order in which the data analyses were conducted but in a way that makes sense to the story you want to tell.

The "Results" section should include (a) descriptive statistics, which summarize the data in a readily comprehensible form, and (b) inferential statistics, which test the likelihood that the results were obtained due to chance alone. Techniques you used for data analysis should be reported with sufficient clarity that someone else could replicate them on the basis of your description. If you had a choice of which statistical methods to employ, give a rationale for what you did. If you plan to present a large number of results, divide the "Results" section into subsections. The particular subsections used will depend on the nature of the experiment.

It is expected that authors provide effect sizes as well as significance values. The field is divided regarding the value of conventional significance testing, but it nevertheless is the most commonly used basis for reporting results.

As in the previous sections, you should make an effort to report the right amount of information, neither underreporting nor over-reporting your results. Also as in the previous sections, it is usually better to report a result if you are uncertain as to whether to include it. The criteria you should follow are to report (a) all data that are directly relevant to your hypotheses and (b) other data that may be peripheral to your hypotheses but are of particular interest in their own right. Do not present data for individual participants unless (a) you used an $N = 1$ (single-subject) design, (b) the individual data show trends that are masked in the group data, or (c) your hypotheses are relevant to each individual's data rather than to the group data.

It is often convenient to summarize your data in the form of one or more tables or figures. In planning tables and figures, keep in mind that you should not repeat in the text information that is contained in tables and figures and that tables and figures should be largely self-explanatory, although you should certainly discuss them in the text. Two more considerations are relevant, but only if you plan to submit a paper to a journal: (a) large numbers of tables and figures are discouraged (because they are expensive to reproduce in journals), and (b) one or two sentences often can summarize data that initially seem to require a table or figure.

In deciding between presenting data in a table versus a figure, you face a trade-off. On the one hand, figures tend to give the reader a better global sense of the data; on the other hand, tables convey information to the reader more precisely. In general, tables are preferred, but your own judgment of what best conveys your message should be the arbiter of how you present the data.

In reporting tests of statistical significance, include (a) the name of the test, (b) the value of the test statistic, (c) the degrees of freedom (if relevant), and (d) the significance level of the test. Readers should also be informed of whether or not the test is directional and what the direction of the effect was. Assume that your reader is knowledgeable about basic statistics, but describe briefly the assumptions and theory underlying unconventional tests, if possible giving a reference to which readers can refer. Editors may also require you to indicate the power of the significance test.

### 5.5.7 Discussion

The "Discussion" section should include the following: (a) an explanation of how well your data fit your original hypotheses, (b) an explanation of how your data fit in with the existing body of literature, (c) a statement of your conclusions, and (d) a discussion of theoretical and, if relevant, practical implications of the results.

It is appropriate to include in the discussion a consideration of why the findings are important; why the topic itself and the problems within it are important; why you chose the level of analysis you did; and how, if at all, the findings can be applied.

You may open the discussion with a paragraph that summarizes the purpose of your study, your hypotheses, and most important findings.

Then continue with a general statement of how well the data fit your hypotheses. If the data fit your hypotheses, your task is straightforward. If the data do not fit your hypotheses, then you can approach the data from either of two angles. One angle is an acceptance of the data as uninterpretable; the other angle is an interpretation of the data as fitting hypotheses different from the ones you originally suggested. In either case, you should be as clear in describing lack of fit as you are in describing fit. Typically, authors reconceptualize papers that originally were designed to show one thing but end up showing another, thereby writing up the papers in a way different from that originally planned.

If your data are uninterpretable or only partially interpretable, say so. Convoluted explanations of unexpected data are easily recognized as rationalizations of failures. If you have good reason to believe that some aspect of your experiment was responsible for the uninterpretable results, say so briefly, and let matters stand there. Do not, however, waste space listing possible reasons for the uninterpretable results: Such lists can go on forever and are boring to read.

As a guideline, use about one paragraph or more for each main point in your discussion. Make sure that you do not merely reiterate results but also integrate them somehow (Calfee, 2000).

If your data are unexpected but interpretable, it is permissible to interpret them in light of new, reformulated hypotheses. You must make clear, however, that your explanation is post hoc and speculative. There is a fine line between reformulation of hypotheses and empty rationalization, so you must convince your readers that your post hoc explanation provides a compelling account of the data.

Afterward, comment on how your data fit into the existing literature. Where do your results differ, and where do they fit right in? What do the discrepancies and parallels suggest?

After you have discussed the fit of your data to the original hypotheses as well as existing literature, and any new hypotheses you might have, a concise statement of your conclusions should be presented. Because the conclusions are the major message of your paper, you should phrase them with great care, thereby ensuring that readers will interpret them as you intended.

Finally, discuss theoretical and possibly practical implications of the results. Consider internal and external validity in your discussion. If you have drawn conclusions different from those of your original hypotheses, you might suggest ways in which the conclusions could be verified in future research. Do not merely say, however, that future research will be needed to clarify the issues, without giving readers any inkling of what form such research might take. Every reader knows that more research can be done on any topic. What readers want to learn from you is what direction this research should take.

## 5.5.8 An Alternative: "Results and Discussion"

The "Results" and "Discussion" sections are sometimes combined into one section called "Results and Discussion," especially when each section is relatively short. We recommend this combination even when the individual sections are not short. The problem with a "Results" section standing by itself is that it is difficult to follow and makes for dry reading. The reader is confronted with masses of statistics without being told what the statistics mean or why they are important. Meaningful discussion is deferred until later.

Reconsider our discussion in the previous chapter of thematic versus nonthematic organization. In the present context, one's choices are the following:

| Nonthematic Organization | Thematic Organization |
|---|---|
| III. Results | III. Results and Discussion |
|   A. Presentation of Result A |   A. Result A |
|   B. Presentation of Result B |     1. Presentation |
|   C. Presentation of Result C |     2. Discussion |
| IV. Discussion |   B. Result B |
|   A. Discussion of Result A |     1. Presentation |
|   B. Discussion of Result B |     2. Discussion |
|   C. Discussion of Result C |   C. Result C |
| |     1. Presentation |
| |     2. Discussion |

In the format on the left, readers almost certainly will have to refer back to the results from the discussion, unless the results are re-presented in the "Discussion" section, an undesirable redundancy. Readers are unlikely to remember all the results from the "Results" section if they have been presented in an unmotivated fashion with no interpretation to make them meaningful.

In the format on the right, there is no need for paging backward. The results are discussed as they are presented, so that readers can understand why they are important when they are presented. They do not have to wait until later to discover why the author bothered to present those particular results and not others. Consequently, readers can form a more integrated and coherent representation of the author's results-discussion package.

If the thematic organization on the right in the next example is easier to follow than the nonthematic organization on the left, why is the organization on the left the more widely used? We suspect that it is because of a tacit fear that, in a joint presentation of results and discussion, the discussion will somehow contaminate the results – that combining the sections will blur the distinction between objective and subjective information. This argument, although understandable, is weak. Even slightly skilled writers can interweave data and discussion of the data in a way that makes clear the distinction between the two. Writers can, of course, be dishonest and try to pass off their opinions as facts. But such writers can distort their data regardless of the way in which the paper is organized.

Regardless of which organization you choose, related results may be presented and discussed in clusters to increase the meaningfulness of the presentation. For example, Results A and B might be clustered together in the following ways:

| Nonthematic Organization | Thematic Organization |
|---|---|
| III. Results | III. Results and Discussion |
|   A. Presentation of Result cluster (A, B) |   A. Result cluster (A, B) |
|   B. Presentation of Result C |     1. Presentation |
| IV. Discussion |     2. Discussion |
|   A. Discussion of result cluster (A, B) |   B. Result C |
|   B. Discussion of Result C |     1. Presentation |
| |     2. Discussion |

### 5.5.9 References

The references provide a complete list of the sources you cite in your paper. The format of the references is discussed further in Chapters 4 and 8. Be sure your references are accurate. Incorrect citations are a disservice to readers and show sloppy scholarship.

### 5.5.10 Appendix

An appendix is rarely used in psychological papers, although it is valuable in certain cases. It is appropriate for (a) computer programs designed explicitly for your research, unavailable elsewhere, and possibly valuable to others, (b) unpublished tests, (c) mathematical proofs that are relevant to your paper but would distract the reader if included in the text, and (d) lists of stimulus materials, if the materials are unusual or particularly important to your conclusions (American Psychological Association, 2009). The appendix should be included only if it is especially enlightening or helpful to others in replicating your study. Sometimes multiple appendices are used. In this case, label each appendix with a capital letter (e.g., Appendix A, Appendix B). If you have only one appendix, name it *Appendix*. Multiple tables per appendix must be labeled with the capital letter of the appendix and a number (e.g., A1, A2, A3, B1, B2). Note that even if you have only one appendix, you still have to label your tables in the appendix A1, A2, and so forth, to indicate that they are located in the appendix. Appendices sometimes are presented via the web.

## 5.5.11 Order of Sections

Once you are ready to write your paper in final form, you should order the sections in the following way:

1. Title page (including your name and affiliation)
2. Author identification notes
3. Abstract
4. Text
5. References
6. Footnotes
7. Tables (one table per page)
8. Figure captions
9. Figures (one figure per page)

This ordering is to facilitate editing and printing. It is not the order in which the various parts will appear. Pages should be numbered consecutively using arabic numerals, beginning with the title page and ending with the figure captions. Place page numbers in the upper right corner of each page. Immediately above the page number, write the first few words of your title, or the whole title if the title is short. This way, the pages can be returned to a manuscript in case they are temporarily misplaced.

The preceding ordering applies to papers written for submission to journals. For course papers, the following exceptions should be noted. First, footnotes usually should be placed at the bottom of the page on which they are cited. Second, tables and figures should be placed near where they are cited in the text rather than at the end. Third, figure captions should be placed immediately below the appropriate figures rather than in a separate section.

Once you have finished ordering and numbering your pages, the paper is complete. Once you have proofread it (see Chapter 13), you are ready to hand it in or send it off.

## CHECKLIST FOR EXPERIMENTAL PAPERS

☐ Is your title simple, concise, and self-explanatory? Does it contain keywords?

☐ Have you decided on a name under which you will publish all your professional publications?

☐ Is your abstract self-explanatory, and does it include major hypotheses, a summary of the method, the main results, and the conclusions?

☐ Will your introduction appeal to readers and animate them to continue reading?

☐ Does your introduction state what previous theory and research led to your own research, what your research adds and how, and why your research and the question it answers are important?

☐ Does your "Method" section contain all necessary information concerning subjects, materials, apparatus, design, and procedure?

☐ Does the "Design" subsection, in particular, include information on the type of design, the independent and dependent variables, and how participants were assigned to groups?

☐ Have you presented your results in a way that makes sense and supports your story rather than in the order in which you conducted the data analyses?

☐ Have you made an effort to report the "right" number of results – neither too many nor too few? Have you ensured that your data are directly relevant to your hypotheses, or that they are at least interesting in their own right?

☐ Does your discussion include (a) an explanation of how well your data fit your hypotheses, (b) how your data fit with the literature,

(c) your conclusions, and (d) a discussion of theoretical and practical (if applicable) implications of your results?

☐ Have you used about one paragraph per main point in your discussion?

☐ Have you named all sources and listed them in the references list?

☐ Are the parts of your manuscript in the right order?

# 6 A Word About Content, Language, and Style

In the previous chapters, we have described what belongs in a literature review or an experimental paper. You have learned how to do literature research, what the goals of the two different kinds of papers are, and how to report your findings. To write an appealing paper that maximizes your chances of getting your research published, it is important not only that your studies have substance but also that you well explain about that substance. This chapter provides you with some guidelines on how to write a paper that conveys your findings in an attractive, easily readable, and convincing way. We have divided the guidelines into three parts: Part 1 explains how to present your content in a way that is compelling and convincing. Part 2 deals with style issues, and Part 3 deals with language and grammar issues.

## 6.1 CONTENT GUIDELINES

1. State clearly the problem you are addressing, and then organize the article around the problem.

2. Start strong.

3. Make clear up front what the new and valuable contribution of your article is, and make sure you are right.

4. Tell readers why they should be interested.

5. Make sure the article does what it says it will do.

6. Make sure that the literature review is focused, reasonably complete, and balanced.

7. Make clear how your work builds on that of others.

8. Check your data analyses and interpretations.

9. Always explain what your results mean – don't force the reader to decipher them.

10. Make sure that your conclusions follow from your data.

11. Make clear what the limitations of your work are.

12. Be sure to consider alternative interpretations of the data.

13. End strongly and state a clear take-home message.

## 1. State clearly the problem you are addressing and then organize the article around the problem.

Sometimes it is hard to figure out exactly what problem authors of an article thought they were trying to solve. This phenomenon can occur because an author does not know what problem the article is supposed to solve or because the nature of the problem was not clearly communicated. It is the author's responsibility to make clear early in the article what problem or problems the article tackles.

Once you have stated the problem, organize the article around it. Show why the problem is important, why it should matter to anyone beside you. If you do not know, why should a reviewer? In the literature review, use relevance to the problem tackled as the major basis for deciding what to cite. In the "Methods" section, tell the story of how the successive analyses help solve the problem that you originally posed. And then, in the "Discussion" section, summarize what you did and discuss its implications.

A clearly focused, tightly organized article has a great advantage in the review process. You are helping the referee understand what your goals are and how you are trying to reach them. If you leave it to the referees to figure these things out, there is a good chance that the conclusions they come to will differ from your own.

## 2. Start strong.

"Smith and Jones (2009) found that 83% of readers never got beyond the first paragraph of the majority of articles they began to read." This opening is an example of how to be boring, as are these opening sentences: "Past research shows..." or "It is interesting to note that..." (says who?). A stronger start asks a question or states a problem pertinent to the theme of your article: "Why are so many psychology articles safe and cheap substitutes for sleeping pills?" for example, or "Dullness blunts the impact of many potentially interesting articles." Tell readers what the article is about in a provocative way that catches their attention.

### 3. Make clear up front what the new and valuable contribution of your article is, and make sure you are right.

Our conversations with journal editors suggest that the No. 1 reason for rejection of journal articles is lack of substance – there just is not enough new information in the article to justify its publication in a journal. Reviewers, too, are on the lookout for articles that have little or nothing new to say.

It therefore behooves you to ask yourself what the new and valuable contribution of your article is and to make clear near the beginning of the article what it is. Do not expect reviewers to figure it out for themselves. If you cannot figure it out, you cannot expect them to. If you cannot find such a contribution, either do more research or do more thinking before you submit the article.

### 4. Tell readers why they should be interested.

"These findings are interesting and important. Therefore, you should support my promotion to tenure." Don't expect readers to know why you find a topic interesting or why they should find it interesting. Show them! Keep your audience in mind: The more you can relate your topic to concerns of your readers, the more interest you will generate. If you are writing for perceptual psychologists, make contact with the theoretical issues that concern people in that field. If you are writing for teachers, show how your findings can be used to improve teaching.

### 5. Make sure that the article does what it says it will do.

"In this article, I will characterize the meaning of life, solve the problem of world hunger, and reveal at long last Richard Nixon's secret plan to end the Vietnam War." Many articles are rejected by journals because they do not deliver what they promise. They claim much but deliver little. For example, experiments should follow from the theory you present. Make sure that you frame your article in terms of what you have really accomplished, not in terms of what you wished you had accomplished.

## 6. Make sure that the literature review is focused, reasonably complete, and balanced.

"Thus, both studies showed that high levels of reasoning performance require people to wear propeller beanies on their heads. Other studies, showing that high levels of reasoning performance require pocket protectors, are irrelevant." Reviewers are infuriated by literature reviews that are biased in favor of a single point of view, especially if it's not their own (and chances are good that at least some of the reviewers will have views different from your own). Reviewers are even more upset when their own work is clearly relevant but not cited (you can say *Sayonara* to your acceptance). And reviewers do not want to read about every marginally relevant study ever done. Make your review complete and current, but also keep it focused and concise so that it encompasses but does not overwhelm what you are studying.

## 7. Make clear how your work builds on that of others.

No one likes a credit hog – someone who makes a contribution and then acts as though no one else has ever had any idea of value in the area of work. Sharing credit goes beyond citing potential reviewers. It involves showing how your work builds on their work and the work of many others. Scholarship always requires drawing connections between what is new and what is old.

It also is important in citing references that you are up to date. Referees generally are not happy to see reference lists that would have been up to date a decade earlier. So check recent literature in the area in which you are working. In this way, you also are less likely to repeat what someone already has done.

Some authors may feel that, in setting out in a bold new direction, they really owe almost nothing to anybody else. But it is important to realize that, even when you oppose old ideas, you still are using those ideas as a base from which to map your campaign of opposition. And even when you move away from what others have done, had they not done what they had done, you would not have had their work to move away from. Thus, it is important to show how you build on, not just how you go beyond, past work.

### 8. Check your data analyses and interpretations.

If your article makes a substantial contribution, there is a good chance that someone will ask for your data, which you are obliged to provide. This "someone" may be a referee or someone who later reads the article. One of the more embarrassing events in the life of an academic is to have the interpretation of one's data analyses demolished. It is therefore important to check that you have used the correct forms of analysis and to ensure that you have transcribed the statistics correctly.

Also, make sure that your interpretations are correct. For example, more stringent levels of significance do not indicate stronger effects but rather decrease likelihoods that a given result would have been obtained under the null hypothesis.

### 9. Always explain what your results mean – don't force readers to decipher them.

"Finally, we obtained a seven-way interaction among the independent variables, clearly showing that the variables need to be considered in terms of their interactive as well as their additive effects." Interpret your results. With enough time, readers could figure out the meaning for themselves, but who has time? Don't leave the interpretation for the "Discussion." Speculation and ideas that relate your work to that of others should go in the "Discussion" section. Basic interpretations should accompany the results – while people still remember what they are.

### 10. Make sure that your conclusions follow from your data.

High up on the list of annoyances to referees are authors whose claims go well beyond their data. Such authors are all too common. They may have a modest finding and then write about that finding as though they have changed the face of the earth. If your conclusions go beyond your data, chances are that referees will notice this and lash out at the conclusion and at you.

There is a place in most articles for speculation that goes beyond the boundaries of the data. This place is the "Discussion" section. But when you go beyond the boundaries of the data, make clear that you are speculating. Do not assume that referees or other readers will know that you are in a speculative state of mind.

## 11. Make clear what the limitations of your work are.

Any good "Discussion" section includes at least some frank acknowledgment of the limitations of the study. Did you use just a single methodology or type of stimulus material? Did you use a restricted range of types of participants? Did you look at behavior only in one kind of situation, perhaps an artificially contrived one? Referees and all readers appreciate honesty. Most important, referees are less likely to mention in reviews limitations that you already have mentioned, unless the referees see them as fatal flaws.

Many authors nurse the hope that referees will not notice the flaws. Such a hope is likely to be wishful thinking. Moreover, it is a misguided wish. Worse even than getting a paper rejected before publication is having to retract it after publication or having to resist an onslaught of published criticism for flaws that you should have noticed. Save yourself the trouble by acknowledging the flaws yourself.

## 12. Be sure to consider alternative interpretations of the data.

"Thus, the data overwhelmingly support the XYZ theory, and if you can't see it, you need to have your head examined." No data set is unequivocal. Sooner or later, someone will see one or more alternative interpretations. You are much better off recognizing and trying to discount the alternatives yourself than leaving the task to the reviewers or to your potential readers. Even if you cannot discount every alternative, readers will appreciate your honesty in recognizing that other explanations may exist. If the results are too inconclusive, your article may be turned down. But even published articles are not fully definitive, and readers expect you to admit as much.

## 13. End strongly and state a clear take-home message.

"In sum, there is a need for further research to clarify the issues." What a snooze! There's always room for further research; readers don't have to be told that. Readers want a punch line. They want to go away from a paper with a clear conclusion, preferably a snappy one (which may or may not be in the last sentence). When readers later try to remember your article, they will probably do so by means of your conclusion. Leave readers with what you most want them to remember.

## 6.2 STYLE GUIDELINES

In this section, we first give you an overview of the guidelines and subsequently explain them in more detail:

| |
|---|
| 1. Your paper should interest, inform, and persuade your readers. |
| 2. Place yourself in the background. |
| 3. Write for your readers. |
| 4. Emphasize logical flow and organization. |
| 5. Be creative, and give concrete examples. |
| 6. Write sentences that are clear, readable, and concise. |
| 7. Prefer simpler to more complicated sentences. |
| 8. Use summary statements. |
| 9. Use transitions. |
| 10. Avoid digressions. |
| 11. Don't overexplain. |
| 12. Don't assume that people will know what you mean or be familiar with abbreviations or jargon. |
| 13. Write for a somewhat broader and technically less skilled audience than you expect to read the article. |
| 14. Avoid overstatement. |
| 15. Eliminate unnecessary redundancy. |
| 16. Don't bother to say that your results are "interesting" or "important." |
| 17. Cite sources as well as findings. |
| 18. Don't end your article by saying, "More research is needed." |
| 19. Proofread your paper. |
| 20. Request a critical reading of your paper from an adviser or colleague. |

### 1. Your paper should interest, inform, and persuade your reader.

Psychological writing should not be dull or stuffy. An article tells a story. Like a story, it should capture readers' interest. You must interest your readers in your paper; otherwise, readers will find some-thing else to do. Even teachers reading course papers will often read boring papers more quickly and less carefully than they will read interesting papers. Although you can lose a reader at any time, the major decision points for the reader are the title, abstract, and introduction.

An optimal title is one that concisely informs readers of what the article is about. Such a title will minimize the number of people who start the article only to find that the topic doesn't interest them and maximize the number of people who start the article because the topic does interest them. The abstract should summarize the article while conveying to the reader why the topic, hypotheses, and results are of theoretical or practical interest. The introduction should fur-ther motivate readers by pointing out why the research is a necessary next step in putting together the pieces of an as-yet-unsolved puz-zle. The reader should finish the introduction believing that you have (a) put together one or more pieces of the puzzle and (b) pointed the way toward further pieces being put together. The second accom-plishment is as important as the first. No one likes to come to the end of an article only to find that the research has hit a dead end.

The best way to inform your readers is to tell them what they are likely to want to know – no more and no less. Experienced writers acquire a knack for knowing what to include and what not to include. Ask yourself which points are central to your main arguments and which are peripheral details possibly of interest to you but not to your readers.

The major means of persuasion is tight logic. Tight logic is more convincing to readers of psychological papers than rhetorical devices. Remember that you must sell your ideas but not oversell them, and you must be persuasive without being condescending. In attacking alternative positions, stick to substance, avoiding ad hominem or irrelevant attacks. (People who disagree with this advice don't know what they're talking about!)

## 2. Place yourself in the background.

There was a time when it was considered bad form for writers to place themselves anywhere near the foreground of a paper. Writers avoided first-person references at all costs. When strictures against first-person references started to ease, sole authors often started referring to themselves as *we*, even though they were sole authors of papers. Today, references to oneself as *we* are discouraged. If you are the sole author of a paper and use the word *we*, you should use it only to refer to yourself and your readers, not just to yourself. If you mean *I*, then use *I*. Overuse of the first-person singular, however, tends to distract the reader, calling attention to you rather than to what you are saying. Stay in the background, surfacing only when you have good reason to draw attention to yourself, as in emphasizing that an idea is your own speculation rather than a conclusion closely following from a set of data.

In some schools, you are expected to tell the story of your life when you write a paper, especially a dissertation. This story includes all your false starts, blind alleys, and tales of woe. You even may be expected to explain all the reasons your manipulation didn't work out the way it was supposed to. Journal space is precious, however, and there just isn't room for these autobiographical details. Therefore, journal articles are usually written in a manner that bears little resemblance to the way the research was actually conducted. This difference is not dishonesty: Professionals simply know how the system works.

(The first author first learned this fact when he was in graduate school. It was a dark and stormy night. He'd just received an editor's letter. For further details, see his *Complete Life and Works*, Vol. 21, published by Narcismo Press.)

### 3. Write for your reader.

Writing for your readers means keeping in mind four things. First, take into account the extent of their technical vocabulary. Terms that are familiar to professional psychologists may be unfamiliar to members of a general audience. Even within the field of psychology, specialists in different fields have different technical vocabularies. Whenever you can replace a complicated word with a simple word, do it. If you must use technical words, define them. It is most annoying to find a technical term used repeatedly without first having been defined. Second, maintain a level of formality in your writing that is appropriate for your audience. A book addressed to students can be more informal than a book addressed to professional psychologists. Remember, though, more formal writing need not and should not be stilted. Formality is not a substitute for readability. Third, include only those details that are appropriate for your audience. Readers of a popular journal such as *Psychology Today* will probably be less interested in methodological and statistical details than will readers of the scholarly journal *Psychological Review*. Fourth, avoid abbreviations. They can be annoying, and often interfere with the reader's comprehension of the text (QED!).

## 4. Emphasize logical flow and organization.

Don't expect readers to decipher the logical sequence of your ideas. It is important that the prose flow and that the organization emerge clearly. Write your ideas down in a sensible sequence. Readers should concentrate on what you say, not on how you say it. Logical organization can mean the difference between confusion and clarity.

## 5. Be creative, and give concrete examples.

Some academic writers harbor the illusion that the more abstract and highbrow their writing is, the more readers will be impressed. On the contrary, most readers need concrete examples or analogies to understand other people's ideas. The more abstract the points, the more it is that readers need examples. Readers are busy: Don't expect them to generate the examples. It's your responsibility. You have all read papers that have left you drowning in abstractions. We'll leave it to you to think of specific examples.

## 6. Write sentences that are readable, clear, and concise.

You know an unclear sentence when you read it. Why, then, don't authors know unclear sentences when they write them? A major reason is their personal involvement in their own work. If authors omit or poorly describe certain details, they can subconsciously insert or clarify them. Because readers do not share authors' cognitive structure, readers cannot do the same. A large amount of unclear writing would never pass beyond authors' eyes if all authors were willing to reread their papers in the role of naive readers. A major reason for lack of clarity in writing is an author's unwillingness to go back over what has been written and rewrite it. One reason for this unwillingness is a delusion that readers won't notice unclear sentences. Authors hope that the imperfections in their writing will pass by readers unnoticed. Unfortunately, the typical outcome is the opposite of what authors desire. Readers stumble over the unclear sentence and then reread it, trying to make sense of it. Instead of the sentence blending into the background, it sticks out like a sore thumb. If there are enough unclear sentences, what started out as temporary confusion may be come permanent. Hence, do not succumb to the delusion that you will get away with poor writing. Assume that your readers are as likely to detect an unclear sentence as you are to write one. (For the ideation of unclarity is the worst form of self-indulgence, and an ideological facsimile!)

## 7. Prefer simpler to more complicated sentences.

Sentence structure is largely a matter of style, and you should write in a style that is comfortable to you. Some major writers, like Ernest Hemingway, preferred short sentences; others, like William Faulkner, preferred long sentences. The advantages of short sentences, from a journalistic point of view, are that they are (a) easier to understand and (b) less likely to contain errors of grammar or diction. When you find yourself becoming bogged down in a complicated construction, try to restate in two or more sentences what you had planned to state in one. You will probably find that you are able to say better what you wanted to say. (Having thought about this, you will realize as you read this sentence at the end of the paragraph why complexity in an already long sentence creates bewilderment!)

## 8. Use summary statements.

Explain what you're going to say, say it, and then restate what you've said. In this way, you provide an advance organization for the reader, explicate the main content, and emphasize to readers what you want them to remember.

Psychologists frequently divide long papers into sections and subsections. It is often helpful to include one or two brief summary statements at the end of each section or at the end of a long argument. Such statements improve comprehensibility at very little cost in additional space. Summaries help readers (a) quickly absorb the main point of each section as they complete it and (b) keep track of where they are. A long summary in the middle of a paper is unnecessary and inadvisable, because it is redundant with the abstract and possibly the conclusions. (To summarize, a summary at this point in the chapter is unnecessary!)

## 9. Use transitions.

Have you ever noticed that some people write clear sentences, and yet their writing nevertheless appears disjointed? A common cause of disjointed and choppy writing is missing transitions between ideas. Missing transitions are sometimes caused by careless thinking: The writer goes from Step A to Step C without thinking of the necessary, intervening Step B. More often, though, missing transitions are caused by quick thinking: Authors think faster than they write. As authors write Sentence A, they are already thinking about Sentence B. By the time they finish writing Sentence A, they have started thinking about Sentence C and so proceed to write Sentence C, forgetting to insert the necessary transitional Sentence B. No matter how clearly Sentences A and C are stated, readers will pause in reading Sentence C, wondering whether they missed something in Sentence A or even in some sentence further back. You can insert missing transitions if you reread your paper and check carefully whether each sentence follows logically from the sentence immediately preceding it. (The price of rice also increased in China during this past year!)

## 10. Avoid digressions.

Papers are usually difficult enough to follow without the added encumbrance of digressions. Digressions lead readers away from the main points of your paper. Once readers' attention is diverted from the main points, there is always a risk that their attention will never find its way back to the main point. Occasionally, a digression may be needed to clarify a point. Minor digressions of this kind can be incorporated into footnotes. Major digressions can be incorporated into an appendix. But keep the digressions out of the basic text, where they will distract readers unnecessarily. (It's off the subject, but all this reminds us about a joke we heard. Two guys walk into a bar, and the first one says . . . )

## 11. Don't overexplain.

Students learning how to write psychology papers often explain too much. This problem is especially apparent in their "Method" sections.

Students doing a simple free-recall experiment can end up explaining (a) why they used visual rather than auditory presentation of words, (b) why they used nouns instead of other parts of speech, (c) why they used 18-word lists rather than lists of some other length, (d) why they presented words at a rate of one word per second rather than some other rate, and so on. Assume that readers of your paper (if they are professionals) are familiar with standard procedures and will be interested only in explanations of nonstandard ones. Exclusive use of people's names, for example, would be nonstandard in a free-recall experiment.

The same warning is relevant to the presentation and discussion of results. If your experiment has only a few results, then you need not select among them. If your experiment has many results or if you have analyzed the same data in many different ways, select the important results or analyses and concentrate on those. Your selection procedure must be honest: It would be unethical and unscientific to report and discuss only those results that support your hypotheses. The importance of a result should not be determined by its fit to your preconceived notions. (All of this will become clearer when we write our 1,000-page tome on how to avoid overexplanation!)

## 12. Don't assume that people will know what you mean or be familiar with abbreviations or jargon.

Sometimes when we're writing an article, we notice a sentence or paragraph that isn't clear. Occasionally, we're too lazy to change the offending text and hope no one will notice. We're particularly likely to hope that people will know what we mean when we're not sure what we mean ourselves, so that perhaps later they can tell us. Almost without fail, however, readers don't understand what we've said any better than we do. Reviewers complain about what they don't understand – and that includes abbreviations or jargon. (QED!)

## 13. Write for a somewhat broader and technically less skilled audience than you expect to read the article.

Writers tend to overestimate the knowledge and technical sophistication of their readers, as well as the extent to which readers share their exact interests. You should therefore write for a slightly broader and less knowledgeable audience than you expect will read the article, keeping in mind that you don't want to insult your audience, either. Somewhere between *"Visualize Maculation Decamp"* and *"See Spot Run"* lies both your audience and the Land of Acceptance Letters.

## 14. Avoid overstatement.

Scientific writing should be conservative in its claims. By overstating your case, you undermine your credibility and put your readers on guard. Once on guard, readers may cease to accept at face value anything you say. Consider, for example, the psychological phenomenon of writing a letter of recommendation for an undergraduate applying to graduate school or for a graduate student applying for a job. On the one hand, you want to do what you can to ensure that a good student obtains the best possible placement. On the other hand, you know that if your claims sound extravagant, you run the risk of damaging your case. Hoping that the major strengths will sell the candidate, writers of letters frequently look for minor weaknesses in their candidates so that their letters appear impartial. Persons writing and reading letters know that some letter writers have reputations for writing inflated letters, and as a result, their letters are taken less seriously than the letters of others with greater credibility. The same reputations can be acquired by writers of psychology papers. Authors who are known to overstate their case will find others taking their claims less seriously than they would have taken the identical claims coming from someone else. (Everyone caught overstating their case ought certainly to be hanged on the spot!)

## 15. Eliminate unnecessary redundancy.

Elimination of redundancy from a paper is a difficult task, because one is never certain of how much redundancy should be eliminated. On the one hand, redundancy can reinforce your points. Readers may comprehend the second time a point that had eluded them the first time. On the other hand, redundancy can obscure your points. When a paper is highly redundant and readers become aware of its redundancy, they may start reading the paper more quickly and less carefully, assuming that they will have read before and will read again much of what they are reading. Readers assume that if they do not quite understand a point the first time, they will have another chance when the author repeats the point in a slightly different way. Readers may then fail to understand the point because it is not in fact presented again or because its second presentation is no more enlightening than was the first.

Because redundancy is a double-edged sword, you are better off attaining emphasis through other means. There are three alternative means you can use. First, you can discuss in more detail the points you wish to emphasize. Instead of repeating the points several times at different places in the paper, you give them additional space the first time you make them. Second, you can make important points at strategic places in the paper. People tend to remember best what they read at the beginning or the end of a paper. Third, you can state explicitly that one or more points are of special importance and thus merit more careful attention. It may be obvious to you which points are your important ones, but it may not be obvious to your readers. Simply telling readers which points are important can help guide their attention in an optimal way.

Writers usually find it much easier to spot redundancy in others' writing than in their own, because they have difficulty distinguishing what they have thought about from what they have written about. They may repeat a point for a second or third time, unaware that they have made the point before. Even in rereading their work, they may have trouble distinguishing their thoughts from their writing. It is therefore a good idea to have someone else read your paper and deliberately seek out repetitious material. (Because other people usually will not have thought about your topic in the same way you have, they are more likely to recognize redundancy, repetition, reiteration, rehashing, restating, and duplication!)

### 16. Don't bother to say that your results are "interesting" or "important."

Let the results speak for themselves.

### 17. Cite sources as well as findings.

When you cite a finding, cite its source. There are four reasons you should supply this information. First, readers can check whether you have cited the source accurately. They may doubt the finding and want to verify that you properly cited it. Second, readers can check whether the source is credible. If you merely cite a finding, readers have no way of checking the quality of the evidence in support of that finding. Third, readers can learn about a reference that they may have been unaware of and that they then want to read. Fourth, you show your readers that you are familiar with the literature on your topic, thereby increasing your own credibility as a source of information. (In fact, research has shown that citing sources of research findings does improve credibility!)

### 18. Don't end your article by saying, "More research is needed."

This statement has become a cliché. There is almost always room for further research.

### 19. Proofread your paper.

We estimate that fewer than half the papers we receive have been proofread by their authors. Fewer than one quarter are proofread carefully. We think that authors often fail to proofread their work because they are afraid they won't like what they read. But other readers of your paper will like it even less if they have to put up with errors that the author easily could have corrected. We cannot emphasize enough the importance of proofreading. The time it takes to proofread a paper is a small fraction of the time it takes to write the paper. And there is probably no other thing you can do in so little time that will as much improve others' evaluations of your work.

The best method of proofreading is to have someone read the text to you from the original while you check the final copy line by line. In following the text, read only for errors in spelling, punctuation, capitalization, and the like. Do not read for meaning. You should read the paper an additional time to make sure that you have said what you wanted to say in the way you wanted to say it. (Typografikal erors are uneccesary!)

### 20. Request a critical reading of your paper from an adviser or colleague.

Because people are so involved in their own work, they find it much easier to criticize the work of others than to criticize their own work. It is therefore to your advantage to seek the advice of others on any paper you write. When asking people to read your paper, ask them to read it critically, indeed, ruthlessly. It is a common experience for authors to receive compliments from their colleagues on their papers and then to find them torn to shreds by journal reviewers. One reason for the discrepancy is that colleagues you ask to read your paper may not willingly sacrifice the time or risk the loss of friendship that might be involved in a very critical reading of your work. Encourage your readers to be critical, perhaps offering your own critical paper-reading services in return.

## 6.3 LANGUAGE AND GRAMMAR GUIDELINES

| 1. Use the precise word. |
| 2. Prefer simpler to more complicated words. |
| 3. Use concrete words and examples. |
| 4. Use the active voice. |
| 5. Prefer affirmative to negative constructions. |
| 6. Avoid unnecessary qualifiers. |
| 7. Avoid dangling constructions. |
| 8. Avoid participles without referents. |
| 9. Avoid pronouns without antecedents. |
| 10. Avoid use of the indefinite *this*. |
| 11. Avoid split infinitives. |
| 12. Avoid gender-biased language |

### 1. Use the precise word.

In the course of writing your paper, you will probably find yourself occasionally stumbling over words, unable to choose a word that expresses the precise meaning you want to convey. Do not settle for an approximate word when a precise word is available. While you are writing, have available both a dictionary and a thesaurus, so that you can search for the optimal word. Settle for a suboptimal one only if you are unable to find the optimal one after diligent searching. (It is to your advance to alleviate use of ill-chosen words!)

## 2. Prefer simpler to more complicated words.

The main purpose of writing is communication, and simpler words usually communicate more effectively than do complicated ones. The reaction of readers coming across a complicated word they do not know is not awe for the writer's vocabulary but annoyance that communication has broken down. The reaction of readers coming across a complicated word that they know doesn't fit the context in which it is being used is often one of even greater annoyance. Every year, we encounter at least one author who seems to write papers not to communicate thoughts but to communicate vocabulary. More often than not, this communication is unsuccessful: The writer misuses complicated words. The most important decision regarding words is always to use the one that best expresses your meaning. (If you find that two words express your meaning equally well, use the simpler one, not the more reticular one!)

## 3. Use concrete words and examples.

Much psychological writing is of necessity abstract. Whenever you have a choice, though, between an abstract and a concrete word, choose the concrete one. People will understand you better. When taking your readers through an abstract argument, use examples. If the argument is a long one, don't wait until the end to supply the example. Readers may have gotten lost in your argument a long time before, so that in reading your example they will have to go back through the argument anyway. Your argument will be clearer if you weave examples into the argument, alternating between the abstract and the concrete. Readers will then be able to understand your argument as they read it rather than when (or if) they reread it. (Indeed, this paragraph would have been clearer if it had provided an example of what it was talking about.)

## 4. Use the active voice.

Use of the impersonal third person in psychological articles encourages overuse of the passive voice. Psychology papers are replete with expressions like "it was found," "it can be concluded," "the tests were administered," "the subjects were told," and "the session was completed." Expressions stated in the passive voice are harder to read and make for duller reading than expressions stated in the active voice. Whenever you use a passive construction, try to restate it as an active one. (Although it will be found that this cannot always be done by you, it will be appreciated by your reader, whose understanding of your prose will be enhanced!)

## 5. Prefer affirmative to negative constructions.

Psychologists have established that negative constructions are harder to understand than affirmative ones (Clark & Chase, 1972). Your writing will therefore be easier to understand if you use affirmative rather than negative constructions wherever possible. In some cases, you will have a choice between an implicit and an explicit negation. For example, you might say either "Writers should avoid negative constructions" or "Writers should not use negative constructions." Similarly, you might say either "Six children were absent from school the day the testing took place" or "Six children were not present in school the day the testing took place." Implicit negations like the first example in each pair are easier to understand than explicit negations (Clark, 1974), and hence are preferred. (Wherever possible, do not fail to avoid explicit negations!)

## 6. Avoid unnecessary qualifiers.

Qualifiers serve a useful purpose when they honestly limit the scope of a statement. For example, if only some participants showed the effect of a certain treatment, then the effect of the treatment should be qualified as limited only to those subjects. Qualifiers serve no purpose, however, if they do not honestly limit scope. A somewhat noticeable tremor is not distinguishably different from a noticeable tremor; a rather loud pulse is not distinguishably different from a loud pulse. The use of *somewhat* and *rather* in those contexts draws life from the prose without giving anything in return. In using qualifiers such as *somewhat*, *rather*, *mostly*, *largely*, and *for the most part*, check that they make an honest addition to the sentence. If they don't, throw them out.

Sometimes authors use qualifiers to hedge their bets. Because psychology is an inductive science, proceeding from the specific to the general, psychologists can never draw conclusions with certainty. Psychologists may therefore express their uncertainty by qualifying their conclusions. For example, suppose that in a series of experiments, psychologists find that recall of a list of words always increases with practice. They conclude that "at least under some circumstances, certain participants tend to recall more words after more free-recall trials." The qualifications are correct: There are indeed circumstances under which recall will not improve with practice; there are some participants who will not show increasing recall over trials (e.g., dead ones); and because a given participant's recall may occasionally decrease from one trial to the next (if only by chance), one is safe in referring to a tendency toward increasing recall. The psychologists' successive qualifications, however, have left the statement moribund and have not told readers anything they don't already know. Had the authors simply stated that "the results indicate that free recall increases over trials," they would have made the point without bogging readers down in excess words. (For the most part, it is usually true that, in most cases, absolutely unnecessary qualifiers can often impede communication!)

## 7. Avoid dangling constructions.

Dangling constructions make sentences ambiguous, including this one. The preceding sentence is ambiguous because it is not clear whether *one* refers to dangling constructions or to sentences. The source of the ambiguity is the phrase "including this one," which dangles at the end of the sentence. Suppose a "Method" section informs you that "the participants were falsely debriefed by the confederates after they finished their task." You cannot be certain whether *they* and *their* refer to the participants or to the confederates. This sentence could be improved by eliminating the dangling construction. Depending on who finished the task, authors might write either "after they finished their task, the confederates falsely debriefed the participants" or "after they finished their task, the participants were falsely debriefed by the confederates." Consider another example from a "Discussion" section: "The result would have been more easily interpretable if all the participants had answered all the questions affirmatively, not just the first five." In this sentence, it is not clear whether just the first five participants answered all the questions affirmatively or whether all the participants answered just the first five questions affirmatively. The sentence should be rewritten in one of two ways, depending on the author's intent: (a) "The result would have been more easily interpretable if all the participants, not just the first five, had answered all the questions affirmatively" or

(b) "The results would have been more easily interpretable if all the participants had answered all the questions, not just the first five, affirmatively."

## 8. Avoid participles without referents.

Suppose you read in a paper, "The rat was found dead while cleaning the cage." You probably would be correct to assume that an experimenter or a technician, not the dead rat, cleaned the cage. The sentence is ambiguous, however, because it lacks a referent for the participle. Less extreme examples of participles without referents abound in psychological writing. Consider the following sentence from a "Method" section: "While monitoring the participant's heartbeat, adrenaline was injected into the participant's left arm." The sentence is unacceptable because it does not state who monitored the participant's heartbeat. Obviously, it wasn't the adrenaline that did the monitoring. But who did? The sentence should be revised to read, "While monitoring the participant's heartbeat, the experimenter injected adrenaline into the participant's left arm." In general, if you use active constructions when you use participles, you will eliminate participles without referents.

## 9. Avoid pronouns without antecedents.

Students learn the rule to avoid pronouns without antecedents early in their schooling, and yet they continue to violate it, usually in subtle ways. For example, many people will not recognize the following statement from a "Method" section as ungrammatical: "After the participant's task was completed, he or she was free to leave." To whom does "he or she" refer? Obviously not to *task*, but there is no other noun in the sentence, and the antecedent of a pronoun must be a noun. The author could reword the statement to say, "After the participant's task was completed, the participant was free to leave," or better, "After the participant completed the task, he or she was free to leave."

A possessive pronoun needs an antecedent as much as does any other pronoun. Consider, for example, a slight variant of an earlier sentence: "While monitoring the participant's heartbeat, the experimenter injected epinephrine into his or her left arm." The grammatical antecedent for *his* is *experimenter*, although it is obvious that the author intended otherwise. The author should rephrase the sentence: "While monitoring the participant's heartbeat, the experimenter injected epinephrine into the participant's left arm."

## 10. Avoid use of the indefinite *this*.

A common problem in writing is use of the word *this* without a definite antecedent. You will find this even in otherwise well-written prose, such as this sentence. The first use of *this* in the preceding sentence is indicative of sloppy prose. Note that there are two possible antecedents of *this* in the second sentence of this paragraph, *problem* and *use of the word*. The ambiguity is eliminated by changing *this* from a pronoun to an adjective: "You will find this problem even in otherwise well-written prose."

## 11. Avoid split infinitives.

Split infinitives seem to evoke two reactions. Some people use them regularly and barely notice when they read them. Other people never use them and wince every time they see or hear them. Usually, split infinitives make sentences less graceful without adding any clarity. To carefully weigh the evidence is the same as to weigh the evidence carefully, but the latter way of expressing the idea is more readable than the former. If the adverb with which you want to split the infinitive seems to fit nowhere else, consider rewriting the sentence in a different way. (Try to always follow this advice!)

## 12. Avoid gender-biased language.

Do not use the pronoun *he* when you mean *he* or *she*. Excessive use of *he or she* is awkward and can be irritating as well. Use of plurals and rephrasing of sentences can often help eliminate both sexist language and excessive use of *he or she*.

### CHECKLIST FOR CONTENT

- [ ] Have you stated the problem clearly?
- [ ] Is the article organized around the problem?
- [ ] Have you made clear early on what the contribution of your paper is?
- [ ] Have you told readers why your paper is of interest to them?
- [ ] Is your literature review focused, reasonably complete, and balanced?

☐ Have you checked your data analyses and interpretations?
☐ Have you explained the meaning of your results?
☐ Do your conclusions follow from your data?
☐ Have you made the limitations of your work clear?
☐ Have you considered alternative interpretations of the data?
☐ Have you provided a take-home message?

## CHECKLIST FOR STYLE

☐ Have you placed yourself in the background?
☐ Is your paper logical and organized?
☐ Have you given concrete examples?
☐ Are your sentences clear, readable, and concise?
☐ Are your sentences as simple as possible?
☐ Have you used summary statements?
☐ Have you used transitions?
☐ Have you avoided digressions?
☐ Have you explained abbreviations?
☐ Have you avoided jargon?
☐ Have you eliminated unnecessary redundancy?
☐ Have you cited sources and findings?
☐ Have you requested a critical reading of your paper by a colleague or adviser?

## CHECKLIST FOR LANGUAGE AND GRAMMAR

**Whenever possible, have you**
☐ used precise words?
☐ used simple words?
☐ used concrete words and examples?
☐ used the active voice?
☐ used affirmative constructions?
☐ avoided unnecessary qualifiers?
☐ avoided dangling constructions?
☐ avoided participles without referents?
☐ avoided pronouns without antecedents?
☐ avoided use of the indefinite *this*?
☐ avoided split infinitives?
☐ avoided gender-biased language?

# 7 Commonly Misused Words

This chapter explains the meanings of some of the most commonly misused words in student papers. The chapter is divided into two parts. The first part deals with meanings of nontechnical terms. Dowling (2008) provides an extensive overview of misused words, and Garner (2003) provides a complete dictionary of American usage. The second part of the chapter deals with meanings of technical terms. The psychological dictionaries and encyclopedias described in Chapter 3 provide much more extensive lists of psychological terms.

## 7.1 NONTECHNICAL TERMS

1. **adapt, adopt.** To adapt is to accommodate, to adjust, to bring into correspondence. To adopt is to embrace, to take on, to make one's own.
   a. Organisms adapt to their environment.
   b. Children adopt the attitudes of their peers.
2. **adopt.** See (1).
3. **affect, effect.** Both words can be used either as nouns or as verbs. An affect is an emotion or something that tends to arouse an emotion. An effect is a result or outcome of some cause. To affect is to influence or to have an effect on something. To effect is to accomplish or to bring about.
   a. His display of affect in response to the TAT (Thematic Apperception Test) picture seemed artificial and contrived to gain the psychologist's sympathy.
   b. The effect of the experimental treatment was negligible.
   c. Shoddy procedures affect the outcome of an experiment.

    d. She was able to effect a change in behavior by desensitizing the patient to snakes.

4. **aggravate, irritate.** To aggravate is to intensify, to heighten, or to magnify. To irritate is to annoy, to inflame, to provoke.
    a. Don't aggravate his frustration by telling him that he answered all the questions incorrectly.
    b. Experimenters who deceive subjects often irritate the subjects.

5. **allusion.** An allusion is an indirect reference. An explicit statement about X is not an allusion to X.
    a. The first experimenter made an allusion to a reward for exceptional performance, but she never came out and directly told the subject that the subject would receive a reward.
    b. The second experimenter told the subject he would receive a reward for exceptional performance. (He did not allude to a reward.)

6. **among, between.** *Between* refers to a relation between two things and *among* refers to a relation among two or more than two things. The term *between* can be used for a relation involving more than two things if reciprocity is involved in the relation. When in doubt regarding relations among more than two things, use *among*.
    a. The subject had to decide between the button on the left and the button on the right.
    b. The subject had to decide among the left, middle, and right buttons.
    c. The agreement between the three members of the group broke down quickly when the experimental manipulation was introduced.

7. **amount of, number of.** An amount of something is a sum total or aggregate. A number of something is a quantity of it. Use *amount of* when dealing with quantities that can't be counted. Use *number of* when dealing with quantities that can be counted. Monetary terms are exceptions to this generalization.
    a. The amount of liquid in the tall jar was the same as the amount in the fat jar.
    b. The number of stimuli was too small.
    c. The subject was dissatisfied with the amount of money she received for participating in the experiment.

8. **and/or.** Avoid this expression, which means that a relation is either conjunctive (*and*) or disjunctive (*or*). The expression

disrupts the flow of prose, is ambiguous, and often indicates that authors couldn't decide which conjunction to use, so they used both.

9. **as to whether.** Avoid this expression. Say *whether*.

10. **between.** See (6).

11. **bring, take.** To bring something is to carry it toward the speaker or listener. To take something is to carry it away from the speaker or listener.
    a. Take this incomprehensible book back to the library.
    b. Bring me a better book from the library.

12. **certainly.** Use the word *certainly* only if you mean "with 100% probability." Don't use the word loosely to connote near certainty.
    a. She certainly won't eat her hat.

13. **compare to, compare with.** To compare *to* is to point out or emphasize similarities between different things. To compare *with* is to point out or emphasize differences between similar things.
    a. The student compared the predictions of the continuous learning model to those of the discrete learning model and showed that they were indistinguishable.
    b. The student compared Freud's conception of the ego with Erikson's conception and showed that the two conceptions differed in fundamental respects.

14. **comprise.** To comprise is to consist of or to embrace. This word has the dubious distinction of being misused more often than it is properly used in student papers. A whole comprises its parts; parts constitute (form or compose) a whole.
    a. This book comprises 15 fascinating chapters.

15. **continual, continuous.** Continual means often repeated. Continuous means without stop.
    a. Continual interruptions forced the experimenter to terminate the session early.
    b. Continuous background music improved employees' morale.

16. **continuous.** See (15).

17. **data.** *Data* is a plural noun and should take a plural verb. The singular form is *datum*, which is used infrequently.
    a. The professor's data were far from perfect.
    b. One datum was inconsistent with all the rest.

18. **different from, different than.** If two things differ, they are *different from* each other. The expression *different than* is nonstandard.

19. **discover, invent.** To discover something is to find something that was there before. To invent something is to create something new.
    a. No one has discovered a single gene for intelligence.
    b. Some people would like to invent a pill to increase intelligence.
20. **disinterested, uninterested.** To be disinterested is to be impartial. To be uninterested is to lack interest.
    a. There seem to be few disinterested investigators studying the heritability of intelligence. Most of them have obvious biases.
    b. Psychoanalysts are generally uninterested in stimulus-response explanations of behavior.
21. **effect.** See (3).
22. **enormity, enormousness.** The former word refers to extreme wickedness, the latter to extreme size or volume.
    a. The enormity of the tyrant's crimes could not be simulated in an experimentally controlled setting.
    b. The enormousness of the giant scared the children.
23. **enormousness.** See (22).
24. **fact.** A fact should be directly verifiable either empirically or logically. Do not refer to judgments or probable outcomes as facts.
25. **factor.** Because this word has at least two technical meanings in psychology (see the next part of this chapter), it is best not to use it in a loose, nontechnical sense. Instead of saying, for example, that "several factors contributed to the subject's euphoria," say that "the subject was euphoric for several reasons."
26. **farther, further.** The word *farther* should be used to refer to greater distance; the word *further* should be used to refer to quantity or time.
    a. Further jokes were to no avail; the subject refused to laugh.
    b. The patient explained to the psychologist that the farther he traveled from his home, the more anxious he felt.
27. **fewer, less.** *Fewer* refers to number, *less* to amount or degree.
    a. The patient had fewer nightmares after she began therapy.
    b. The patient's nightmares became less frightening after she began therapy.
28. **former, latter.** *Former* refers to the first item in a series, *latter* to the second. These words are applicable when the series consists of just two items or when a longer series is divided into two parts. In series with more than two items, refer to the end points of the series as the first and last items.

    a. The male and female confederates entered the room together, the former carrying a live alligator and the latter carrying a dead rattlesnake.

    b. Of the three people who interviewed for the job, only the first was qualified but only the last was willing to take the job after finding out what it entailed.

29. **fortuitous, fortunate.** A fortuitous event is one that occurs by chance. A fortunate event is one that is favored by fortune.

    a. The simultaneous appearance of the two rivals was made to appear fortuitous, but it was in fact contrived.

    b. The appearance of all the subjects at the testing session was most fortunate because the machine controlling the testing exploded at the end of the session and thereafter was incapable of further use.

30. **fortunate.** See (29).

31. **further.** See (26).

32. **hopefully.** This word means *full of hope*. It does not mean *it is to be hoped*. Today, this word is more often used incorrectly than correctly.

    a. He started the experiment hopefully but ended it discouraged.

33. **imply, infer.** To imply something is to suggest it indirectly. To infer something is to conclude or deduce it from the information available. The two words are not interchangeable.

    a. The patient implied that she still felt like strangling anyone who got in her way.

    b. The therapist thus inferred that the patient was not yet cured.

34. **infer.** See (33).

35. **interesting.** This word is overused. Saying that something is interesting is not a substitute for making it interesting.

36. **invent.** See (19).

37. **irregardless.** This word does not exist in English. The proper word is *regardless*.

    a. The rat receives a sugar pellet after pressing the bar regardless of how long the rat takes to press it.

38. **irritate.** See (4).

39. **its, it's.** The word *its* is a pronoun that indicates *belonging* or *pertaining*. The word *it's* means *it is* or *it has*.

    a. The investigator knew the fear manipulation had failed when the monster shook its tail and the children laughed in response.

    b. After seeing the children's response, the investigator thought to himself: "It's all over."

40. **latter.** See (28).
41. **lay, lie.** *Lay* and *lie* both have a number of meanings. Confusion regarding which word to use arises from one meaning of each word. For *lay*, that meaning is *to put or place something*. For *lie*, that meaning is *to recline*. The past tense of *lay* is *laid* and the present perfect is *have laid*. The past tense of *lie* is *lay* and the present perfect is *have lain*. *Lay* always takes an object; *lie* never does.

    a.   i.  When the experimenter enters the room, he lays the booklets on the table.

         ii.  The experimenter laid the booklets on the table.

       iii.  The experimenter has laid the booklets on the table.

    b.   i.  The patient lies down on a couch when she enters the therapist's office.

         ii.  The patient lay down on a couch after she entered the therapist's office.

       iii.  After the patient has lain down, the therapist begins the session.

42. **less.** See (27).
43. **lie.** See (41).
44. **literally.** If something is literally true, then it is true in fact. Use *literally* only if you mean it. Do not use the expression *literally true* if you mean figuratively true or almost true.
45. **number.** See (7).
46. **one.** Do not follow *one* by *his*. Follow it by *one's*.

    a. To communicate effectively, one must organize one's papers carefully.

47. **only.** Imprecise placement of *only* in a sentence can change the meaning of the sentence. Place *only* immediately before the word or clause it modifies. Do not say, for example, "I only tested five participants" if you mean, "I tested only five participants." Consider how the meaning of a sentence changes depending on the placement of *only*:

    a. Only I will treat the patient in my office tomorrow.

    b. I only will treat the patient in my office tomorrow.

    c. I will only treat the patient in my office tomorrow.

    d. I will treat only the patient in my office tomorrow.

    e. I will treat the only patient in my office tomorrow.

    f. I will treat the patient only in my office tomorrow.

    g. I will treat the patient in only my office tomorrow.

    h. I will treat the patient in my only office tomorrow.

    i. I will treat the patient in my office only tomorrow.

    j. I will treat the patient in my office tomorrow only.

48. **principal, principle.** Used as an adjective, *principal* means *chief*, *dominant*, *main*, *major*. Used as a noun, it means a *person* or *thing of* importance or rank. *Principle* can be used only as a noun, and it refers to a general truth or law.

    a. The principal reason for not scoring the subject's test was that the subject had cheated in answering the last two problems.

    b. This book presents many principles for writing psychology papers.

49. **principle.** See (48).

50. **relevant.** Use this word only if you can specify a precise relationship. Do not use it to express a vague connection to everyday life or your experience, as in "clinical psychology is relevant." If you make the connection clear, then the word is appropriate:

    a. Clinical psychology is relevant to everyday life.

51. **since.** APA recommends that in formal writing for its journals, authors use this word only in its temporal sense, not as a substitute for *because*. If you mean *because*, use *because*.

    a. Since leaving therapy, the patient has shown no recurrence of symptoms.

52. **take.** See (11).

53. **that, which.** *That* is used for restrictive clauses, *which* for nonrestrictive clauses. Restrictive clauses limit the possible meaning of a preceding subject of a sentence. For example, "The paper that he wrote was a great success." Here, "that" refers to a specific paper. Nonrestrictive clauses contain information regarding a preceding subject in the sentence, but they do not limit (restrict) the meaning of that subject. For example, "The paper, which he wrote, was a great success." Note that here, in this second use, the fact that he wrote the paper tells us more about the paper rather than pointing to a specific (restricted) paper. Clauses using *which*, therefore, are surrounded by commas. The use of *which* for *that* is common in psychological (and other) writing but is inadvisable. Excessive use of *which* makes sentences cumbersome and difficult to read. The advice of Strunk and White (2008) is most appropriate: "The careful writer, watchful for small

conveniences, goes *which*-hunting, removes the defining *whiches*, and by doing so improves his work" (p. 53).

    a. The experiment that he designed is a gem. (This sentence tells which experiment is a gem. It was his experiment, not someone else's.)

    b. The experiment, which he designed, is a gem. (This sentence tells something about the one experiment in question.)

54. **try.** Say "try to," not "try and."

    a. Before she showed the picture of the snake to the patient, the therapist told the patient to try to relax.

55. **uninterested.** See (20).

56. **unique.** Something that is unique is one of a kind. It is not merely unusual or extraordinary. There can be no degrees of uniqueness.

    a. The psychologist employed a unique combination of therapeutic techniques in treating his patients.

57. **utilize.** *Use* is simpler, and usually serves just as well.

    a. The participant used the process of elimination to answer the multiple-choice test questions.

58. **which.** See (53).

59. **while.** This word is best used to mean "at the same time that." It is frequently used as a substitute for *whereas*, *but*, and *although*. The word does not serve well as a substitute, because it is not clear whether the author intends to imply simultaneity. The sentence, "I went east while he went west," is unambiguous if the reader knows that the author uses *while* only to mean *at the same time that*. But if the author sometimes uses *while* to mean *whereas*, the sentence is ambiguous: The reader does not know whether the two individuals went in opposite directions at the same time. Similarly, in reading the sentence "the subject answered test questions while the examiner scored them," readers will want to infer that answering and scoring occurred simultaneously.

    a. The experimenter appeared nonchalant while the subject finished the task.

60. **Whom.** This word is often used incorrectly before expressions like *he said*, when *who* should serve as the subject of the verb following the expression.

    a. The graduate student who the professor said would come to Yale went to Squeedunk instead. (*Who* is the subject of *would come*.)

    b. The graduate student whom the professor telephoned was not at home.

61. **Whose.** This word can serve as the possessive case of either *who* or *which*. Hence, it can refer to inanimate as well as animate objects.

    a. The subject was upset when the machine whose buttons she pressed disintegrated in fewer than five seconds.

    b. The experimenter, however, knew whose fault the disintegration was and had trouble holding back a smile.

## 7.2 TECHNICAL TERMS

1. **ability, capacity.** Capacity is innate potential. Ability is developed capacity. One's ability may not reflect one's capacity if environmental circumstances have been unfavorable to the development of that capacity. Only ability can be measured; hence, we cannot assess the degree to which one's ability reflects one's capacity.

    a. The child's test scores indicated only marginal ability to succeed in school work.

    b. The child's unhappy childhood suggested to the psychologist that the child's capacity for school work might not be reflected in his scores on ability tests.

2. **algorithm, heuristic.** An algorithm is a systematic routine for solving a problem that will eventually solve the problem, even if the solution involves consideration of all possible answers to the problem. A heuristic is a short cut or informal routine for solving a problem that may or may not eventually solve the problem. An algorithm may be slow, but it is guaranteed eventually to reach an answer. A heuristic is relatively fast but does not guarantee solution. Some problems can be solved only by heuristics. No algorithm is available, for example, that guarantees that a given move in a game of chess is the optimal move.

    a. The subject discovered an algorithm for solving the jigsaw puzzle, but the algorithm required 752,964 arrangements of the pieces of the puzzle to guarantee a solution.

    b. Another subject discovered a heuristic for solving the puzzle that she estimated gave her a 75% chance of solving the puzzle after only 55 arrangements of the pieces.

3. **anxiety, fear.** Anxiety is a state (or trait) of apprehension or uneasiness with no well-defined object. Fear is a state of apprehension in response to a well-defined threat.

   a. The executive felt a constant sense of anxiety, and yet was unable to pinpoint anything in his environment that threatened his well-being.

   b. The hunter was filled with fear when her rifle failed to fire and the bear started charging toward her.

4. **applied research, basic research.** Applied research strives for findings of practical value, regardless of whether or not they have theoretical value. Basic research strives for findings of theoretical value, regardless of whether they have practical value. Applied research may yield findings of theoretical value, and basic research may yield findings of practical value, although such findings are incidental to the major goals of each type of research.

   a. Research on consumer preferences for different kinds of cosmetic products has been almost exclusively applied research.

   b. Research on serial learning of nonsense syllables has been primarily basic research.

5. **artificial intelligence, simulation.** Artificial-intelligence researchers seek to build machines or instructions for machines that solve in an optimal way problems usually thought to require intelligence. Little or no attempt is made to have these machines or instructions correspond to the human mind or to the strategies used by the human mind. Simulation research seeks to build machines or instructions for machines that solve problems in ways analogous to those used by humans. Little or no attempt is made to achieve optimal performance. Indeed, if human performance is suboptimal, then an attempt is made to imitate this suboptimal performance.

   a. Using the techniques of artificial intelligence, the computer scientist was able to program a computer to solve algebra problems far more efficiently than human beings solve them.

   b. The psychologist wrote a simulation program that closely matched the techniques of Algebra I students in solving algebra problems.

6. **average.** As a statistical term, this word is used in two ways. The more specific way is as a synonym for *mean*. Used in this way, the average is the sum of a set of values divided by the number of values. The more general way is as a generic term for all measures

of central tendency (cf. mean, median, mode). Used in this way, the average is the central value, however defined. In order to avoid confusion, the word *average* is best used only in its more specific meaning.

    a. The five children taking the test had scores of 2, 4, 4, 6, and 14, giving an average of 6.

7. **avoidance learning, escape learning.** Avoidance learning is motivated by avoidance of punishment. The learner is punished only if learning does not take place. Escape learning is motivated by escape from punishment. The learner is punished until learning takes place.

    a. After being suspended from school for a third time, the mischievous child learned not to play practical jokes on his classmates. (This situation provides an example of avoidance learning.)

    b. The rat learned to jump on the pedestal whenever the floor to its cage was electrified (This situation provides an example of escape learning.)

8. **basic research.** See (4).

9. **classical conditioning, operant conditioning.** In classical conditioning, an originally neutral stimulus is repeatedly paired with a stimulus that evokes a certain response. This latter stimulus is called the *unconditioned stimulus* or *US*. The response given to the stimulus is called the *unconditioned response* or *UR*. As a result of the repeated pairing, the originally neutral stimulus eventually starts to evoke the same response as the unconditioned stimulus, even if it is not paired with the *US* any more. At this point, the originally neutral stimulus becomes a *conditioned stimulus* or *CS*. The response given to this stimulus is called the *conditioned response* or *CR*. In operant conditioning, a learner is rewarded (reinforced) when a desired response takes place. Eventually, the learned response occurs even without paired presentation of the reward.

    a. Every time the salesman visited his Southeast Asian client, the salesman became ill from the change in climate; the salesman was surprised, though, when the client came to visit him and he became sick without exposure to the different climate. (This situation provides an example of classical conditioning.)

    b. As a child, she was given a lollipop every time she took her vitamins without complaining, and as an adult, she continued to take her vitamins without complaining, even though the lollipop no longer accompanied the vitamins. (This situation provides an example of operant conditioning.)

10. **compulsion, obsession.** A compulsion is an irresistible urge to perform repeatedly a stereotyped act that serves no apparent purpose. An obsession is a recurrent thought that the thinker is powerless to control.

    a. The therapist suggested to the patient that the patient's desire to wash her hands every 15 minutes might be a compulsion rather than a reasonable wish for cleanliness.

    b. As a soldier during the Gulf War, he had seen a little girl shot to death on the battlefield. Since then he was obsessed: A vision of the little girl being shot plagued him at least twice every waking hour.

11. **control group, experimental group.** A control group is one that does not receive the experimental treatment of interest. An experimental group is one that does receive the treatment. The effect of the treatment can then be assessed by comparing performance in the experimental group with that in the control group. The term *experimental group* is sometimes used in a more general sense to refer to any group in an experiment. In order to avoid confusion, the term is better restricted to the more limited, contrastive usage.

    a. Members of the experimental group were told that they had been selected because their teachers had rated them unusually likely to succeed in difficult reasoning tasks.

    b. Members of one control group were told that they had been selected at random, whereas members of a second control group were not told anything about selection procedures. The first group served as a control for telling subjects that they were rated unusually likely to succeed, and the second group served as a control for telling subjects anything at all about selection procedures.

12. **culture-fair test, culture-free test.** A culture-fair test is one that attempts to minimize the *differential* effects of different cultural experiences upon performance. A culture-free test is one that attempts to minimize the *absolute* effects of any cultural experiences upon performance. Construction of a culture-fair test is a sensible goal, although one that probably only can be approached. Construction of a culture-free test is not a sensible

goal, (a) because the very act of taking a test is culture-bound and (b) because we have no culture-free baseline against which to assess the success of a culture-free test. In other words, we have no way of knowing what *culture-free* means.

a. By using only pictures of naturally and commonly occurring objects, the investigator hoped to attain a culture-fair test.

b. The investigator set out to make a culture-free test by stripping away from her culture-bound test everything that in any way reflected cultural experiences; when she finished her task, she realized she had nothing left.

13. **culture-free.** See (12).

14. **deduction, induction** Deduction is reasoning from the general to the specific. Given general principles, one deduces specific outcomes. A characteristic of deduction is that one can attain certainty in one's conclusions. If the premises are valid and the reasoning correct, then the conclusions must be valid. Mathematical and logical proofs are usually deductive. Induction is reasoning from the specific to the general. Given specific outcomes, one induces general principles. A characteristic of induction is that one can never attain certainty in one's conclusions. One can disconfirm but never confirm with certainty an inductive argument.

a. From just a few basic axioms, Euclid was able to deduce all the theorems that constitute what we now call Euclidean geometry.

b. A jeweler observed that all emeralds he had ever seen were green. He induced on the basis of his extensive observations that all emeralds are green, regardless of whether he had ever seen them. He realized, though, that the induction could be disconfirmed by the subsequent appearance of just a single nongreen emerald, but that the induction could not be confirmed because the next emerald he saw might be nongreen.

15. **delusion, hallucination, illusion.** A delusion is a false belief. A hallucination is a sensory experience in the absence of an appropriate external stimulus. An illusion is a misperception of a stimulus.

a. The psychologist tried to convince the patient that her belief that her friends were secretly plotting against her was a delusion.

    b. After 3 days without water in the desert, the explorer saw an oasis ahead; but when he reached the point where he had seen the oasis, and saw only dry sand, he realized he had suffered a hallucination.

    c. The clever student knew that her perception of the train tracks as meeting each other on the horizon was an illusion.

16. **dependent variable, independent variable.** A dependent variable is one whose value is affected by (is dependent upon) the value of some other variables(s). These other variables, which are the variables under experimental control, are the independent variables.

    a. The dependent variable in the experiment was reaction time to a visually presented stimulus.

    b. The independent variables in the experiment were length of stimulus presentation and clarity of the visual stimulus.

17. **descriptive statistics, inferential statistics.** Descriptive statistics summarize data. They include indices such as the mean, median, standard deviation, and correlation coefficient. Each of these statistics tells us some important property of the data under consideration. Inferential statistics provide tests of hypotheses about data or simply permit generalizations about populations from sample data. They include such indices as $t$, $z$, and $F$. Each of these statistics is used to test hypotheses about differences between one value (or set of values) and another.

    a. The author first presented descriptive statistics so that readers could get a feeling for the data.

    b. Then he presented inferential statistics so that readers could see the extent to which the data were consistent with his hypotheses.

18. **deviation IQ, ratio IQ.** The IQ, or intelligence quotient, was originally conceived of as a ratio of mental age to chronological age. This ratio (or quotient) was soon perceived to have several disadvantages. First, it seemed to assume that mental age kept increasing as long as chronological age increased, whereas in fact mental age increases very slowly after a person reaches a chronological age of 16, and eventually it begins to decrease. Second, the ratio assumed that increases in mental age are continuous in the same way that increases in chronological age are continuous, although the research of Piaget (1952) and others indicates that this assumption is not the case. In order to correct for these

undesirable properties of the ratio IQ, deviation IQs were introduced. These IQs are not actually quotients, although the designation "IQ" was retained. The concept of mental age is not used in the calculation of deviation IQs. Instead, the IQs are fixed at a certain mean, usually 100, as is a certain standard deviation, usually 15 or 16. IQs are then computed on the basis of each person's standardized deviation from the mean. If the mean IQ is set to 100 and the standard deviation to 15, the deviation IQ is equal to $\{[(\text{Raw Score} - \text{Mean Score})/(\text{Standard Deviation})] \times 15\} + 100$.

a. The child's raw score on the intelligence test was 50. Because the mean on the test was 40, and the standard deviation was 10, her deviation IQ was $\{[(50 - 40)/10] \times 15\} + 100$, or 115.

b. The child's raw score of 50 corresponded to a mental age of 12 years, 0 months. Because her chronological age was 10 years, 0 months, her ratio IQ was $(12/10) \times 100 = 120$.

19. **escape learning.** See (7).

20. **empiricism, nativism.** Empiricism is a view that behavior is learned primarily as a result of experience. In its extreme form, it claims that all behavior is acquired through experience. Nativism makes the claim that most behavior is innately determined. In its extreme form, it claims that all behavior is innately determined.

a. Empiricists such as Skinner have claimed that language acquisition can be explained by operant conditioning.

b. Nativists such as Chomsky have claimed that language acquisition can be understood only if one postulates an innate competence for learning (sometimes called a language acquisition device).

21. **experimental group.** See (11).

22. **experimental psychology.** This term is used in two different ways. Properly used, it refers to a methodology – the use of experiments to collect data. Thus, psychologists who collect data via experiments are referred to as experimental psychologists. A second and less desirable use of the term is as referring to a substantive area of psychology embracing sensation, perception, learning, memory, and thinking. This latter usage developed because researchers interested in these processes have long (although not always) used experimental methods. Because investigators in other areas of psychology (e.g., personality, social, developmental) may also use experimental methods, the term *experimental psychology* is better used in its first meaning.

    a. Using experimental methods, the investigator concluded that introverts were more likely to complete his boring task than were extroverts.

23. **extrinsic motivation, intrinsic motivation.** Extrinsic motivation is motivation controlled by the possibilities of reward or punishment other than those directly achieved by engaging in a behavior or by the outcome of that behavior. Intrinsic motivation is motivation controlled by the possibilities of reward or punishment that are achieved directly by engaging in a behavior or by the outcome of that behavior.

    a. The student's motivation to learn geometry was extrinsic: She wanted to receive an A in her geometry course.

    b. Her friend's motivation to learn geometry was intrinsic: He enjoyed learning how all of geometry could be deduced from a few simple axioms.

24. **factor.** This word has two common technical meanings in psychology. First, it can refer to an independent variable in an experiment. A three-factor experiment is one with three independent variables. In such cases, you are better off referring to *variables* rather than *factors* in order to avoid confusion with the second meaning of *factor*. Second, the word can refer to a mathematical representation of a hypothetical psychological construct. This mathematical representation is obtained through a statistical technique called factor analysis.

    a. The student manipulated two factors in her experiment, attractiveness and sex of the confederate.

    b. According to Spearman's theory of intelligence, intelligence comprises one general factor common to performance on all intellectual tasks and many specific factors, each limited to performance on a single intellectual task.

25. **fear.** See (3).

26. **fixation, regression.** Fixation refers to arrested development at some stage, usually a stage earlier than the one an individual should be in. Regression refers to a return to an earlier stage of development.

    a. The 5-year-old child's continual sucking of anything she could get into her mouth suggested to the psychologist that the child had fixated at the oral stage of development.

    b. The soldier seemed perfectly normal until he entered the battlefield, at which time he showed regression toward infantile behaviors that he had not exhibited for more than two decades.

27. **genotype, phenotype.** A genotype is a set of inherited characteristics that may or may not be displayed. A phenotype is the set of characteristics that is displayed.
    a. The woman's phenotype revealed brown eyes.
    b. When the brown-eyed woman had a child with blue eyes, it became apparent that her genotype included the recessive gene for blue eyes as well as the dominant gene for brown eyes.

28. **hallucination.** See (15).

29. **heritability.** Heritability is the proportion of the total variance of a trait in a population that is attributable to genetic differences among individuals in that population. Heritability is thus the ratio of (variance due to genetic causes)/(total variance). (See item 70.)
    a. Height is a characteristic with high heritability, whereas temperament is a characteristic with low heritability.

30. **identification, imitation.** In identification, a person (often a child) acquires the social role of another person by modeling the behavior of that person. In imitation, the person models the behavior of another person, not necessarily acquiring that person's social role.
    a. Because the man identified with his lazy and irresponsible father, he found himself unable to cope with any of his family responsibilities.
    b. The young boy often imitated the actions of his mother, but he eventually identified with his father.

31. **illusion.** See (15).

32. **imitation.** See (30).

33. **independent variable.** See (16).

34. **induction.** See (14).

35. **inferential statistics.** See (17).

36. **intrinsic motivation.** See (23).

37. **latent content, manifest content.** The latent content of a dream is its deeper, hidden meaning. The manifest content of a dream is its apparent meaning.
    a. The manifest content of the dream consisted of the patient's being chased out of a luxurious palace across a moat by an angry older man wielding a big stick.

b. The psychologist believed the latent content of the dream was sexual, and that the man exhibited through the dream an unresolved Oedipal conflict.

38. **learning, maturation, performance.** Learning is often distinguished both from maturation and from performance. Learning is an increment in knowledge that occurs as a result of practice. Maturation is a change in behavior resulting from a growth process that is independent of practice. Performance is overt behavior. Note that *learning* takes place only with practice; *maturation* takes place regardless of whether or not it is preceded by practice. Note also that learning may occur without showing itself through a change in performance.

a. The child repeatedly failed to understand that the amount of liquid in the tall jar was the same as the amount obtained when the contents of the tall jar were poured into the fat jar. Eventually, her cognitive abilities matured to the point at which she could understand the principle of conservation, and thus the equality between the two amounts of liquid.

b. Although the subject had learned all the words in the list, his recall performance was far from perfect; it was not until the subject was given a test of recognition performance that he showed that he was familiar with all of the words.

39. **manifest content.** See (37).

40. **maturation.** See (38).

41. **mean, median, mode.** The mean (average) is the sum of a set of values divided by the number of values. The median is the middle value: Half the values are higher and half are lower. The mode is the most frequently occurring value.

a. The mean of the numbers 2, 2, 4, 6, and 16 is 6.

b. The median of the numbers 2, 2, 4, 6, and 16 is 4.

c. The mode of the numbers 2, 2, 4, 6, and 16 is 2.

42. **median.** See (41).

43. **mode.** See (41).

44. **nativism.** See (20).

45. **nature–nurture.** The nature–nurture distinction refers to the relative proportions of variance in traits or behaviors attributable to heredity (nature) versus environment (nurture).

a. In the nature–nurture debate, hereditarians favor nature and environmentalists favor nurture as the primary source of differences in behavior.

46. **neurosis, psychosis.** A neurosis is a minor disorder in which a person exhibits maladaptive behavior patterns (symptoms) that avoid rather than cope with underlying problems. A psychosis is a major disorder in which a person exhibits severely maladaptive behavior patterns that usually require treatment in a hospital.
    a. The neurotic woman counted her money every hour-on-the-hour to make sure it hadn't fallen out of her pocket.
    b. The psychotic man continually saw robbers reaching out to grab his wallet, but when he chased the robbers, they always disappeared into thin air.
47. **null hypothesis.** The null hypothesis is a hypothesis of no difference. It is not *no* hypothesis.
    a. The investigator's null hypothesis was that the treatment would produce no effect on the experimental group relative to the control group.
48. **obsession.** See (10).
49. **operant conditioning.** See (9).
50. **parameter, statistic.** A parameter is a constant value that describes a characteristic of a population. A statistic is a variable value that describes a characteristic of a sample from a population.
    a. A psychologist tested the IQs of all 25 students in Ms. Blakeley's 2009 fourth-grade class. He found that the mean IQ was 105. If this class were the population of interest, then the mean of 105 would be a population parameter. (See item 54 for definition of *population*.)
    b. If, in the above example, Ms. Blakeley's 2009 fourth-grade class were viewed as a sample of fourth-grade classes throughout the United States, then the mean of 105 would be a sample statistic. (See item 54 for the definition of *sample*.)
51. **participant, subject.** At various times, the word "subject" or "participant" has been preferred in referring to human beings involved in studies. Currently, the words are used largely interchangeably, except when testing animals other than humans, in which case the term "subject" should be used.
52. **performance.** See (38).
53. **phenotype.** See (27).
54. **population, sample.** A population is the universe of cases to which an investigator wants to generalize his results. A sample is a subset of a population.

a. If an investigator views Ms. Blakeley's 2009 fourth-grade class as a population, then any generalizations he makes from data obtained from the class will be limited to that class only.

b. If an investigator views Ms. Blakeley's 2009 fourth-grade class as a sample, then generalizations he makes from data obtained from the class will be to the population of which Ms. Blakeley's class is a subject. The more diverse the population, the less likely is Ms. Blakeley's class to be representative of the population and, thus, the less likely are the data to be generalizable. One could have more confidence in generalizations to the entire fourth grade at Ms. Blakeley's school than in generalizations to the fourth grades of the entire United States.

55. **Primacy/recency.** Primacy effects are effects that occur at the beginning of some temporal sequence. Recency effects are effects that occur at the end of some temporal sequence.

a. The primacy effect in free recall is the tendency for people to remember items from the beginning of a list better than they remember items from the middle of a list.

b. The recency effect in free recall is the tendency for people to remember items from the end of a list better than they remember items from the middle of a list.

56. **ratio IQ.** See (18).

57. **recency.** See (55).

58. **regression.** See (26).

59. **reliability, validity.** Reliability refers to how well or consistently a test measures whatever the test measures. Validity refers to how well a test measures what it is supposed to measure. Thus, a perfectly reliable test can be completely invalid if it measures something well but not what it is intended to measure. A perfectly valid test, however, must be perfectly reliable, because if the test measures what it is supposed to measure perfectly, it must measure what it does in fact measure perfectly.

a. The test of finger-tapping speed proved to be highly reliable, providing consistent estimates of people's finger-tapping abilities. The test of intelligence proved to be only moderately reliable, providing only somewhat consistent estimates of people's measured intelligence.

b. The highly reliable test of finger-tapping speed proved to be invalid as a predictor of school achievement. The moderately reliable intelligence test proved to be moderately valid as a predictor of school achievement. In this case, the more reliable test was less valid for a specific purpose to which it was poorly suited. Although reliability places an upper bound on validity, it is no guarantee of validity.

60. **repression, suppression.** Repression is a defense mechanism whereby a thought or feeling is removed from consciousness. Suppression is a defense mechanism whereby a thought or feeling remains in consciousness but is not overtly expressed. People are aware of suppressed but not repressed material.

    a. The patient had long ago repressed all memories of his brutal grandfather. At the therapy sessions, he honestly denied ever even having known his grandfather.

    b. The psychologist's therapy sessions with the student were getting nowhere, because the student suppressed any information that she thought might embarrass her in the psychologist's eyes.

61. **significant.** A statistically significant result is one that enables an investigator to reject a null hypothesis (see item 47). Statistical significance is sometimes contrasted with practical significance. A result can be statistically significant but not practically significant. Whenever the term *significant* is used by itself, it should be used only to refer to the technical meaning of *statistical significance.* Do not use the word to refer to any result that you think is important.

    a. The large difference between means in the two groups was statistically significant, enabling the psychologist to reject the null hypothesis of no difference between the groups.

62. **simulation.** See (5).

63. **state, trait.** A state is a temporary mood or frame of mind. A trait is a permanent disposition.

    a. Anxiety as a state refers to a temporary frame of mind in which the individual feels uneasy or apprehensive for no clear reason.

    b. Anxiety as a trait refers to a permanent disposition of an individual to feel uneasy or apprehensive for no clear reason.

64. **preconscious, unconscious.** The preconscious contains cognitions that are not conscious but can be brought into consciousness with little or no effort. The unconscious (subconscious) contains cognitions and feelings of which we are unaware and that can be brought into consciousness only with difficulty.

    a. As she completed the first sentence of her paper, the ideas for her second sentence glided from her preconscious to her conscious thoughts.

    b. The girl's desire to excel over her three sisters was unconscious and showed itself only in her behavior and in her repeated dreams of athletic conquests over three familiar but not quite recognizable opponents.

65. **subject.** See (51).

66. **suppression.** See (60).

67. **trait.** See (63).

68. **unconscious.** See (64).

69. **validity.** See (59).

70. **variability, variance.** The variability of a set of observations refers to the amount of dispersion or spread in the observations. The variance of a set of observations refers to a specific measure of the amount of dispersion: $\Sigma(x^2)/N$, where $x$ is the deviation of each score from the mean and $N$ the number of cases. The term *variance* should be used only to refer to this specific measure, not to refer loosely to the amount of dispersion in the observations.

    a. The scores in the sample showed very little variability.

    b. The variance of the scores in the sample was only 4 points.

71. **variance.** See (70).

72. **white noise.** White noise is noise composed of sounds of all frequencies. It is called white noise as an analogy to white color, which is composed of colors of all wavelengths. It otherwise has no relation to white or any other color.

    a. White noise was piped into the testing room in order to distract subjects from the difficult memory task.

# 8 | American Psychological Association Guidelines for Psychology Papers

This chapter summarizes the guidelines for preparing a psychology paper presented in the *Publication Manual of the American Psychological Association*, Sixth Edition (2009). You should consult this manual for a complete list of guidelines. If you intend to submit a paper for publication, then you cannot afford to be without this manual. It can be obtained from any bookstore or online book retailer, or directly from the American Psychological Association at www.apastyle.org.

Journals of the British Psychological Society (BPS) adopted the APA style as of October 2001. Publications other than journal articles of the BPS follow the *Style Guide* that can be found online by entering the search words "BPS style" in a search engine. Many other non-APA journals will accept papers prepared in accordance with APA guidelines as well, even though there are minor differences in style. You should always consult the guidelines of the journal to which you plan to submit to make sure you are adhering to its style regulations.

All examples used to illustrate principles in this chapter are fictitious. Note that the formatting of this book, as printed, does not always follow the conventions described in this chapter. The conventions in the chapter are for preparing manuscripts, not for printed versions of books and articles.

## 8.1 FORMATTING THE PAPER

■ Margins

Set your margins to leave 1 inch at the top, bottom, and both sides of each page. Each line should be no longer than $6\frac{1}{2}$ inches. Use flush-left style. In other words, the right margin should be "ragged." Do not use your word processor's automatic hyphenation option, and do not hyphenate words at the ends of lines yourself.

■ **Vertical Spacing**

Double space between all lines, without exception. There may be times when you are tempted to single space – in writing references, footnotes, block quotations, and the like. Do not succumb to the temptation. Your paper should be double spaced throughout with the exception of tables and figures.

■ **Horizontal Spacing**

Begin each new paragraph by indenting a half inch, or using a tab key, which you should set to default at a half inch. Type all other lines starting from a uniform left margin: (a) the abstract, (b) block quotations, (c) titles and headings, (d) table titles and notes, and (e) figure captions. Furthermore, leave no space after internal periods in abbreviations (e.g., U.S., U.K.) and in ratios. Leave one space after commas, colons, semicolons, and periods ending sentences, as well as after internal periods in first and middle initials (e.g., H. B. Hinkelmeyer).

■ **Numbering Pages**

Number pages consecutively, starting with the title page. Use Arabic numerals. If pages are accidentally separated from the manuscript, the page numbers together with the running head help identify where they belong.

■ **Font**

For the text, use a 12-point font size with an easily readable font such as Times New Roman, Arial, or Courier (the preferred font for APA publications is Times New Roman). For figures, use a sans-serif typeface.

## 8.2 GRAMMAR

### 8.2.1 Punctuation

#### 8.2.1.1 Comma

A comma should be used

1. before *and* and *or* in a series of three or more items:

   The participant, confederate, and experimenter all entered the room together.

2. before and after a nonrestrictive clause (i.e., a clause that is nonessential to the sentence):

The empty box, which had been rigged to look like a lie detector, was placed on a table next to the participant.

The empty box that had been rigged to look like a lie detector was placed on a table next to the participant.

3. to separate two coordinate clauses joined by a conjunction:

The experimenter pretended to activate the lie detector, and the confederate disappeared into an adjoining room with a one-way mirror.

A comma should **not** be used

1. before or after a restrictive clause (i.e., a clause that limits or further defines the word it modifies):

The button that the experimenter pushed served only to impress the participant.

2. between two parts of a compound predicate:

The experimenter attached two fake electrodes to the participant's wrists and told the participant that the machine would record the truth or falsity of each response.

3. to separate two independent clauses not joined by a conjunction:

First, the participant was asked to answer each question; then he was told that he would receive double pay at the end of the experiment if he succeeded in fooling the "lie detector."

4. to separate parts of measurement:

The participant was exposed to the white noise for exactly 5 min 15 s.

### 8.2.1.2 Semicolon

A semicolon should be used to

1. separate two independent clauses that are not joined by a conjunction:

The experimenter then proceeded to ask the participant a series of embarrassing questions; she pretended to be surprised at the participant's responses.

2. separate items that already contain commas:

The sets of questions asked by the experimenter dealt with sex, swearing, and bathroom habits; masculinity, undressing habits, and thumbsucking; or private fantasies, nightmares, and academic failures.

### 8.2.1.3 Colon

A colon should be used

1. before a final phrase or clause that amplifies the material that comes before it:

Most participants initially hesitated to answer the questions: They stared at the experimenter in disbelief.

2. in ratios and proportions:

The proportions of participants answering the questions honestly were 15:25, 13:37, and 18:26 in the three groups receiving the different sets of questions.

### 8.2.1.4 Hyphen

A hyphen should be used in

1. a compound with a participle if the compound precedes a noun it modifies:

The truth-telling participants showed less fidgeting than the lie-telling ones.

2. a phrase used as an adjective if the phrase precedes a noun it modifies:

A subject-by-subject analysis of the results showed strong differences in the honesty with which various individuals answered the questions.

3. a compound adjective comprising an adjective and a noun that precedes and modifies another noun:

High-anxiety participants were less honest in their answers than were low-anxiety participants.

4. all compounds involving the prefix *self*:

Self-report data indicated that high-anxiety subjects were more worried than low-anxiety participants that honest answers would later be used against them.

5. fractions that are used as adjectives:

To get approval for his high-risk study, he needs a two-thirds majority from the Institutional Review Board.

A hyphen should **not** be used in

1. a compound with an adverb ending in *–ly:*

A widely expressed fear was that the participants' responses would not really be kept confidential.

2. a compound involving a comparative or superlative:

A less common fear was that the experimenter would know from the "lie detector" which responses were truthful and which were not.

3. a modifier with a letter or numeral as the second term:

The Session 2 data seem to have been affected less by these fears than were the Session 1 data.

4. foreign phrases used as adjectives/adverbs:

The a posteriori test revealed that the means for all three groups differed significantly.

5. fractions that are used as nouns:

Participants missed about one fourth of the stimuli.

There are several symbols that can be confused with a hyphen but are used in different circumstances. These symbols are as follows:

■ **em dash**
The em dash is longer than an en dash or hyphen – it is the width of the letter *M*, the widest letter in a font set. As with the hyphen, do not use a space before or after the em dash. If you do not have an em dash on your keyboard, you may use two hyphens instead (again, with no space before or after them). The em dash is used to delimit

elements from the main clause that are used to amplify or digress. For example:

The subjects who lied in answering every question—all of them members of the high-anxiety group—confessed that they thought the "lie detector" was nothing more than an empty box.

■ **en dash**
An en dash is longer is longer and not as thick as a hyphen – it is the width of the letter *N* in a font set. If you do not have an en dash on your keyboard, use a hyphen with no space before or after. En dashes are used between words of equal weight in a compound adjective:

The Freud–Einstein exchange of letters is still of highest significance today.

■ **minus sign**
The minus sign is the same length as the en dash but somewhat thicker and higher. Should you not have a minus sign, you can use hyphen with spaces on both sides. Note, however, that negative values should be typed using a hyphen rather than a minus sign, with a space before but not after the hyphen, for example, -7.23.

### 8.2.1.5 Double Quotation Marks

Double quotation marks should be used

1. to introduce a word or phrase used in a special or unusual way (use quotation marks only the first time a word is used):

   The experimenter divided the participants into two groups: the "con artists" and the "apple polishers."

2. to reproduce material that is quoted verbatim:

   The con artists had taken to heart the experimental instruction, "You should lie whenever you think you can get away with it." The apple polishers seem to have ignored or disbelieved this instruction and almost always told the truth.

3. for names of articles:

   The experimenter planned to name the article "An Experimental Investigation of Con Artistry."

Double quotation marks should **not** be used

1. to qualify statements or to hedge bets:

   The apple polishers were relieved when the experiment was over; the con artists begged for more (not "begged" for more).

2. for quotations of 40 words or more; instead, use block format:

   The experimenter debriefed the participants at the end of the experiment:

   > The purpose of this experiment was to provide a source of examples for *The Psychologist's Companion*. The experiment itself made no sense and had no purpose other than to provide the examples. We hope you enjoyed this meaningful activity.

3. to cite linguistic examples up to the length of a sentence; instead, use italics:

   The use of *which* for *that* is common in psychological writing but is inadvisable.

4. to introduce an important technical term; instead, use italics:

   *Schnallkraker's syndrome* is a serious disease (or would be were there such a thing).

Observe the following rules in using quotations:

1. Omission of material within a sentence of a quotation is indicated by the use of three ellipsis points ( . . . ). Omission of material between sentences of a quotation is indicated by four ellipsis points. Ellipsis points should not be used at the beginning or end of a quotation:

   According to McGoof (2009), "The difference between groups . . . was statistically but not practically significant" (p. 303).

   As he left the room, the participant said to the experimenter, "I hope I wasn't really supposed to write down the words in the order in which they were read. . . . I know the instructions said to, but I didn't see the point."

2. Insertion of material within a sentence of a quotation is indicated by brackets. Such insertions are usually used to clarify the quotation for the reader or to make the grammar of the

quotation consistent with the sentence or paragraph in which it is embedded:

According to the instructions, "this test [should be] timed for 30 minutes."

3. Three kinds of changes are permissible in quotations without any indication to the reader: (a) The first letter of the first quoted word may be changed from a capital to a small letter, or vice versa; (b) the punctuation mark at the end of the quotation may be changed to fit the syntax of the sentence in which you have embedded the quotation; and (c) single quotation marks may be changed to double quotation marks, and vice versa. All other changes must be indicated by ellipses or brackets.

The sentence, "She ate the cheese," may be cited as, "she ate the cheese."

4. The source of a direct quotation should always be cited. Include in the citation the author(s), year, and page number(s) of the quotation. If the quotation is in the middle of a sentence, cite the source of the quotation in parentheses immediately after the quotation. If the quotation is at the end of a sentence, cite the page number in parentheses after the end of the quotation but before the final punctuation mark. If the quotation is in block format, cite the page number in parentheses after the end of the quotation and after the final punctuation mark:

According to the author, "None of the mice ate the cheese until they had finished the task" (Rattsky, 2008, p. 108), so they were hungry.

Rattsky (2008) found that "none of the mice ate the cheese until they had finished the task" (p. 108).

According to Rattsky (2008),
> None of the mice ate the cheese until they had finished the task. After they ate the cheese, six mice proceeded to redo the task, while the other nine mice marched back to their cages. (p. 108)

5. In general, commas and periods are placed inside quotation marks and other marks of punctuation are placed outside, unless they are part of the quoted material, in which case they are placed inside:

"Eat the banana," he screamed at the monkey.
Did he scream at the monkey, "Eat the banana"?

6. Long quotations may require permission from the owner of the copyright on the material. APA policy permits use of up to 400 words in single text extracts and up to 800 words for a series of text extracts without permission. Copyright owners vary in the number of words permitted, however, so for quotations of 100 or more words it is wise to check the policy of the copyright owner. Even if the copyright owner is a journal or book company, it is a common courtesy to request permission from the author as well as the company. If multiple authors are involved, request permission only of the lead author.

### 8.2.1.6 Single Quotation Marks

Single quotation marks should be used for quotations within quotations:

The experimenter, as if to emphasize the pointlessness of the experiment, said to the participants, "Remember the well-known proverb: 'All's well that ends well.'"

### 8.2.1.7 Parentheses

Parentheses should be used to

1. set off items that are structurally independent from the rest of the sentence:

   After debriefing, participants were given a questionnaire in which they were asked their reactions to the experiment (see Table 1).

2. enclose the date of references cited in the text or references:

   The questionnaire was adopted with minor modifications from one used by Bozo (2007).
   Bozo, B. B. (2007). A questionnaire for measuring slapstick tendencies. *Humor, 3*, 26–31.

3. enclose abbreviations:

   Subjects were also given the Toliver Test of Tolerance for Trauma (TTTT).

4. enclose letters or numbers enumerating items in a series:

   Finally, participants were given three ability tests: (a) the Penultimate Test of Pencil-Pushing Power, (b) the Scofield Scale of Hand–Foot Coordination, and (c) the Williams Test of Willpower.

5. enclose the page number of a cited quotation:

   The Williams test seemed particularly appropriate for this experiment, because it is described in the manual as "an invalid test of practically anything an investigator might want to measure" (p. 26).

6. group terms in mathematical expressions:

   On the Williams test, there is a correction for guessing, so that overall score is a function of both right and wrong answers:

   $$R - (W/4).$$

7. enclose enumeration of equations:

   The overall score on the Williams test can be converted to a standard score

   $$z = (X - \overline{X})/SD. \tag{1}$$

   In this notation, z is the standard score, $X$ the overall score, $\overline{X}$ the mean of the scores, and $SD$ the standard deviation of the scores.

8. to enclose statistical values:

   The means of the two different experimental groups did not differ significantly ($p = .12$).

9. to enclose degrees of freedom:

   $$F(3, 87) = 2.57$$

### 8.2.1.8 Brackets

Brackets should be used to

1. enclose material inserted in a quotation by someone other than the quoted writer or speaker:

   A participant remarked as he left the experiment, "This is the most pointless [experiment] I've ever been in."

2. enclose parenthetical material within parentheses:

   (The confederate [see "Method" section] was inclined to agree.)

## 8.2.2 Capitalization

### 8.2.2.1 Titles and Headings

1. Capitalize major words in titles of books and journal articles mentioned in the text of a psychology paper:

   The article reporting the experiment was to be titled "A Factor Analysis of Pencil-Pushing Power."

2. In references, capitalize the first word in titles of books and articles cited:

   Muddlehead, M. M. (2008). A factor analysis of pencil-pushing power. *Journal of Junky Experiments, 5*, 406–409.

3. In references, capitalize all major words of journal names:

   Muddlehead, M. M. (2008). A factor analysis of pencil-pushing power. *Journal of Junky Experiments, 5*, 406–409.

4. Capitalize major words of table titles and figure legends:

   Table 1
   Loadings of Ability Tests on Pencil-Pushing Speed Factor

5. Capitalize the first letter of first words and proper nouns of figure captions and table headings:

   Figure 1. A typical sample of copied material.

### 8.2.2.2 Proper Nouns and Trade Names

1. Capitalize trade and brand names:

   Subjects used a Pengo Permapencil to do their copying.

2. Capitalize names of university departments referring to specific departments in specific universities:

   The experiment was conducted under the auspices of the Department of Psychology, Zingo University.

3. Do not capitalize names of general laws, theories, and hypotheses:

   The experimenter used a unifactor theory of pencil pushing to explain her results.

**8.2.2.3** Titles of Tests

    1. Capitalize exact, complete titles of tests:

      Three tests of pencil pushing were administered: (a) the Penultimate Test of Pencil-Pushing Power, (b) the Staley Push-a-Pencil Test, and (c) the Pennsylvania Pencil Inventory.

    2. Do not capitalize shortened or inexact titles of tests or titles of unpublished tests:

      Scores on the Staley test showed no practice effect.

**8.2.2.4** Nouns Followed by Numerals or Letters

    1. Capitalize nouns followed by numerals or letters indicating membership in an enumerated series (except for enumeration of pages, chapters, rows, and columns):

      In Session 1 of a new experiment on pencil pushing, participants were asked to copy on page 1 of their booklets a paragraph of printed material.

    2. Nouns preceding a variable are not capitalized:

      Scores in session $n$ were no higher on average than were scores in session $n - 1$.

**8.2.2.5** Names of Factors, Variables, and Effects

    1. Capitalize names of factors from a factor analysis:

      A factor analysis of the tests revealed just one reliable factor, which the experimenter called Pencil-Pushing Speed.

    2. Do not capitalize names of effects taken from analyses of variance, unless they refer to an interaction (with $\times$):

      An analysis of variance revealed no difference in school achievement as a function of pencil-pushing speed (but the Sex $\times$ Speed interaction was statistically significant).

**8.2.2.6** Names of Conditions or Groups in Experiments

Do **not** capitalize names of conditions or groups in an experiment:

Participants in the experiment were divided into two groups, fast pencil pushers and slow pencil pushers.

### 8.2.3 Italics

Italics should be used for

1. titles of books, periodicals, and microfilms:

   The article relating bumps on the head to claustrophobia was published in the journal *Phrenology Today*.

   The author didn't think a book titled *Bump It or Lump It* would sell enough copies to make writing the book worthwhile.

2. introducing new, technical, or important terms:

   All participants in the experiment were told the meaning of *sociopathy*.

3. letters, words, phrases, or sentences cited as linguistic examples:

   Some participants did not even realize that *phrenology* was a noun.

4. letters used as statistical symbols or algebraic variables:

   The difference in number of bumps on the head between claustrophobic and nonclaustrophobic subjects was not significant, $t(32) = 0.26, p > .05$.

   The phrenologist still argued that the relation between degree of claustrophobia ($y$) and number of bumps on the head ($x$) could be expressed by the equation $y = 7x + 2$.

5. volume numbers in reference lists:

   Bumpo, B. P. (2003). The relation between bumps on the head and claustrophobia. *Phrenology Today*, *13*, 402–406.

6. anchors of a scale:

   A 5-point scale was used ranging from 1 (*do not agree at all*) to 5 (*completely agree*).

Italics should **not** be used for

1. common foreign words and abbreviations:

   The a priori likelihood of a relation between number of bumps on the head and degree of claustrophobia seemed remote.

   The remarks of Zootz et al. (2006) vis-à-vis errors in counting number of bumps are still relevant today.

2. names of Greek letters:

   Zootz and his colleagues noted that there are two kinds of bumps, alpha ($\alpha$) bumps and beta ($\beta$) bumps, and that only alpha bumps should be counted.

3. emphasis, unless the emphasis would be lost without italics:

   Zootz and his colleagues emphasized that there was no known relation between number of beta bumps and claustrophobia.

4. abbreviations:

   The National Phrenological Society (NPS) dissociated itself from the work of both Bumpo and Zootz.

## 8.2.4 Spelling

The standard reference used by American Psychological Association journals for spelling is *Merriam-Webster's Collegiate Dictionary*, 11th ed. (2005). *Webster's Third New International Dictionary* (2002) should be consulted for spellings of words not in the collegiate volume. In cases where two or more spellings are acceptable, use the first, preferred spelling. You can also consult www.apastyle.org for the latest information on certain spellings not found in the dictionary.

## 8.2.5 Abbreviations

Use abbreviations sparingly. Explain each abbreviation the first time it is used (except in Example 1 here). Here are some general rules:

1. Abbreviations do not need to be explained if they are listed as word entries (i.e., are not labeled *abbr*) in *Merriam-Webster's Collegiate Dictionary* (2005):

   The participant scored 108 on the IQ test.

2. Abbreviations need to be explained when they are used for the first time:

   The participant's average response time (RT) in responding to test items was 6.52 s.

3. Latin abbreviations should be used only in parenthetical material; their English translation should be used in non-parenthetical material. However, the abbreviation *et al.* should be used both in parenthetical and non-parenthetical text:

   The procedure required the subjects to complete a variety of different assessments (e.g., a questionnaire to assess their state anxiety and an IQ test).

4. Metric and nonmetric units should be abbreviated when appearing together with a numerical value:

   To give readers an idea of the length of the test, the authors noted that the test booklet was 2 cm thick.

5. Units of time that should not be abbreviated are *year*, *month*, *week*, and *day*. Abbreviations can be used for *hour* (hr), *minute* (min), *second* (s), *millisecond* (ms), and *nanosecond* (ns):

   The participant's average response time in responding to test items was 6.52 s.

Abbreviations should **not** be used

1. if you use nonstandard abbreviations that you have made up, and
2. to abbreviate the words *subject* (S), *experimenter* (E), or *observer* (O). Although these abbreviations were once standard, they are no longer used.

## Periods in Abbreviations

Periods should be used with

1. initials of names:

   A. C. Acney discovered the little known Acney effect.

2. Latin abbreviations:

   The discovery was made at exactly 8:00 a.m.

3. reference abbreviations:

The effect is described in the *Autobiography of A. C. Acney (Vol. 3)*.

Periods should **not** be used with

1. capital-letter abbreviations, including acronyms:

The now discredited Acney effect relates IQ to facial complexion. Acney was unsuccessful in getting the report of his findings into any APA journal.

2. abbreviations of metric units:

Expressed in metric units, the weight of Vol. 3 of Acney's autobiography is 1.4 kg, 1.4 kg more than the book is worth.

3. abbreviations of nonmetric measurement:

This lengthy book weighs 3 lb and can be used to press leaves.

4. abbreviations of state and territory names:

He discovered the effect in his little lab in Washington, DC.

## 8.3 HEADINGS

APA editorial guidelines provide for five levels of headings:

1. a centered, boldface heading typed in uppercase and lowercase letters;
2. a flush left, boldface heading typed in uppercase and lowercase letters;
3. an indented, boldface heading typed in lowercase letters with a period at the end;
4. an indented, boldface, italicized heading typed in lowercase letters with a period at the end;
5. an indented, italicized heading typed in lowercase letters with a period at the end.

The complete set of five headings is usually needed only in very long articles, for example, reports of multiple experiments. Always start with the highest level of heading and work your way down to whatever number of levels you may need. This book does not follow this sequence of headings.

An example using all five levels of headings is the following:

Experiment I

Collection of Norms
   Method.
   *Design.*
   *Independent variables.*

## 8.4 QUANTITATIVE ISSUES

### 8.4.1 Units of Measurement

The American Psychological Association has adopted the metric system in all APA journals, and other journals have generally followed suit. Authors therefore should express measurements in metric units wherever possible. If measurements are expressed in other kinds of units, metric equivalents should be given. When a metric unit appears with a numeric value, use the metric symbol (without a period after the symbol); when it appears without a numerical value, spell it out in lowercase letters.

### 8.4.2 Statistics

Statistics can be presented in the text, tables, or figures. Authors must choose the means that most effectively communicate their data. Frequently used statistics (e.g., the mean, $t$, $F$) can be used without explanation. Infrequently used statistics (e.g., $c_p$) should be explained, and a reference for the statistic cited. A reference should also be given for use of a statistic in a controversial way (e.g., the $F$ statistic when sample variances are widely discrepant).

The standard format for presentation of inferential statistics in text calls for inclusion of the name of the statistic, the degrees of freedom for the statistic (if relevant), the value of the statistic, and the probability level associated with the statistic. This information is presented in the following way:

Participants informed of the relation between lists recalled significantly more words than participants not informed of this relation, $t(68) = 2.93$, $p = .014$.

The personality scale did not differentiate among compulsive, hysterical, and normal participants, $F(2, 28) = 1.18, p > .05$.

Report exact $p$ values unless the value is less than .001, in which case it is preferable to report as $p < .001$.

### 8.4.3 Equations

#### 8.4.3.1 General Principles

Several general principles apply to the presentation of equations:

1. Space mathematical expressions as you would space words, keeping in mind that the primary consideration is legibility:

$$y = a/(b + c)$$

2. Align mathematical expressions carefully. Subscripts generally precede superscripts, but primes occur immediately following the primed letter or symbol:

$$y = x_p{}^3 + x'_q{}^2$$

3. Punctuate all equations, however presented, as you would any expression, mathematical or not:

The standard formula was used for computing IQ:
$$IQ = MA/CA.$$

4. Parentheses ( ), brackets [ ], and braces { } should be used in that order to avoid ambiguity:

$$y = a/(b + c)$$
$$y = a/[(b + c) \cdot (d - e)]$$
$$y = \{a/[(b + c) \cdot (d - e)]\} + f$$

5. Use the percentage symbol (%) only when a number precedes it. Otherwise, use the word *percentage*:

Only 18% of the sample responded to the questionnaire. The percentage of respondents was disappointing.

**8.4.3.2** Equations Merged with Text

Short and simple equations that will not have to be referred to later in the text can be placed in the midst of a line of text. Follow these rules:

1. Fractions presented in the midst of a line of text should be indicated by use of a slash:

   The data indicated that for any values of $a$ and $b$, $y = a/b$.

2. The equation should not project above or below the line. If it does, use the format for equations described below.

**8.4.3.3** Equations Separated from Text

Equations should be separated from the text if (a) they are referred to later, (b) they are complex, or (c) they project above or below a single line of text. Equations separated from the text should be numbered consecutively, with the number enclosed in parentheses and near the right margin of the page:

$$RT = 5x^2 + \frac{y+8}{2n} + \frac{z^3+5}{y} \qquad (1)$$

## 8.4.4 Numbers

**8.4.4.1** General Principles

Several general principles apply to the use of numbers in text:

1. Rules for cardinal numbers (e.g., *two*) and ordinal numbers (e.g., *second*) are the same (see below), except for percentiles and quartiles. Percentiles and quartiles should always be expressed in figures:

   The boy's score placed him in the 5th percentile.

2. Use Arabic rather than roman numerals wherever possible. Use roman numerals, however, where convention calls for their use:

   The probability of a Type I error was less than 5%.

3. For numbers greater than or equal to 1,000, use commas between every group of three digits:

   Her response was timed at 1,185 ms.

4. In writing decimals, place a 0 before the decimal point if the number is less than 1, unless the number *must* be less than one:

The average score on the test was a pitiful 0.73.
The proportion of participants finishing the task was .86.

5. Use decimal notation instead of mixed fractions wherever possible. Do not use decimals, though, if their use is awkward:

The maximum score on the test was 8.5 out of 10.
The oldest child in the experimental group was $5\frac{1}{2}$ years old.

6. Round numbers, in most cases, to two decimal digits, not more (e.g., a correlation of .53, not .5297).

### 8.4.4.2 Numbers Expressed in Words

Numbers should be expressed in words if

1. they are between zero and nine inclusive (with exceptions described in the next section):

There were only six children in the sample.

2. they begin a sentence, regardless of whether or not they are less than 10:

Eleven children were tested.

3. they are common fractions:

One sixth of the participants failed to complete the given tasks in under 1 hour.

### 8.4.4.3 Numbers Expressed in Figures

Numbers should be expressed in figures if they satisfy any of the following conditions. Notice that all conditions except the first are exceptions to Rule 1 above for expressing numbers in words. Express numbers in figures if they are

1. greater than or equal to 10:

There were 18 adults in the sample.

2. ages:

   All of the adults were older than 21 years of age.

3. times and dates:

   The experiment took place between the hours of 8 a.m. and 10 a.m. on October 6, 2009.

4. percentages:

   More than 90% of the participants finished the task.

5. ratios:

   This was a ratio of 9:1.

6. fractions or decimals:

   The corresponding fraction was 9/10, and the corresponding decimal, .9.

7. exact sums of money:

   Participants were each paid $3 for participating in the experiment.

8. scores and points on scales:

   The student received a score of 8.32 on a scale ranging from 0 to 9.

9. references to numerals as numerals:

   The numeral 0 was placed next to each true item; the numeral 1 was placed next to each false item.

10. page numbers:

    The students were told to write their identification numbers on page 1.

11. series of four or more items:

    Students were assigned consecutive identification numbers: The first four students, for example, were assigned the numbers 1, 2, 3, and 4, respectively.

12. numbers grouped for comparison either between or within sentences if any of the numbers is 10 or greater:

There were 11 participants in the first group, but only 9 participants in the second group.

13. sample or population sizes:

The experiment involved 8 participants, half of them male and half of them female.

## 8.5 SERIATION

### Within a Paragraph

Seriation within a paragraph is indicated by lowercase letters written in parentheses. Do not italicize the letters.

The five categories of words to be recalled were (a) fruits, (b) animals, (c) nuts, (d) countries, and (e) oceans.

If the elements within the seriation have commas, the elements are separated by semicolons.

The four categories of words to be recalled contained (a) fruits, vegetables, and nuts; (b) mammals, insects, and birds; (c) lakes, rivers, and oceans; and (d) countries and continents.

### Of Paragraphs

Seriation of paragraphs is indicated by Arabic numerals followed by periods. Do not enclose the numbers in parentheses.

The experimenter used a three-step procedure:

1. The experimenter greeted the subject as the participant entered the room.
2. A confederate entered the room and asked for the time of day. He appeared to be in a state of great confusion.
3. The confederate noticed the participant, and struck up a conversation with him.

## 8.6 REFERENCES

### 8.6.1 Citations in Text

#### 8.6.1.1 Standard Formats

References that are generally available may be cited either directly or indirectly.

1. If the author is cited directly, the date follows the author citation in parentheses:

   Nimbus (2008) found that cloud formations can be used to predict persons' moods.

2. If the author is cited indirectly, both the author's name and the date are placed in parentheses:

   It has been found that cloud formations can be used to predict persons' moods (Nimbus, 2008). This result has since been replicated (Nimbus, 2009; Stratus, 2009).

3. If the date is mentioned in the text, it need not be repeated in parentheses:

   In 2008, Nimbus found that cloud formations can be used to predict people's moods.

4. If a work is cited more than once within the same paragraph, the date need not be repeated if there is no resulting ambiguity:

   Nimbus's (2008) work on cloud formations and mood has received little attention. The lack of attention may be due to Nimbus's opening sentence: "Only a fool would take the work reported here seriously" (p. 1).

5. Multiple references to work of the same author published in the same year are assigned lowercase letters to distinguish them when they are cited. The letters should be assigned alphabetically, by title name:

   Snow (2005a) has concluded that precipitation can dampen people's spirits. Snow (2005b) has argued that frozen precipitation is most demoralizing.

**8.6.1.2** Multiple Authors

Follow these rules in citing work of multiple authors:

1. If a work has just two authors, cite both names and the date every time you make a citation:

   McLeod and O'Dowd (2007) found an artifact in Nimbus's (2008) study. (First citation)

   McLeod and O'Dowd (2007) corrected the artifact. (Later citation)

2. If a work has up to five authors, cite all names and the date the first time you make the citation – in later citations, you need only cite the first author, followed by "et al." and the date. If a work has six or more authors, only cite the surname of the first author followed by the "et al." statement, regardless of how many there are. If two different pieces of work shorten to the same form, then always cite as many surnames as needed to distinguish the two different sources:

   McLeod, O'Dowd, and Giroud (2007) found no relation between cloud formations and mood. (First citation)

   McLeod et al. (2007) did not investigate cloud formations during tornadoes or hurricanes, however. (Later citations)

3. If citations with multiple authors are made directly, the names of the authors are connected by *and*. If citations are made indirectly (i.e., parenthetically), the names of the authors are connected by an ampersand (&):

   McLeod and O'Dowd (2008) found the artifact.
   An artifact was discovered (McLeod & O'Dowd, 2008).

**8.6.1.3** No Author

If you cite a reference with no author, use the first two or three words of the entry as described in the references. In this case, the entry will usually be cited by title.

The pamphlet suggests ways of improving one's memory ("Tips on Memory," 2001).

**8.6.1.4** Corporate Author

A corporate author may be cited instead of a personal one. Lengthy corporate names should be abbreviated only if they are readily identifiable in the reference list:

The book presented 15 ways to make friends (Golden Friendship Society, 2008).

**8.6.1.5** Authors with the Same Surname

If you refer to more than one author with the same surname, include each author's initials each time you cite the author:

S. Jones (2009) disagreed with the interpretations of E. Jones (2007).

**8.6.1.6** Electronic Sources

If available, provide the digital object identifier (DOI) number as an article identifier for electronic version of works you are citing. The DOI is an alphanumeric string that starts with a 10. If no DOI exists, cite the home page URL of the journal or publisher:

Firestone, N. Z. (2007). You can prevent pyromania. *Journal of Exotic Ailments, 15,* 63–68. doi:10.1023/4587-6667.22.3.345
Lazynik, C. C. (August 15, 2009). How to make every day a Sunday. *The Lazy Times.* Retrieved from http://www.lazytimes.com

## 8.6.2 The Reference List

The References section of a paper contains an alphabetical list of the references cited in the text of the paper. References to more than one work by the same author are arranged by order of date of publication, with earlier works listed first. Each reference should include the author(s), title, and facts of publication. Details regarding format are given in Chapter 4 of this book: The format for the references is the same as the format for the author notes described in that chapter. There are so many different kinds of reference formats that it is not possible to include them all in this book. Please consult the *APA Manual* (2009) for a complete list of formats.

Note the use of the hanging indent in reference entries, whereby the first line of each reference is flush with the left margin and other lines are indented. Here are some examples of different kinds of references:

## REFERENCES

Balderdash, H. Q. (2008). *Writing for meaning*. Los Angeles: Perfection Press.

Crumpet, C. D., & Donut, D. C. (2009). *Sugar tastes good and is good for you* (Vol. 1). Honolulu: Sugar Promotion Press.

Finn, D., Jr. (2008). Breathing in fish. In G. Trout & H. Bass (Eds.), *The physiology of fish*. San Francisco: Fisherman's Press.

Firestone, N. Z. (2007). You can prevent pyromania. *Journal of Exotic Ailments, 15*, 63–68.

*Gambling for fun and profit*. (2009). Las Vegas, NV: American Gambling Institute.

Lemon, B. J. (2002). *Vitamin C in your diet* (2nd ed.). Miami: Citrus Press.

Lohne, E. Z., & Sharke, P. P. (in press). Should usury be a crime? *Money Minder's Digest*.

Pompus, V. Q. (Ed.). (2004). *Encyclopedia of knowledge* (16 vols.). San Francisco: Worldwide.

## 8.7  AUTHOR NOTES

The author note (a) provides information about the authors' complete departmental affiliation, (b) notes a change of an author's affiliation, (c) acknowledges financial support for a study, (d) acknowledges assistance in preparing, conducting, analyzing, or reporting a study, (e) explains special agreements with regard to authorship, (f) reports on any special circumstances (e.g., the data used as a basis for the paper have been used for a prior publication, or a conflict of interest), and (g) provides an address for correspondence. All of the above functions can be combined in a single author note; the order of statements should be as listed above. Author identification notes are not numbered. They are placed on the title page below the title, byline, and affiliation.

Phineas Phlom, Department of Psychology, Lazy State University at Slow River. The author is now at Rocky Ridge State College. The research was supported by grant G1O7H5 to the author from the National Institute of

Rodent Research. I thank Whyte Meise for assistance in conducting the study. Correspondence regarding this article should be sent to Phineas Phlom, Department of Psychology, Rocky Ridge State College, Small Town, Vermont.

E-mail: pphlom@rrsc.edu

## 8.8 FOOTNOTES

### 8.8.1 Kinds of Footnotes

#### 8.8.1.1 Content Footnotes

Content footnotes are used for material that elaborates on the text but is not directly relevant to it. When citing a footnote in the text, place the note citation after all punctuation (except dashes).

  Because footnotes can distract the reader, they should be used sparingly. Before using a footnote, you should decide whether the material might be better incorporated into the text or deleted.

[1]The only ill effect on the subject resulting from the treatment was a deep fear of furry animals, a fear we hope eventually to eradicate.

#### 8.8.1.2 Reference Footnotes

Reference footnotes are used only rarely in psychological reporting. Almost all citations should be made through references. Reference footnotes may be used, however, for legal citations and copyright permissions.

[1]From *Writing for Meaning* (p. 113), by H. Q. Balderdash, 2009, Los Angeles: Perfection Press. Copyright by Perfection Press. Reprinted with permission.

#### 8.8.1.3 Table Footnotes

Table footnotes amplify information contained in tables. These footnotes are of three kinds.

**1. General notes**
A general note provides further information about the table as a whole and explains any abbreviations and symbols.

## 2. Specific notes

A specific note provides further information about one or more entries in the table. Such notes are indicated by letter superscripts attached to the appropriate entries. If there is more than one note, the notes are ordered horizontally by rows.

## 3. Probability levels

Probability levels are used to ascertain the significance of statistical tests. A single asterisk should be used for the highest probability level, and an additional asterisk should be used for each lower probability level.

The number of asterisks used for a given probability level should be consistent across tables. The most common use of asterisks is for one to represent $p < .05$, two to represent $p < .01$, and three to represent $p < .001$. When possible, authors should report exact $p$ values (e.g., $p = .03$) rather than ranges (e.g., $p < .05$)

When more than one kind of footnote appears in a single table, general footnotes precede specific ones, and specific ones precede probability levels. The footnotes to a single table might look like this:

*Note.* All subjects were veterans.
[a] Two subjects were caught copying from each other, and were eliminated from this group. [b] One subject in this group refused to finish the task and was eliminated.
*$p < .05$, **$p < .01$, ***$p < .001$

Observe that multiple footnotes of a given kind follow each other on a single line, where possible.

### 8.8.2 Numbering of Footnotes

Content and reference footnotes are numbered consecutively throughout a paper. Footnotes are indicated by Arabic numeral superscripts. If a footnote is referred to more than once, subsequent references should use a parenthetical statement rather than a superscript. Footnotes to a table should be lettered consecutively within each table.

Jones (2008) found that subjects suffered from few ill aftereffects.[1] Critics have lambasted Jones's (2008) alleged insensitivity to subjects (see Footnote 1).

### 8.8.3 Placement of Footnotes

In papers to be submitted for publication, footnotes are placed on a separate page after the references (see Chapter 5 of this book). In student papers, however, it is often more convenient for the reader if the footnotes are placed at the bottom of the page on which each footnote is cited.

## 8.9 CREDITING SOURCES AND PERMISSIONS

All direct quotations need to be accompanied by a reference citation, regardless of the length of those quotations. If you quote, you must supply an exact citation, including page numbers, even for short quotes. You also need permission from the rights holder for longer quotes. The length of the quote for which you need to express permission varies by copyright holder. Hence, you may need to check whether written permission is needed. The same rules apply to use of electronic material and for use of material in an electronic medium. The APA requires permission for quotes of more than 400 words in length for single text extracts and more than 800 words for series of text extracts.

## 8.10 CONFLICT OF INTEREST

When you go to publish an article, you may be asked to sign a form either stating that no conflicts of interest are involved in the research or else stating what they are or may be. For example, if a drug company has funded you to test the psychological effects of a drug that the company produces, you are in a potential conflict-of-interest situation. You must report all such conflicts or potential conflicts fully and accurately.

## 8.11 A FINAL WORD

You should adhere to these rules diligently, whether you submit your paper to a course instructor or to a journal editor. In the former case, your instructor will appreciate your concern for correct format, even if he or she has not explicitly requested it. In the latter case, a journal editor will expect strict adherence to the rules and may send back a paper that does not conform to them. The *APA Manual* (2009) provides a very useful checklist on pages 241–243 that helps you determine whether you have conformed to all the formal requirements. A sample student paper typed according to the APA rules is presented in the Appendix of this book.

# 9 Guidelines for Data Presentation

The goal of this chapter is to help you understand how optimally to present data. The chapter draws heavily on three sources to which we refer readers for more details. For the presentation of data in the form of tables, Andrew Ehrenberg's *Data Reduction* and *A Primer in Data Reduction* (1978, 1982) contain much good sound advice. For the use of figures, William Cleveland's *The Elements of Graphing Data* (1994) is a style guide that is required reading for anyone considering using a graph, from the most junior undergraduate to the most experienced researcher. Good advice is also available in the works of Tufte (2001) and Wainer (1984) as well as in the sixth edition of the *APA Manual* (American Psychological Association, 2009).

Tables and figures allow large amounts of material to be presented concisely. Well presented, they often enable readers to understand at a glance patterns of data and exceptions that would be obscured if presented in the text. Tables and figures are more expensive for journals to produce than text, however, so if you plan to submit a paper for publication, you should present in this form only your most important sets of data. Do not duplicate data from one table or figure to another unless it is essential for comprehension. Extensive sets of data should be reported in appendices rather than in the body of the paper, or should be made available online with an appropriate note in the paper indicating the Web address at which the data can be obtained.

The same principles that apply to the effective presentation of tables and figures also apply to effective scientific writing. The basic rule is to aim for a simple, direct presentation, without clutter.

Parts of this chapter have been prepared by Chris Leach.

Stylistic excesses like the moiré pattern graphics that appear on many histograms hinder rather than help, because they often direct attention away from the data. Edward Tufte (2001) uses the term *chartjunk* to refer to such unnecessary elements of graphs and has good advice on how to avoid it.

Care in preparing tables and figures helps you to understand your data. As you produce better versions, you explore your data and tease out meanings as well as choose how best to communicate the data. For this reason, tables and figures should be constructed first. Together with their captions, they should be able to communicate much of the information in the paper, without one's even having to read the text.

## 9.1 RELATION BETWEEN TABLES OR FIGURES AND TEXT

Three common mistakes in the use of tables and figures are the following:

1. Duplication in the text of material presented in tables and figures;
2. Presentation of tables and figures that are unintelligible without reference to the text; and
3. Presentation of tables and figures with no or minimal discussion.

First, data presented in tables and figures should be discussed in the text, and not just re-presented. Give brief verbal summaries to lead readers to the main patterns and exceptions, but do not repeat values that they easily can read from tables or figures. Second, construct each table and figure and the caption accompanying it so that readers are able to understand it without reference to the text. Third, remember that, even if readers are able to understand the table or figure by itself, they may not see the conclusions you want to draw. If data are important enough to present in tabular or graphical form, they are important enough to discuss.

## 9.2 SOME GENERAL TIPS FOR DESIGNING YOUR DATA DISPLAYS

No matter what kinds of data displays you are planning to use in your paper, there are a few guidelines that are always worth considering when you start designing your displays to ensure that your displays are as reader-friendly as possible (see also American Psychological Association, 2009):

- If your readers are supposed to compare different numbers or columns, place the items that need to be compared right beside each other.
- Be sure that all text in your display is legible without the use of a magnifying glass.
- Include all information in your display that is necessary to understand it – that is, make use of table notes, explain uncommon abbreviations, and so on.
- Keep the look of your display factual, and avoid using elements just for decorative purposes.

## 9.3 TABLES

### 9.3.1 When to Use Tables

Tables are preferable to figures for many small data sets. For larger, more complex data sets, a good choice of graph may do a better job of showing the patterns and exceptions. Tables also may be preferable if it is important to show precise values.

### 9.3.2 Four Rules for Constructing Tables

Compare Tables 9.1 and 9.2, which show the same crime figures for 15 states over a 3-year period. Table 9.2 was produced using four guiding principles suggested by Andrew Ehrenberg that make it much easier to understand than Table 9.1. (See Ehrenberg, 1982, for a more comprehensive account of this example.)

**1.** Order rows and columns by size.

Table 9.2 has the rows ordered by the three-year average for each state. In Table 9.1, they are ordered alphabetically. The only advantage of alphabetical ordering is that it is easier to find a given state. The columns have not been reordered because the yearly averages do not differ much, and there is some interest in year-to-year fluctuation. It is clear from Table 9.2 that the ordering of the crime figures is similar to the ordering of the states' population sizes. Although it may seem obvious that the larger states would have higher crime rates, this fact is not obvious from Table 9.1. Rather than using the row averages to order the table, we could have used population size.

Table 9.1. The Number of Murders and Non-negligent Manslaughters by States, 2005–2007 (First 15 States Alphabetically)

| | Murder and non-negligent manslaughter | | |
| | Number | | |
| | 2007 | 2006 | 2005 |
| --- | --- | --- | --- |
| Alabama | 412 | 382 | 374 |
| Alaska | 44 | 36 | 32 |
| Arizona | 468 | 465 | 445 |
| Arkansas | 191 | 205 | 186 |
| California | 2260 | 2485 | 2503 |
| Colorado | 153 | 158 | 173 |
| Connecticut | 106 | 108 | 102 |
| Delaware | 37 | 42 | 37 |
| District of Columbia | 181 | 169 | 195 |
| Florida | 1201 | 1129 | 883 |
| Georgia | 718 | 600 | 564 |
| Hawaii | 22 | 21 | 24 |
| Idaho | 49 | 36 | 35 |
| Illinois | 752 | 780 | 766 |
| Indiana | 356 | 369 | 356 |

*Source:* Federal Bureau of Investigation (2005, 2006, 2007).

Using such an external criterion is helpful if a number of tables are to be compared, because the same fixed order can be used for each table. Of course, the external criterion should be one that is likely to be of help in making sense of the data, as population size is here.

**2.** Use averages to summarize or provide a focus.

Table 9.2 has both row and column averages. Where the individual numbers do not differ much, the average provides a good summary. For example, the average of 360 murders and non-negligent manslaughters per year summarizes the numbers for Indiana in this period quite well. Where the numbers differ, the average provides a focus for comparison, as with the column averages. In Table 9.2, we can see that crime was fairly stable over this period, and that this stability applies equally to states with low and high crime rates. We can also see exceptions clearly. The numbers are, on average, higher in 2006 than in 2005, although Hawaii, Colorado, the District

Table 9.2. Murder and Non-negligent Manslaughter: States Ordered by 3-year Averages[a]

| | Murder and non-negligent manslaughter | | | |
| --- | --- | --- | --- | --- |
| | 2007 | 2006 | 2005 | Average |
| California | 2260 | 2485 | 2503 | 2416 |
| Florida | 1201 | 1129 | 883 | 1071 |
| Illinois | 752 | 780 | 766 | 766 |
| Georgia | 718 | 600 | 564 | 627 |
| Arizona | 468 | 465 | 445 | 459 |
| Alabama | 412 | 382 | 374 | 389 |
| Indiana | 356 | 369 | 356 | 360 |
| Arkansas | 191 | 205 | 186 | 194 |
| D.C. | 181 | 169 | 195 | 182 |
| Colorado | 153 | 158 | 173 | 161 |
| Connecticut | 106 | 108 | 102 | 105 |
| Idaho | 49 | 36 | 35 | 40 |
| Delaware | 37 | 42 | 37 | 39 |
| Alaska | 44 | 36 | 32 | 37 |
| Hawaii | 22 | 21 | 24 | 22 |
| Average | 463 | 466 | 445 | 458 |

*Source:* Federal Bureau of Investigation (2005, 2006, 2007).
[a]Reordered data from Table 9.1.

of Columbia, and California had lower crime rates in 2006 than in the previous year.

**3.** Round numbers to two effective digits.

Rounding numbers sensibly is practically always helpful, because it saves on memory load, thus making it easier to do quick calculations. For example, we can quickly see that 740 is about three times 250, but comparing 737 and 245 takes longer. We also rarely need the greater accuracy. Rounding to two effective digits gives sufficient accuracy for most purposes. Effective digits are digits that vary in that sort of number. Numbers like percentages vary in tens and units, so 18.3 and 35.8 are rounded to 18 and 36. With numbers like 1,836.7, 1,639.3, 1,234.2, and 1,122.8, the decimal numbers are not effective in distinguishing the numbers. The rounded versions are 1,847, 1,639, 1,234, and 1,123.

**4.** Table layout should make it easy to compare relevant numbers.

The main principle of table layout is that numbers to be compared should be close together. In Table 9.2, it is easier to compare the numbers in any column than in any row. This is because the leading digits are close to each other, allowing for quicker calculations. The larger numbers have also been put at the top, as we are more used to doing subtractions that way. Other aspects of table layout are also important. Widely spaced rows prevent easy comparison, as does irregular spacing of rows and columns. However, occasional regular gaps help emphasize the patterns, as in Table 9.2. If tables need to be compared to each other, put them next to each other.

### 9.3.3 Placement of Tables

In articles submitted for publication, tables are placed after footnotes (see Chapter 5). In the text, refer to table numbers but do not say "table above" or "table below" as you do not know exactly where the typesetter will place the tables.

In student papers, it is often more convenient to insert the tables at the appropriate places in the text for easier reading.

### 9.3.4 Table Numbers

Tables are numbered consecutively with Arabic numerals, starting with Table 1. Suffixes (e.g., Tables 5 and 5a) should not be used. Tables should have numbers only, so Tables 5 and 5a should be numbered Table 5 and Table 6. If you present tables in an appendix, identify them with a combination of capital letters and Arabic numerals. The second table of Appendix A is Table A2, for example, and the fifth table of Appendix C is Table C5. The table number is written at the top of the table. It is typed flush against the left side of the page.

### 9.3.5 Table Titles

The title of a table should describe concisely what the table is supposed to show and should be understandable without reference to the text. In addition, it should be as brief as possible. Type it below the table number, flush against the left side of the page.

### 9.3.6 Ruling of Tables

Table 9.1 has both vertical and horizontal rules, whereas Table 9.2 has only horizontal rules. Most journals have standard formats. For example, vertical rules are almost never used in APA or British Psychology Society (BPS) journals. The variable spacing in Table 9.2 achieves the same effect without reducing the clarity of the table.

### 9.3.7 Formatting of Tables

Some tables have standard forms for data presentation. The *APA Manual* (American Psychological Association, 2009) lists and exemplifies those different tables. There are standards for regression tables, descriptive statistics, and word tables, among others. It will facilitate the design of your tables significantly if you comply with the APA guidelines. In addition, it is hardly possible to forget to report an important variable in a series of numbers when using a template.

There are also some general guidelines that should always be followed:

- Table headings should be as short as possible and not be much wider than the longest entry
- You can use standard abbreviations without explaining them (e.g., *M* for mean or *N* for number). Non-standard abbreviations should be explained in the table heading or table notes.
- Only the first letter of the first word in each heading should be capitalized.
- When a cell of the table is empty because data were not measured, insert a dash in the cell. If the data are not applicable to that cell, however, leave the cell blank.
- A dash in the main diagonal of a correlation matrix indicated the correlation of a variable with itself, which is 1.
- Tables can be submitted in either single- or double-spaced format.

## 9.4 FIGURES

### 9.4.1 When to Use Figures

A figure is any type of illustration other than a table. Figures include stem-and-leaf displays, graphs, charts, photographs, and drawings.

Table 9.3. Sensation seeking scores for 32 parachutists

| SSQ | 1 | 4 | 6 | 8 | 9 | 11 | 12 | 13 | 14 | 15 | 16 | 17 | 18 | 19 | 20 |
|---|---|---|---|---|---|---|---|---|---|---|---|---|---|---|---|
| Frequency | 1 | 1 | 2 | 2 | 1 | 2 | 3 | 2 | 3 | 4 | 3 | 3 | 2 | 2 | 1 |

Before making a figure, consider which type of figure will present your information most effectively.

Figures, like tables, allow large amounts of data to be presented concisely. Their advantage over tables is that they often enable the reader to see at a glance trends that otherwise would not be readily apparent. With the exception of stem-and-leaf displays, figures have the disadvantage, however, that they do not convey precise values of data.

Use figures when they augment rather than duplicate the text, and then only to convey essential facts. Omit visually distracting details. Make sure your figures are easy to read and understand, and use a consistent style for presenting figures throughout the paper.

### 9.4.2 Stem-and-Leaf Displays

Table 9.3 shows the scores on a Sensation Seeking Questionnaire (SSQ) of 32 hobby parachutists who have completed at least 15 jumps.

The distribution is skewed to the left. This skewness makes it misleading to report just means and standard deviations as summary statistics. Both will be heavily influenced by the two or three unusually high scores (or outliers). In this case, the outliers are particularly interesting, raising questions about why a person that is not high in sensation seeking would engage in such thrill-providing activities like parachuting. Reporting robust estimates of location and spread (e.g., median and interquartile range instead of mean and standard deviation) will reduce the impact of the outliers. However, a more comprehensive report of the data, rather than just summary statistics, would be more informative, particularly if outliers are considered potentially interesting cases rather than just nuisance values that mess up the calculation of summary statistics.

The frequency distribution given in Table 9.3 is one compact way of presenting all the data. A better way is to use a stem-and-leaf display, which combines the advantages of tables and graphs

(a)  2 | 0
     1 | 11222334444555556667778899
     . | 1466889

(b)  2  | 0
     1* | 55556667778899
     1. | 1122233444
     *  | 66889
     .  | 14

(c)  1   2  | 0
     5   1* | 8899
     11  1s | 666777
     7   1f | 4445555
     14  1t | 22233
     9   1. | 11
     7   *  | 889
     4   s  | 66
     2   f  | 4
         t  |
     1   .  | 1

**Figure 9.1.** Stem-and-leaf displays of SSQ scores. *Notes:* (a) Stem widths of 10 SSQ points; (b) stem widths of 5 SSQ points; (c) stem widths of 2 SSQ points, with a cumulative count from either end to the middle.

by retaining all the numerical information as well as showing clearly the shape of the distribution of numbers. Stem-and-leaf displays were developed by John Tukey (1977). The simplest type is produced by first rounding the numbers to two effective digits. The 32 scores in Table 9.3 are already in this form. Each score is now broken into two parts, the part up to and including the first effective digit (the tens in this case) forming the stem and the second effective digit (the units) forming the leaf. So 18 has 1 as stem and 8 as leaf.

The stems determine which row of the display the score appears in and the leaves are written alongside the appropriate stem to identify the individual scores, as shown in Figure 9.1a. This display makes clear the skewness of the distribution, but it is too short and fat to give a clear view of the bulk of the distribution. In this case, it helps to have narrower stems to spread out the display. Figure 9.1b uses stem widths of 5 SSQ points, with the *s containing leaves between 5 and 9 and the ·s containing leaves between 0 and 4. The 14 is therefore placed alongside the 1·stem, whereas the 8 goes with the 1* stem.

Figure 9.1c gives an even more spread-out display, drawing attention to the outliers more effectively than do the other displays. Here the stem widths are 2 GHQ points, with the stems identified by •

(for leaves 0 and 1), t (for two and three), f (for four and five), s (for six and seven), and * (for 8 and 9). So 4 and 8 now go in stems 1f and 1*. These displays are helpful for exploring data and also give a compact way of communicating complete data sets when summary statistics are not sufficient.

### 9.4.3 Box Plots and Quartile Plots

For cases in which the data are too extensive to report the full stem-and-leaf display, Tukey's (1977) box plot is a convenient way of reporting summary statistics. Tufte's (2001) quartile plot is a more compact version of a box plot. The quartile and box plots both plot a five-number summary of the data, including the two extremes (highest and lowest scores), the first and third quartiles (called lower and upper hinges by Tukey), and the median. For the SSQ data, the extremes are 1 and 20, the hinges are 11 and 16.5, and the median is 14.

These five values can be obtained easily from the stem-and-leaf display. First, it helps to add a cumulative count from either end in toward the middle of the display, as has been done in Figure 9.1c. From this panel, we can see that there are 11 scores of 16 or higher, 14 of 12 or lower, and seven in the middle stem with values of 14 or 15. The lowest and highest scores, 1 and 20, can be read off immediately.

The median is the unique score in the middle if there is an odd number of scores, or the average of the two middle scores if there is an even number of scores. To see how deep we have to count in from either end to hit the median, the general rule is depth of median = (1 + number of scores)/2.

Here, there are 30 scores, so the median depth is $(1 + 32)/2 = 16.5$. The half shows that there is no unique middle score, so the median is the average of the 16th and 17th scores in from either end. Counting from low to high, the cumulative count tells us that there are 14 scores of 12 or less and seven in the middle stem, so the 16th and 17th scores will be the second and third entries in the middle stem. Both those scores are 14, so the median is 14.

The hinges are the scores in the middle of the two halves of the data from the median to the extremes. The middle half of the data lies between the two hinges, so the hinges give a good indication of the spread of the bulk of the data. The simplest general rule for the depth of the two hinges is depth of hinges = (1 + depth of median)/2. For an even number of scores, the half that crops up on the end of the

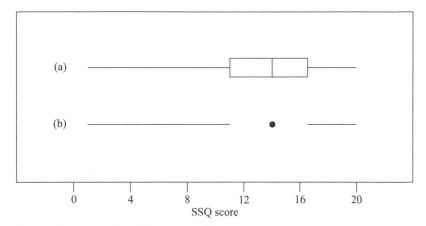

**Figure 9.2.** (a) Box plot; (b) quartile plot of SSQ scores.

median depth should be removed before calculating the hinge depth. For this case, with a median depth of 16.5, the hinge depth will be $(1 + 16)/2 = 8.5$. So the hinges can be computed by taking the eighth and ninth values in from either end and dividing them by two $[(11 + 11)/2 = 11$, and $(16 + 17)/2 = 16.5]$.

Figure 9.2a shows the box plot of this five-number summary. The two hinges form the outer edges of a box, with a line inside the box where the median is. Outside the box, whiskers are extended to the extremes. (Tukey's [1977] original term was *box-and-whisker plot*, now contracted to *box plot*.) From this plot, it can quickly be seen that the middle half of the data lies between scores 11 and 16.5 – the two hinges – with a median score of 14. The fact that the right whisker is longer than the left one suggests the skewness that is actually present in the data.

Figure 9.2b gives the more compact quartile-plot version, with a filled circle for the median and the boxes omitted, but the whiskers the same. This version is the preferred one, particularly when several plots are to be compared.

### 9.4.3.1 Outliers

Information about outliers can be added to these plots very straight-forwardly. Tukey (1977) suggests a simple general procedure for detecting outliers. Calculate the midspread (or interquartile range), which is just the difference between the hinges. Outliers are those scores more than 1.5 midspreads beyond the hinges. Extreme outliers are scores more than 3 midspreads beyond the hinges. In this

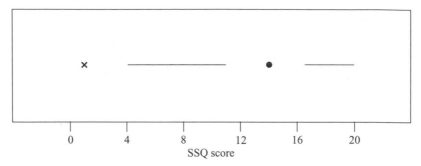

**Figure 9.3.** Quartile plot of SSQ scores with outlier marked.

example, the midspread is $16.5 - 11 = 5.5$, so scores less than 2.75 [$= 11 - (1.5 \times 5.5)$] or greater than 24.75 [$= 16.5 + (1.5 \times 5.5)$] are outliers, whereas scores lower than $-5.5$ or higher than 33 are extreme outliers. The low score of 1 noted earlier now counts as outliers. There are no extreme outliers. On this criterion, none of the high scores is high enough to count as an outlier.

The outliers can be marked on the quartile plot or box plot, using ×s to represent outliers, ⊗s to represent extreme outliers, and extending the whiskers only to the highest (or lowest) scores not counted as outliers. The quartile plot in Figure 9.3 shows the three high outliers, with the whisker extending to 4, the lowest score in Figure 9.1c that is not an outlier.

There are many other methods of detecting outliers. The method given here is a general-purpose rough-and-ready approach that works well in many cases.

### 9.4.3.2 Comparing Data Sets

Stem-and-leaf displays and quartile plots are also helpful in comparing two or more sets of data.

Figure 9.4 shows the depression scores for 20 patients who demonstrated mood improvement after four weeks of cognitive therapy, back-to-back with scores from 13 patients who showed improvement after eight weeks. Figure 9.5 shows the two quartile plots of the data. From each display, it can be seen that the scores for the four-week group are lower, on average, and less spread out than the scores of the eight-week group. Although there are no outliers here, these displays are much more informative than a table of means and standard deviations.

Improvement after Improvement after
four weeks eight weeks

|        |     |      |
|-------:|:---:|------|
|        | 2.  | 0123 |
|   9876 | 1*  | 79   |
|33311100| 1.  | 2334 |
|  98765 | *   | 68   |
|    332 | .   | 0    |

**Figure 9.4.** Back-to-back stem-and-leaf display of depression scores for 20 patients showing improvement after four weeks of cognitive therapy and 13 showing improvement after eight weeks.

## 9.4.4 Graphs

"Above all else show the data" (Tufte, 1983, p. 105). This is the best single principle of graph presentation. William Cleveland's rules, listed in the next section, are good ways of following this advice, aiding both your own understanding and your ability to communicate the data. Before looking at these rules, two graphs will illustrate some of the main points. We have chosen two graphs that already do a reasonable job of communicating the data and suggest some improvements. Most published graphs could be improved; many have worse problems than these two; and many are quite dreadful. For some examples of the dreadful ones, see Wainer (1984).

Figure 9.6 shows a grouped bar chart that depicts the mean number of correct answers in an intelligence test under conditions of noise and silence by three age groups. The main point being communicated is that, whereas the three age groups did not significantly differ in

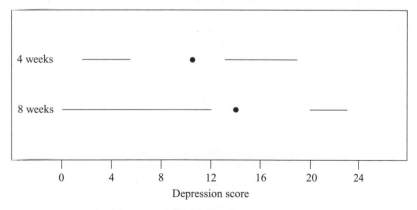

**Figure 9.5.** Quartile plots of depression scores for patients showing mood improvement after four or eight weeks of cognitive therapy.

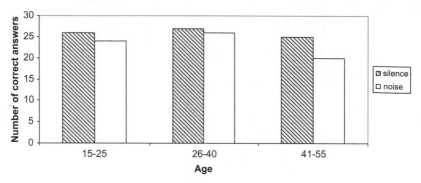

**Figure 9.6.** Bar chart of mean number of correct answers in an intelligence test by three age groups under conditions of silence or noise.

their performance when working under conditions of silence, the age group of 41- to 55-year-olds had much more trouble keeping up their performance with noise than did the younger participants.

The first thing to note is that the figure communicates only eight numbers, so a table is likely to do a better job than a graph. If you write a paper that contains many tables, though, you may decide to choose a figure to highlight those data.

How can you do worse than in presenting the data than in Figure 9.6? A common choice is to use a divided bar chart, as in Figure 9.7. This chart makes it difficult to compare the mid-periphery values, because nonaligned length judgments are involved. The only thing worse than a divided bar chart is a pie chart, because such a chart involves judging areas, which people find hard to do accurately. And the only thing worse than a pie chart is several pie charts.

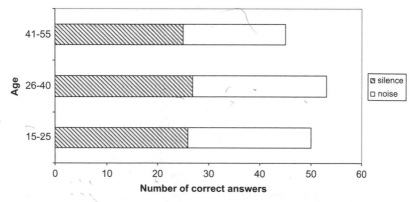

**Figure 9.7.** Divided bar chart version of the data in Figure 9.6.

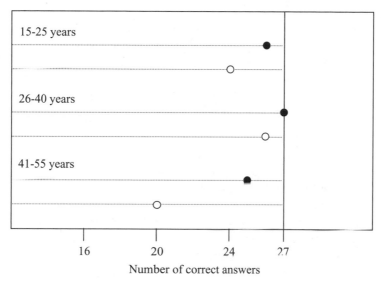

Figure 9.8. Dot chart for the data in Figure 9.6.

Cleveland (1994) reported the results of a number of studies in graphical perception, examining the performance of people at the elementary tasks required for understanding graphs. He reported the following ordering of elementary tasks, from most to least accurate:

1. Position along a common scale;
2. Position along identical, nonaligned scales;
3. Length;
4. Angle or slope;
5. Area;
6. Volume; and
7. Color hue, color saturation, and density

When choosing which type of graph to use, it helps to choose one involving judgments as high up in this ordering as possible. Divided bar charts and pie charts involve judgments low down in the ordering. They can always be replaced by a dot chart of the type shown in Figure 9.8, which involves judgments of position along a common scale. For this reason, divided bar charts and pie charts should never be used.

How can you improve on Figure 9.6? There is no need to use boxes to represent the numbers. If anything, the boxes might be

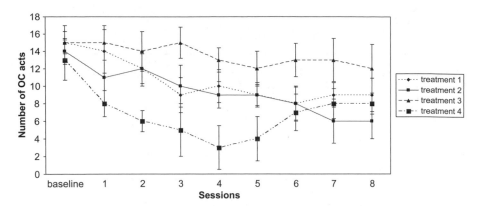

**Figure 9.9.** Cluttered graph of mean number of obsessive-compulsive (OC) acts and standard deviations by treatment sessions.

misleading, as they invite viewers to make area judgments and the areas contain no information about the numbers, particularly as the scale does not start at zero.

Figure 9.8 shows a dot chart for these data. Here the eight dots are visually prominent, with light dotted lines extended across the display up to the maximum value of 27 for easier comparison. Because the scale does not start at zero, it would be misleading to stop the dotted lines at the data points; this procedure would invite viewers to compare lengths rather than positions. The data region is enclosed in a rectangle, with a pair of scale lines marked in, again for easier comparison.

Figure 9.9 gives a comparison of four treatments for obsessive-compulsive behavior. The data are the mean number of obsessive-compulsive acts averaged over the time period from one treatment session to the next. Means and standard deviations for each group on each of nine occasions are presented. The main problem with this graph is that it is incredibly cluttered. With some effort, it is possible to see what is going on. The group receiving Treatment 4 shows a rapid reduction in obsessive-compulsive behaviors, which is not maintained. Treatment Group 3 stays basically the same, whereas the other two groups show a gradual reduction in obsessive-compulsive acts, with a slight advantage to Treatment 2.

The error bars show a fair bit of variation. It is likely, but not absolutely clear, that sample standard deviations rather than standard deviations of the mean (or standard errors) are reported – standard errors would be shorter. Many published graphs that incorporate error bars give less information than in this case, making it difficult to decide whether sample standard deviations, standard errors, or confidence intervals are shown. It is important to state which is being used, because which is used will affect judgments of group differences.

Figure 9.10 shows one way of reducing the clutter. At the top, only the group means are plotted for easier comparisons between groups. The means and error bars for each group are then shown in four separate aligned displays. As in Figure 9.8, the data region is enclosed in a rectangle, with two scale lines for each variable. The light reference line highlighting the baseline measures is optional.

### 9.4.5 Rules for Constructing Graphs

The rules given here are the main principles offered by William Cleveland (1994), with minor modifications. We have divided them into two parts, one with general information on the planning of your chart and one with more specific information on the graphic details of charts. The following sections present some tips for planning the design or your graph.

**1.** Make the data stand out.

The data in Figure 9.9 do not stand out well. Figure 9.10 improves on this situation, although the baseline points are not well discriminated. Using different plotting symbols for the four groups may help a little.

**2.** Avoid superfluity.

Getting rid of unnecessary elements would improve many graphs. The boxes in Figure 9.6 do not hinder communication, but serve no useful purpose beyond what is provided by the dots in Figure 9.8. For the same reason, quartile plots (Figure 9.2b) are often better than box plots (Figure 9.2a).

**3.** A large amount of data can be packed into a small region.

Although clutter and superfluous elements should be avoided, there are many examples of clear graphs with large amounts of data.

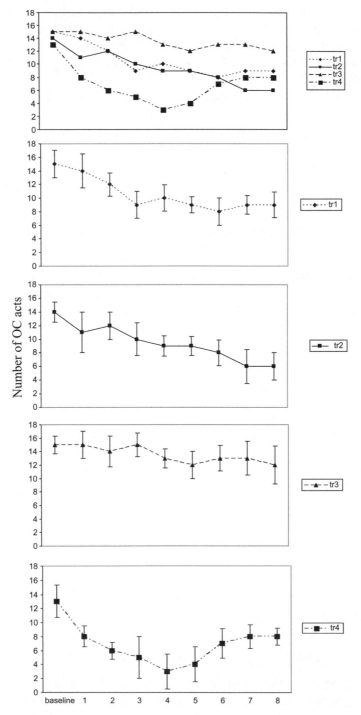

**Figure 9.10.** Redrawing of Figure 9.9 (top panel) to remove the clutter.

Computer graphics allow clear graphics to be produced more easily. See Cleveland (1994) and Tufte (2001) for examples.

4. Graphing data should be an iterative, experimental process.

   Graphing data in several different ways is a good method for exploring the data.

5. Graph data two or more times when necessary.

   If the error bars in Figure 9.9 are worth having, it is better to present them in separate graphs, as in Figure 9.10, rather than to clutter up the display.

6. Many useful graphs require careful, detailed study.

   The messages in the graphs presented here are all straightforward and fairly easy to see. Straightforwardness is not the most important criterion for a good graph. A more important one is whether we can see something using a graph that would have been difficult or impossible to see without a graph. Some of the graphs in Cleveland (1994) or Tufte (2001) deserve careful study.

## 9.4.6 Practical Tips for Designing Graphs

1. Use visually prominent graphical elements to show the data.

   Many published graphs have the data points obscured by lines connecting the data or background grids, or in other ways, simply because the plotting symbols are not prominent enough.

2. Use a pair of scale lines for each variable.

   Make the data region the interior of the rectangle formed by the scale lines. Put tick marks outside the data region. Using two scale lines, as in Figures 9.8 and 9.10, makes it easier to compare points. In addition, Poulton (1985) gave evidence of distorted judgments when only one scale line is used. All the figures here have the tick marks outside the data region, which helps prevent them from obscuring data points.

3. Do not clutter the data region.

Figure 9.9 is too cluttered. Readers should be able to read figures without effort, which is not the case here.

4. Avoid using too many tick marks.

Figure 9.9 has overdone the number of tick marks. Using half as many, as in Figure 9.10, still allows data values to be judged well. From between 3 to 10 tick marks usually suffices to give a broad sense of the measurement scale.

5. Use a reference line when necessary.

Use a reference line when there is an important value that must be seen across the entire graph, but do not let the line interfere with the data.

6. Do not allow data labels in the data region to interfere with the data or to clutter the graph.

The labels in Figure 9.10 do not get in the way of the data. Added to Figure 9.9, they would have increased the clutter. Make sure labels do not decrease the comprehensibility of the graph.

7. Avoid putting notes and keys in the data region.

Put keys to symbols just outside the data region, and put notes in the figure caption or the text.

8. Overlapping plotting symbols must be visually distinguishable.

In Figure 9.10, the baseline measures overlap a little but are distinguishable. Using different symbols for the four groups would help in worse cases.

9. Superimposed data sets must be readily visually discriminated.

The four groups are clearly discriminable in Figure 9.10, although there is a slight problem with the scores of Treatment Groups 1 and 3 in Session 1. Use different plotting symbols where there is poor discrimination.

**10.** Put major conclusions in graphical form.

Make captions comprehensive and informative. Readers often look first at the tables and figures. The captions should communicate most of the major points. Captions should briefly describe what is in the display and bring attention to the important features and the main conclusions you wish to draw.

**11.** Error bars should be clearly explained.

Error bars are useful ways of indicating variability in the data, but only if they are described unambiguously. Say clearly whether you are using (a) sample standard deviations of the data, (b) standard errors of the statistic graphed, or (c) confidence intervals for the statistic graphed.

**12.** Choose the scales wisely.

Choose the scales so that the data fill up as much of the data region as possible.

**13.** Choose appropriate scales when graphs are to be compared.

The graphs in Figure 9.10 are all on the same scale, making it easy to compare them. In some cases, though, using the same scale results in poor resolution.

**14.** Do not insist on zero always being included on a scale showing magnitude.

Including zero often helps comparisons, but it is not necessary to include it if doing so results in poor resolution of the data. Clearly labeled tick marks are essential, though.

**15.** Use a logarithmic scale when it is important to understand percentage change or multiplicative factors.

When magnitudes are converted to logarithms, percentage change and multiplicative factors are easy to understand because equal percentage or multiplicative factors have equal distances on a logarithmic scale. (For explanation and examples, see Cleveland, 1994.)

16. Showing data on a logarithmic scale can improve resolution.

   Many data sets in psychology are skewed to the right. Plotting the data on the original scale will often result in graphs with most of the data bunched together at the low end and just a few points at the high end. This bunching can cause poor resolution. Using logarithms reduces the skewness and improves resolution.

17. Use a scale break only when necessary.

   If a break cannot be avoided, use a full scale break. Do not connect numerical values on two sides of a break. In some cases, scale breaks are needed to improve resolution, although transforming the data (logarithms, again, for data skewed to the right) often removes the need for a break.

### 9.4.7 Placement of Figures

In articles submitted for publication, figures are placed at the end of the article (see Chapter 5). Refer to figures by number. Do not refer to them as "above" or "below" as you can not be sure where the typesetter will place them in the text.

   Figure captions, along with the figure numbers, are typed double-spaced on a separate page, which is placed before the figures. In student papers, it is often more convenient to insert the figures at the appropriate places in the text, with the figure captions directly underneath each figure.

### 9.4.8 Figure Legends

Many figures require a legend or key to symbols. The legend appears within the figure itself and is photographed as part of the figure. The legend should thus be consistent in style and proportion with the rest of the figure. Put the legend just outside the data region so as not to interfere with the data.

### 9.4.9 Figure Numbers

Figures are numbered consecutively with Arabic numerals, starting with Figure 1.

## 9.4.10 Figure Captions

A figure caption should describe concisely what the figure is supposed to show. It should be understandable without reference to the text. If you need to include any further information, add it in parentheses after the figure caption. If you use a figure that is not original, obtain written permission to reprint the figure, and cite the source in the figure caption.

## 9.4.11 Preparing Figures for Publication

If you plan to submit your paper for publication, remember that figures may be reduced in size so that detail becomes harder to see. Be sure, then, to make your figures especially sharp and legible. Follow the particular journal or book publisher's instructions regarding the submission format for electronically prepared figures. If you draw your figures by hand, use black India ink on bright white drawing paper. Most figures these days are computer generated, but it is still important to make sure that their quality meets the standards of the journal:

■ **Graphs**

When plotting values of a dependent variable against values of an independent variable, place the independent variable on the horizontal axis and the dependent variable on the vertical axis. It is usually helpful for the vertical axis to be about two thirds as long as the horizontal (see Tufte, 2001).

■ **Drawings**

Drawings are most effective when kept simple. Drawings with shades of gray, like photos, require halftone processing, which is more expensive than regular processing. Avoid the added expense, when possible, by using patterns of lines or dots to create a shaded effect.

■ **Photographs**

Submit professional-quality black-and-white photographs with high contrast. If necessary, crop the photograph to remove unwanted material. If it is a photograph of a person, obtain written permission to use it.

## 9.4.12 Submitting Figures

For journals, figures should be submitted as electronic files (for those journals that use electronic submissions), as hardcopy laser-printer printouts (not dot matrix), or as 20 × 25 cm glossy photographs. Glossy prints smaller than 20 × 25 cm should be mounted on 22 × 28 cm paper. For other journals, follow the publisher's instructions. On the back of each figure write "TOP" to show which side is the top of the figure, and write the figure number and the article's short title. On a photograph, write lightly in pencil so as not to damage it. Do not use staples or paper clips. Protect prints by covering them with tissue paper and separating them with cardboard if necessary. Before submitting figures, carefully proofread them. You want to make sure that you, not readers, spot the errors!

## CHECKLIST FOR TABLES

☐ Have you assigned Arabic numerals to all tables?
☐ Does every table have a clear title that explains the content?
☐ Have you chosen the design with the reader in mind?
☐ Is the content of the table limited to the essential information?
☐ Are items that need to be compared placed beside each other?
☐ Are the tables discussed in your paper?
☐ Is the table supplementing the text and not duplicating it?
☐ Are no data duplicated in more than one table or figure?
☐ Can fonts be read without magnification?

## CHECKLIST FOR FIGURES

☐ Have you assigned Arabic numerals to all figures?
☐ Does every figure have a clear title that explains the content?
☐ Have you chosen the design with the reader in mind?
☐ Is the content of the figure limited to the essential information?
☐ Are figures that need to be compared placed beside each other?
☐ Are the figures discussed in your paper?
☐ Is the figure supplementing the text and not duplicating it?
☐ Are no data duplicated in more than one figure?
☐ Did you exclude any design detail that does not contribute to the understanding of the figure?
☐ Is your figure consistent in style with other figures in your paper?
☐ Did you explain all elements of your figure?
☐ Are the symbols used easy to differentiate?
☐ Can fonts be read without magnification?

# 10 | What Makes a Good Paper Great? Standards for Evaluating Psychology Papers

In this chapter, we enumerate some of the standards we believe our colleagues use in evaluating the contribution to knowledge made by psychology papers. We then cite three classic articles exemplifying these standards. We have deliberately picked classics that have withstood the test of time. Little has been written about how psychologists evaluate a paper's contribution. Nor have psychologists passed down from one generation to the next a clearly explicated, spoken tradition of evaluative standards. It is therefore remarkable that psychologists find a high level of agreement in their evaluations of one another's papers. In an *Annual Review of Psychology* chapter reviewing the literature on memory and verbal learning, Tulving and Madigan (1970) noted their own remarkable agreement in evaluations of papers and offered some keenly perceptive tongue-in-cheek comments regarding the state of the literature:

In the course of preparation for this chapter, we selected a sample of 540 publications – slightly less than one half of all relevant publications that appeared during the main time-period under review here – and independently rated each paper in terms of its "contribution to knowledge." We agreed to a remarkable extent in classifying all papers into three categories. The first, containing approximately two thirds of all papers, could be labeled "utterly inconsequential." The primary function these papers serve is giving something to do to people who count papers instead of reading them. Future research and understanding of verbal learning and memory would not be affected at all if none of the papers in this category had seen the light of day.

The second category, containing approximately one quarter of all the papers in our test sample, fell into the "run-of-the-mill" category. These represent technically competent variations on well-known themes. Their main purpose lies in providing redundancy and assurance to those readers whose faith in the orderliness of nature with respect to ecphoric [learning and memory] processes needs strengthening. Like the papers in the first category, these articles also do not add anything really new to knowledge, and they, too, will have fallen into oblivion 10 years from now.

Many papers in the first two categories simply demonstrate again something that is already well known. Many others offer one or more of the following conclusions: (a) variable X has an effect on variable Y; (b) the findings do not appear to be entirely inconsistent with the ABC theory; (c) the findings suggest a need for revising the ABC theory (although no inkling is provided as to how); (d) processes under study are extremely complex and cannot be readily understood; (e) the experiment clearly demonstrates the need for further research on this problem; (f) the experiment shows that the method used is useful for doing experiments of this type; and (g) the results do not support the hypothesis, but the experiment now appears to be an inadequate test of it. Apart from providing dull reading, papers with such conclusions share another feature: They contain an implicit promise of more along the same lines in the future. They make one wish that at least some writers, faced with the decision of whether to publish or perish, should have seriously considered the latter alternative.

The third category of papers in our sample, comprising less than 10 percent of the total, was classified as "worthwhile," including a small group of real gems. The papers in this category carry the burden of continuous progress in our field, by clarifying existing problems, opening up new areas of investigation, and providing titillating glimpses into the unknown. In most cases, the contribution that each particular paper makes is of necessity most modest. Nevertheless, the papers in this category unmistakably stand out from the large mass of other publications.[1]

Most psychologists would view the literature on memory and learning less dismally than did Tulving and Madigan. The difference

---

in opinion, however, would more likely reflect lesser severity in applying standards than disagreement over what standards to apply.

In the following section, we provide a short overview of eight standards that we believe separate truly important papers from other papers. Following the standards, we present synopses of three real papers and one imaginary paper. The three real papers are considered by many psychologists to be classics in the field of psychology. As you read the synopses, try to pinpoint the characteristics of these papers that make them classics. The imaginary paper is a prime contender for Tulving and Madigan's first category of "utterly inconsequential" papers. This paper should lack the characteristics you observed in the first three papers. In the last section, we return to the eight standards again and discuss how they apply to the four papers synopsized here.

## 10.1 EIGHT STANDARDS FOR THE EVALUATION OF PSYCHOLOGY PAPERS

In the following, we present eight standards that can help you evaluate the quality of psychology papers. We believe that these standards are what separate out papers that truly make a difference in the field from other papers. In the last part of the chapter, we elaborate more on these standards. For now, they should serve as guidelines to keep in mind when you read the synopses that follow the guidelines:

1. The paper contains one or more surprising results that nevertheless make sense in some theoretical context.
2. The results presented in the paper are of major theoretical or practical significance.
3. The ideas in the paper are new and exciting, and perhaps the paper presents a new way of looking at an old problem.
4. The interpretation of results is unambiguous.
5. The paper integrates into a new, simpler framework data that had previously required a complex, possibly unwieldy framework.
6. The paper contains a major debunking of previously held ideas.
7. The paper presents an experiment with a particularly clever paradigm or experimental manipulation.
8. The findings or theory presented in the paper are general ones.

## 10.2 SYNOPSES OF FOUR PSYCHOLOGY PAPERS

### 10.2.1 A Classic Literature Review: Miller (1956)

George Miller's (1956) "The Magical Number Seven, Plus or Minus Two: Some Limits on our Capacity for Processing Information" is undoubtedly one of the most influential and often cited literature reviews ever published in a psychological journal. Miller opens the paper with a confession:

My problem is that I have been persecuted by an integer. For seven years this number has followed me around, has intruded in my most private data, and has assaulted me from the pages of our most public journals. This number assumes a variety of disguises, being sometimes a little larger and sometimes a little smaller than usual, but never changing so much as to be unrecognizable. The persistence with which this number plagues me is far more than a random accident. There is, to quote a famous senator, a design behind it, some pattern governing its appearances. Either there really is something unusual about the number or else I am suffering from delusions of persecution. (p. 81)

The remainder of the paper is devoted to a case history of the persecution. This case history is summarized in the following pages.

**Span of Absolute Judgments.** In experiments on absolute judgment, subjects are asked to assign a number to represent the amount of some attribute or attributes possessed by a stimulus. Consider some examples of such experiments.

Pollack (1952) had subjects assign numbers to tones of different pitch. The pitches ranged in frequency from 100 to 8,000 cycles per second and were equally spaced along a logarithmic scale of frequencies. The experimenter varied the number of tones among which subjects had to distinguish. The number of alternative tones ranged from 2 to 14. As you would expect, subjects had little difficulty distinguishing between two tones, and a lot of difficulty distinguishing among 14 tones. The main result of interest, however, was that subjects' discrimination failed to increase beyond six different pitches. Whereas subjects were able to discriminate six different pitches with virtually no errors, they were unable consistently to discriminate more than six different pitches. This result was replicated when the range of pitches was changed by a factor of about 20 and when the spacing of tones was varied.

Garner (1953) studied absolute judgments of loudness. He spaced his tones over the intensity range from 15 to 110 decibels and used conditions with 4, 5, 6, 7, 10, and 20 different intensities. He found that the maximum number of stimulus intensities subjects are able to judge without error is about five.

Beebe-Center, Rogers, and O'Connell (1955) studied taste intensities in a similar fashion. The stimuli in their experiment were varying concentrations of salt solution. They found that subjects were able to distinguish among about four different concentrations.

Hake and Garner (1951) had subjects judge the position of a pointer in an interval along a line. Subjects were thus required to divide up the line into subjective intervals. The experimenters presented stimuli at either 5, 10, 20, or 50 different positions along the line. In one condition, subjects were told to use the numbers from 0 to 100 in making their absolute judgments. In a second condition, subjects were told to use the same number of responses as there were different stimuli (5, 10, 20, or 50). Regardless of the rating scale, subjects were found able to distinguish about 10 different positions along the line.

In other experiments, subjects have been found to distinguish about five different categories for hue and six categories for brightness. When vibrators are placed along a subject's chest, the subject is able to distinguish about four different intensities of vibration, five different durations, and seven different locations.

Miller presents further data corroborating the basic pattern of findings: As measured by absolute judgments of unidimensional stimuli, subjects' limitations on processing of information (often called *channel capacity*) range over a remarkably small interval. This interval seems to be about seven plus or minus two categories, regardless of (a) sensory modality, (b) type of stimuli within modality, or (c) range of stimuli within modality.

**Span of Attention.** Suppose a random pattern of dots is flashed on a screen very briefly. How many dots can a subject report without making errors? Kaufman, Lord, Reese, and Volkmann (1949) did this experiment by flashing from 1 to 200 dots on a screen for a period of 0.2 seconds. The subject was required to report the number of dots appearing on the screen. The authors found that subjects made practically no mistakes in reporting patterns containing as many as 5 or

6 dots. Beyond this number of dots, however, subjects made frequent errors. The span of attention for random dot patterns, therefore, also seems to fall into the seven plus or minus two range.

**Span of Immediate Memory.** Suppose you are presented with a sequence of random numbers that you are asked to recall immediately after they are presented to you. Most people are able to recall about seven digits without error. The same limit applies to random sequences of letters or words.

**Limitations on Seven Plus or Minus Two.** The spans of absolute judgment, attention, and memory all seem to be about seven plus or minus two. Yet we know from everyday experience that we are able to distinguish among more than seven faces, words, numbers, letters, and so on. Hence, our limitation to seven categories would itself seem to be limited. How do we increase our ability to distinguish among stimuli? There seem to be three important ways.

First, we can make relative rather than absolute judgments. For example, suppose that we were presented with successive pairs of tone frequencies and were asked to judge which tone in each pair was higher in pitch. We easily would be able to distinguish more than seven distinct tone frequencies. Or suppose that subjects were asked to judge which of two markers on a line was further to the right. We then could distinguish even all 50 different placements of markers in Hake and Garner's experiment. By making relative judgments, we can distinguish far more than seven categories.

Second, we can increase the number of dimensions along which the stimuli differ. In the experiments described previously on spans of absolute judgment, attention, and immediate memory, all the stimuli varied along only a single dimension. In everyday life, however, most stimuli vary along multiple dimensions. For example, discrimination among tones can be increased if pitch and loudness are varied simultaneously. If two perpendicular lines were used rather than just a single one, we could distinguish more than 10 different positions in the plane formed by the two lines. If the random dot patterns of Kaufman et al. (1949) were replaced with dots systematically arranged into a five-by-five square, we would have no trouble counting 25 dots. In each case, multidimensionality increases our capacity to make differentiations among stimuli.

Third, we can arrange the task so that subjects are required to make several absolute judgments in a row. Instead of presenting a single stimulus to the subjects and asking them to make an absolute judgment, we present several stimuli in rapid succession and then ask the subjects to make an absolute judgment. For example, we might present several markers in rapid succession on a line, and then ask the subjects to give an absolute judgment for any one of them. They are now presented with a context for the absolute judgment that was missing in the Hake and Garner (1951) experiment.

**Recording.** Under what circumstances are we limited to seven plus or minus two categories, and under what circumstances are we not so limited? Consideration of the following situations may help elucidate the limiting circumstances:

1. People usually can repeat back only about nine binary digits (0 or 1) presented in a sequence for memorization. Thus, they will probably be able to recall 001011010 after some practice in memorizing such sequences, but they probably won't be able to repeat back 001011010010110. Under a special set of circumstances, however, a person can repeat back as many as 40 binary digits. This set of circumstances involves recoding binary digits into larger chains. In an octal (8-digit) recoding scheme, the subject thoroughly learns the following conversion table:

$$000 = 0 \quad 010 = 2 \quad 100 = 4 \quad 110 = 6$$
$$001 = 1 \quad 011 = 3 \quad 101 = 5 \quad 111 = 7$$

Note that a string of three binary digits now has been recoded into a single octal digit. Subjects master this scheme and are then presented with a long string of binary digits. Every time they hear a consecutive triplet of digits, they convert it into a single octal digit. In reciting back the digits, they decode the recalled octal digit back into a string of three binary digits. If subjects previously could have remembered 10 binary digits, they now can remember about 30 such digits because they have recoded them into groups of three digits.

2. When telegraph operators first learn Morse code, they perceive each dit and dah as a separate chunk, treating it in the same way that the naive subject treats a binary digit. As the telegraph operator learns to group dits and dahs into letters, however, her recall improves dramatically, reaching about the same level as for letters.

3. When you are asked to recall an English sentence, you have no trouble recalling more than seven plus or minus two letters. You

probably also can recall with little difficulty more than seven syllables or even words. Suppose, however, that you are asked to recall a sentence presented in a foreign language with which you are unfamiliar. You may be able to recall more than seven plus or minus two letters, but perhaps not more than seven plus or minus two syllables or words.

The foregoing examples make clear the importance of the unit of encoding in assessing how much is judged, attended to, or remembered. By recoding stimuli into hierarchically organized, higher-order units, we can process large amounts of stimulus information. The processing limit of seven plus or minus two applies not to any unit but only to the highest order unit used to encode a stimulus. Given that restriction, the processing limit is general to a wide variety of task domains, as Miller (1956) has amply shown:

And finally, what about the magical number seven? What about the seven wonders of the world, the seven seas, the seven deadly sins, the seven daughters of Atlas in the Pleiades, the seven ages of man, the seven levels of hell, the seven primary colors, the seven notes of the musical scale, and the seven days of the week? What about the seven-point rating scale, the seven categories for absolute judgment, the seven objects in the span of attention, and the seven digits in the span of immediate memory? For the present I propose to withhold judgment. Perhaps there is something deep and profound behind all these sevens, something just calling out for us to discover it. But I suspect that it is only a pernicious, Pythagorean coincidence. (p. 96)

## 10.2.2 An Experimental Investigation of Forced Compliance

One of the most influential papers ever published in the field of social psychology was Festinger and Carlsmith's (1959) "Cognitive Consequences of Forced Compliance." The paper investigates what happens when people are forced to do or say something contrary to their own privately held opinions. Two theoretical positions had been advanced, each proposing a different outcome.

According to Janis and King (1954), opinion change will increase as a function of mental rehearsal of the previously disputed opinion. The best way to induce opinion change in subjects is to force them to think up and rehearse new arguments in support of the disputed opinion. Janis and King's research seemed to support this position. Subjects forced to improvise a speech that supported an opinion contrary to their own showed more change in favor of this opinion than did (a) subjects who merely heard a speech advocating the disputed opinion, and (b) subjects who delivered a speech prepared by someone else and advocated the disputed opinion.

Festinger (1957) made a different prediction. According to Festinger's theory, opinion change will be maximized if the pressure used to produce opinion change is just sufficient to produce the change. As the amount of pressure increases beyond that sufficient amount, the amount of change toward the new opinion will decrease.

Festinger and Carlsmith's experiment was designed to distinguish between the two preceding theories. The basic idea was simple (although the execution of the experiment, described herein, was rather involved). Three groups of subjects participated in an excruciatingly boring experiment. Each subject in one group was paid $1 to convince a naive subject – one who did not realize the purpose of the experiment – that the experiment, in which the naive subject was about to participate, was interesting and enjoyable. Each subject in a second group was paid $20 to tell the same lie. After they had made the persuasion attempt, subjects in each of the two groups were asked to report on how interesting and enjoyable they had found the experiment. Subjects in the third (control) group were asked only to report on the experiment, not to persuade anyone that the experiment was interesting and enjoyable. According to Janis and King's theory, reports from subjects paid $20 to lie about the experiment should have been more favorable to the experiment than reports from subjects paid $1, if one assumes that the subjects paid $20 felt more rewarded for doing the task and therefore rehearsed more favorable thoughts about it. According to Festinger's theory, reports from subjects paid $1 to lie about the experiment should have been more favorable, as $1 provided only a minimally adequate incentive to lie. Both theories predicted more favorable reports from subjects in the experimental groups than from subjects in the control group. Let's see how the experiment was executed and how it turned out.

**Method.** Seventy-one male students in the introductory psychology course at Stanford University participated in an experiment on "Measures of Performance." The subjects were presented with two tasks chosen to be as boring and monotonous as possible. In the first task, subjects were told to put 12 spools onto a tray, then to empty the tray, then to refill the tray with the 12 spools, and so on. They continued doing this task for a half hour. In the second task, each subject was presented with a board containing 48 pegs. The subject's task was to turn each peg a quarter turn clockwise, then to turn each peg again a quarter turn clockwise, and so on. Again, the task lasted a half hour. In both tasks, subjects were told to use just one hand and to work at their own speed. While the subject engaged in the task, the experimenter appeared to be taking notes on the subject's performance.

After subjects had completed the second task, the experimenter presented them with a spurious debriefing: The experimenter told each subject that there were two groups in the experiment. In one group, the subject's own, subjects simply came into the room and performed the tasks. In the other group, subjects were told before the experiment by a confederate of the experimenter that the tasks they were about to perform were fun, enjoyable, interesting, intriguing, and exciting.

At this point in the experiment, treatments for the control and experimental groups diverged. Subjects in the control group were asked to rate, among other things, how interesting and enjoyable the experiment had been. Subjects in the experimental ($1 and $20) groups were given further spurious information about the experiment: They were told that, unfortunately, the confederate was unable to appear that day because of another important commitment. This left the experimenter in the predicament of having a particular subject in the "second group" waiting outside with no one to tell him how enjoyable the experiment was. The experimenter then hit on an idea that could resolve the predicament. Perhaps, the experimenter suggested, the subject would be willing to volunteer to be the confederate who would tell the new subject about the experiment. If the subject would be willing to do this, the experimenter would pay him for those services, and also for possible future services as the confederate. The subject was then told either that he would be paid $1 or $20, depending on which experimental group he or she was in. After agreeing to tell the lie, the subject was introduced to the new, "naive" subject, who was in fact a confederate of the experimenter who had no intention of participating in the boring experiment. That confederate's only job was to pretend to be a new, naive subject. After lying to this confederate about the experiment, the subject was taken to another room and asked to rate how interesting and enjoyable the experiment had been.

The rating of the experiment by the subject completed the experiment for all subjects, regardless of group membership. After making this rating (and some others as well), the subject was given a true debriefing about the purpose and execution of the experiment.

**Results.** The results of the experiment supported Festinger's (1957) theory. Ratings of the enjoyableness of the experimental tasks were expressed on a −5 to +5 scale, where negative numbers indicated that the experiment was unenjoyable in various degrees and positive numbers indicated it was enjoyable in various degrees. The mean rating was −.45 in the control group, +1.35 in the $1 group, and −.05 in the $20 group. The mean rating for the $1 group differed significantly from the mean ratings for both of the other groups: These subjects found the experiment more enjoyable than did subjects in either of the other groups. The mean rating for the $20 group did not differ significantly from the mean rating for the control group, although the difference was, of course, in the predicted direction. Festinger and Carlsmith (1959) drew two major conclusions from these results:

1. "If a person is induced to do or say something which is contrary to his private opinion, there will be a tendency for him to change his opinion so as to bring it into correspondence with what he has done or said."
2. "The larger the pressure used to elicit the overt behavior (beyond the minimum needed to elicit it) the weaker will be the abovementioned tendency." (pp. 209–210)

### 10.2.3 An Experimental Investigation of Organization in Memory

Suppose that an experimenter reads to you the following list of words: *dog, carriage, license, clock, light, notion, apple, sojourn, branch, lecture, aluminum,* and *happiness*. After completing the list, the experimenter asks you to recite back in any order the list of words. Suppose, though, that after you have recited back the words, the experimenter reads you the list again, with the words in a different order. The experimenter then asks you to recall the list again and recite back as many words as you can in any order. The chances are excellent that you will recall more words on this second trial than you did on the first one.

It is a well-known fact of learning theory that rehearsal of words in a list improves recall of those words over successive trials in a free-recall experiment. Learning theorists disagree, however, over why recall improves over trials.

For many years, the predominant viewpoint was that of frequency theory. According to this theory, each time a person hears a word, the memory trace for that word is strengthened. The stronger the memory trace, the more likely the person is to recall a word. Hence, repetitions of a word increase recall of that word as a function of the frequency with which the word is repeated.

An alternative point of view is based on Miller's (1956) notions of recoding and unitization. This viewpoint is organization theory. According to this theory, subjects hearing words in a list recode the words into higher order subjective memory units. As subjects receive more trials on a list of words, the size of the subjective units increases. In recalling a list of words, subjects never remember more than about seven plus or minus two subjective units. Because the size of the units increases with rehearsal, however, the number of words recalled over trials increases. According to this theory, then, higher-order subjective organization rather than frequency of repetition determines increases in level of recall.

Tulving (1966) designed an experiment to distinguish between conflicting predictions of the two theories. In particular, Tulving's experiment was intended to show that greater frequency of repetition can actually reduce recall of words if the repetition somehow disrupts subjects' organization of higher order units.

**Method.** All subjects in Tulving's experiment were presented with an initial list of 18 words. They were given eight trials of free-recall learning in which to learn as much of the list as possible. Subjects then received one of two treatments. Subjects in a control group received a second list composed of 36 new words, none of which had appeared on the first list. Subjects in an experimental group received a second list composed of 18 old words (all of them from the original list) plus 18 new words (none of them from the original list). Subjects in both groups received eight trials in which to learn as much of the second list as possible.

The design of the experiment can be summarized in the following way:

| | First list | Second list |
|---|---|---|
| Control group | A | BC |
| Experimental group | A | AB |

All subjects received the same list, A, as the first list. Subjects received different second lists, however. Subjects in the control group received a second list composed of two new sublists, B and C. Subjects in the experimental group received a second list composed of one old sublist, A, and one new sublist, B. Subjects were not told about the structure of the lists or the way in which they were related.

Frequency and organization theories make different predictions regarding performance on the second list. According to frequency theory, performance on the second list should be superior if one has had prior exposure to part of the list's contents. Hence, experimental group subjects should learn the list faster than control group subjects and should show higher recall after the eight trials are completed. According to organization theory, however, learning of the second list by experimental subjects should be slower, and final performance in the experimental group should be inferior to that in the control group. The reason for this prediction is that according to organization theory, the higher order units formed during learning of the first list may have been appropriate for that list, but they will probably be inappropriate for learning the second list. The units for the first list will thus interfere with the formation of new units for the second list. The overlap in words, and hence in subjective units, will thus hinder rather than facilitate recall of the second list.

**Results.** The results of the experiment supported the prediction of organization theory. Subjects in the experimental group (receiving overlapping lists) showed slower learning and poorer final recall than did subjects in the control group (receiving nonoverlapping lists). The identical result was obtained when Tulving replicated the experiment with different subjects and with lists half as long as those used in this experiment. Those data supplied a strong disconfirmation of a basic tenet of frequency theory – that recall increases with increased frequency of repetition.

## 10.2.4 An Imaginary Experiment on Person Perception

Dymond (1949, 1950) developed a scale measuring empathic ability, that is, the ability to make accurate judgments about others. She found that the scale was successful in predicting which persons were more accurate in their interpersonal assessments. She also found that higher empathy scores were associated with higher performance IQs on the Wechsler-Bellevue Adult Intelligence Scale. It is this result that forms the basis for the imaginary experiment described herein.

McDumbo, an obscure and deservedly unknown researcher, observed that the relation between Performance IQ according to the Wechsler-Bellevue Adult Intelligence Scale and empathy scores might be due to two factors. On the one hand, it might represent a genuine relation between Performance IQ and empathy. On the other hand, it might be an artifact attributable to the greater dexterity required to receive higher scores on the Wechsler-Bellevue test. According to this latter hypothesis, the true relation is between manual dexterity and empathy, not between intelligence and empathy. The results are certainly consistent with either hypothesis.

To investigate this hypothesis, McDumbo administered the empathy test to two groups of subjects. Subjects in one group received the Wechsler-Bellevue Performance Scale from the Wechsler-Bellevue Adult Intelligence Scale in addition to the empathy test. Subjects in the other group received homemade pencil-and-paper tests closely resembling the Wechsler-Bellevue Performance Scale but requiring no physical manipulation of objects. If intelligence is responsible for the previously discovered relation between Wechsler-Bellevue and empathy scores, then the association should appear in scores for both groups. However, if manual dexterity is responsible, only the Wechsler-Bellevue group should show a significant association between the ability and empathy tests.

The results of the experiment were ambiguous. Both the pencil-and-paper tests and the Wechsler-Bellevue Performance Scale showed significant associations with the empathy scale, but the degree of association for the pencil-and-paper tests was significantly less than that for the Wechsler-Bellevue. McDumbo therefore concluded that both intelligence and manual dexterity are important components of empathy.

## 10.3 EIGHT STANDARDS FOR EVALUATING THE CONTRIBUTION TO KNOWLEDGE OF PSYCHOLOGY PAPERS

We now return to the eight standards we listed at the beginning of this chapter. We will revisit each standard and see how it applies in each of the four synopses.

**Standard 1.** The paper contains one or more surprising results that nevertheless make sense in some theoretical context (see Sternberg, 2002b, 2002c).

The papers of Miller (1956), Festinger and Carlsmith (1959), and Tulving (1966) all contain surprising, counterintuitive results that make sense when viewed in a new theoretical context. The surprise in Miller's paper is the omnipresence of the number seven (plus or minus two) in a wide variety of tasks measuring humans' information-processing capacity. This result suggests some inherent limit on our capacity to process information of any kind.

In Festinger and Carlsmith's (1959) experiment, it is surprising to find that subjects paid $1 to lie about a boring experiment later feel more positively about the experiment than did subjects paid $20. Common sense and reinforcement theory both would predict the opposite result. But the result makes sense in terms of Festinger's (1957) dissonance theory. Subjects who were paid $20 can justify their lie to themselves with little difficulty: They lied for the money. Subjects paid $1, though, can scarcely justify their lie on the basis of the money received. Hence, they convince themselves that they said the experiment was interesting because it was interesting.

In Tulving's (1966) experiment, the surprising result is that subjects who have already memorized half the words on a list they are about to learn actually learn the new list more slowly than do subjects who have memorized none of the words on the new list. Common sense and frequency theory would predict the opposite result. The result makes sense, however, when viewed in the context of organization theory: The old organization is nonoptimal for the new list and decreases the rate of learning by impeding the formation of new organizational units.

McDumbo's experiment contains no surprises. Because it had been shown previously that the Wechsler-Bellevue Performance Scale correlates with the empathy measure, the replication merely confirms this result. Because the pencil-and-paper tests measure about the same thing as the Wechsler-Bellevue test, it also is unsurprising that the tests correlate significantly with the empathy scale. And because the pencil-and-paper tests probably are inferior to the Wechsler-Bellevue test as measuring instruments, it is not surprising that they show lower correlations with other variables, including the empathy scale.

**Standard 2. The results presented in the paper are of major theoretical or practical significance.**

The first three papers all contain results of major theoretical and practical significance. Miller's (1956) results suggest that humans actually have a low capacity for processing isolated bits of information. They also show, however, that this capacity can be increased greatly by recoding lower order information into higher order units. In Miller's terminology, the number of chunks of information that can be processed remains constant (at about seven), but the amount of information per chunk increases. Thus, although people can recall only about seven isolated letters, they can recall far more letters if they are in chunks of words or sentences.

Festinger and Carlsmith's (1959) findings are of theoretical significance because they suggest the superiority of dissonance theory over reinforcement theory in accounting for effects of forced compliance on private opinions. The practical significance of the results is obvious. To persuade others to adopt your point of view privately, you should not give them the greatest possible reward. Rather, you should give him them minimum possible reward that will entice them to adopt your viewpoint publicly.

Tulving's (1966) findings are of theoretical importance because they suggest that simple frequency principles are inadequate to explain the effect of repetition in learning. Organizational principles seem to be needed in addition to or instead of frequency principles. The findings are of practical importance because they show the importance of effectively organizing the material to be learned. Mere rote drill is a poor way to learn material, and ineffective organization of material can actually impede learning.

McDumbo's experiment contains no results of major theoretical or practical importance. McDumbo presents no theory as to why empathy and performance IQ should be associated, although presumably a post hoc theory could be invented. The association is of some practical interest but seems unlikely to be applied to real-world settings: People are not likely to judge empathic ability on the basis of intelligence test scores.

## Standard 3. The ideas in the paper are new and exciting, and perhaps the paper presents a new way of looking at an old problem.

The first three papers all deal with old problems. Miller's (1956) paper reviews the literatures on absolute judgment, attention span, and memory span. The Festinger and Carlsmith (1959) study forced compliance, a standard topic of investigation in social psychology. Tulving's (1966) paper investigates the effects of repetition on learning, which is probably the oldest and most basic problem in the field of learning. Each paper brings to an old problem a new perspective that seems to provide a better account of basic psychological phenomena than do old perspectives. McDumbo's paper contains no new or exciting ideas – indeed, it contains scarcely any ideas at all. It reports some empirical phenomena and provides an unconvincing explanation of those phenomena.

### Standard 4. The interpretation of results is unambiguous.

Lack of ambiguity is a standard that can be approached but not attained. When each of the first three papers presented here was published, its impact was heightened by the seeming unambiguity in interpretation permitted by the results: The results seemed to demand the interpretation given to them. Nevertheless, the concept of a crucial experiment – an experiment that decides conclusively between two or more competing theories – is a myth. The experiments reviewed or reported in these papers proved no exception. Information theory, on which Miller's (1956) article is based, has all but faded from the psychological scene. Bem (1967) showed that Festinger and Carlsmith's (1959) result can be explained by self-perception theory as well as by dissonance theory. Sternberg and Bower (1974) demonstrated that Tulving's (1966) result and others that followed it are more compatible with list-discrimination theory than with organization theory.

The level of ambiguity in the first three papers can be contrasted with the level of ambiguity in the fourth paper. Many years passed before the first three papers were shown to be amenable to persuasive alternative explanations, and in each case, the alternative explanation is nontrivial. In the case of McDumbo's paper, however, several alternative explanations are immediately apparent, most of them more convincing than McDumbo's explanation. The most plausible explanation is also the most trivial. McDumbo, you will recall, concluded that both performance IQ and manual dexterity are components of empathy. A more likely interpretation of the data is that manual dexterity is unrelated to empathy. The Wechsler-Bellevue test correlated higher with the empathy scale than did the pencil-and-paper tests not because of the added manual dexterity component, but because it is a more reliable and valid measure of performance IQ.

**Standard 5.** The paper integrates into a new, simpler framework data that had previously required a complex, possibly unwieldy framework.

Miller's (1956) paper best exemplifies this characteristic. Prior to publication of the paper, absolute judgment, attention, and memory generally had been viewed as separate phenomena, and had been studied more or less independently. Miller's paper suggested a way in which diverse capacities could be understood (at least to some extent) within a single, unified framework. Miller did not claim that the three capacities were a single capacity. Rather, he claimed that they were subject to the same information-processing limitations – limitations imposed by individuals' ability to handle at one time only seven plus or minus two chunks of information.

**Standard 6.** The paper contains a major debunking of previously held ideas.

Certain ideas become so deeply ingrained in our ways of thinking that we are scarcely aware that we hold these ideas. The ideas serve as unquestioned presuppositions. Festinger and Carlsmith's (1959) major finding flagrantly violated one of these unquestioned presuppositions – that a larger reinforcement for some behavior will work at least as well as a smaller one. Tulving's (1966) major finding also flagrantly violated a generally unquestioned presupposition – that repetition of elements in a to-be-learned list will result in at least as much learning as nonrepetition of those elements.

Timing is of the utmost importance in debunking a theory. Suppose that the theory to be debunked is Theory $X$, and the replacement theory is Theory $Y$. If everyone already believes in the validity of Theory $Y$, a paper debunking Theory $X$ will have little impact. Such a paper will be seen as beating a dead horse. But if most people are deeply committed to Theory $X$, and new results are obtained that cannot be reconciled with Theory $X$ but that are compatible with Theory $Y$, then the paper debunking Theory $X$ can have a great deal of impact.

**Standard 7.** The paper presents an experiment with a particularly clever paradigm or experimental manipulation.

Psychologists admire clever experimental paradigms, even if they are not theoretically motivated. That the paradigms of Festinger and

Carlsmith and of Tulving were both clever and theoretically motivated made them all the more appealing. Paradigms have lives of their own, and their life span sometimes extends well beyond that of the theory that motivated them. Variants of Tulving's part–whole paradigm have continued to appear in the memory literature, even though organization theory now attracts little research.

**Standard 8.** The findings or theory presented in the paper are general ones.

Miller's (1956) theory of chunks and higher order unitization aroused widespread interest among psychologists in part because of its unusual generality: The theory seemed applicable to a wide variety of cognitive performances. Festinger's (1957) dissonance theory also attracted interest because of its generality: It seemed able to explain people's rationalizations in a wide variety of everyday situations. Tulving's (1966) organization theory also seemed quite general and was applied to memory for many different kinds of material. McDumbo, in contrast, has no theory, and the result appears to have little generality: It merely expresses a relation between two specific variables.

A paper that meets all or even some of the standards described here is likely to fall into Tulving and Madigan's (1970) third category. Psychologists should be aware of these standards in evaluating the papers they read, although readers can expect to meet only a small number of them – and those modestly – in their own writing. Whereas the standards for good writing presented earlier in this book are ones that any investigator can and should meet, the standards presented in this chapter are ones to be strived for. The papers that meet these standards are the ones that are remembered when most other papers are long forgotten.

# 11  Ethics in Research and Writing

Ethics are of utmost importance when doing research and later writing about it. There are many ways to get tripped up ethically in both research and writing. This chapter summarizes some of the pitfalls and gives you advice as to how to avoid them.

## 11.1  RESEARCH ISSUES

A number of ethical issues arise in psychological research (as well as in medical and other research). Some of the main issues involve deception, pain, the ethics of research on animals, and confidentiality.

### 11.1.1  Deception

Sometimes, for research to work, participants must be kept unaware of the purpose of the research until it is completed. In some cases, however, psychologists have used extreme forms of deception. Stanley Milgram (1974) led participants to believe that they were delivering painful electric shocks to another person, when in fact they were not. When Milgram carried out his studies, researchers were generally not required to obtain advance approval of their plans to conduct a psychological investigation. Another ethical issue arises when researchers pay participants to indulge in a vice, as when researchers pay alcoholics to drink to study their drinking behavior. Today, deception is permitted in research only when the benefits clearly outweigh the costs.

### 11.1.2 Informed Consent

Before participants begin their involvement in a study, they are required to give informed consent to participate in the research. In the informed-consent procedure, the individuals are told what kinds of tasks they may be expected to perform and what kinds of situations they may expect to encounter, with specific qualifications on the use of deception. They are also told that they may withdraw from the study without penalty. It is unethical to run a study without informed consent. For children or others who are not capable of giving fully informed consent, it may be necessary to obtain informed consent as well from a parent or other guardian.

### 11.1.3 Debriefing

After the research is completed, the participants are fully debriefed about the research. They are told exactly the nature of the experiment, informed of any deception that may have been involved, and given the reason for the deception. Minor deception is usually permitted if the value of the proposed research justifies the deception. But the deception must be necessary for the purpose of the experiment, and it must be fully explained afterward.

### 11.1.4 Pain

In the past, it was not uncommon for experiments to involve mild electric shocks to participants. These shocks were slightly painful but not harmful. In addition, studies sometimes have had the potential to cause psychological damage, because many experiments are stressful. How stressful a study is often depends on the individual as much as on the experiment. What is difficult for one person may be relaxing for another and neutral for yet another. Still, researchers generally try to anticipate and to minimize distress (unless distress itself is the construct under study). Institutions will generally not permit studies that are likely to cause any long-lasting pain or harm. If participating in a study might cause short-term pain or stress, participants must be fully informed in advance about possible consequences, via the informed consent procedure. Moreover, informed consent requires that participants be told that they are free to leave the experiment at any time without fear of any negative repercussions. Thus, if participants thought that they could tolerate the conditions of an experiment beforehand but then found out in the course of it that they could not, they could leave at once.

### 11.1.5 Confidentiality and Anonymity

Most experiments in psychology are conducted on an anonymous basis – participants' names are not associated with their data. Occasionally, however, complete anonymity is not possible. For example, if an experimenter wants to compare students' scores on some standardized test of ability to their freshman grades in college, the experimenter needs to have some means of identifying individual students. Even when participants cannot be anonymous, however, experimenters go to great lengths to ensure that participants' names are known only to the experimenters. Confidentiality can be a particularly important issue when researchers are studying basic characteristics, such as health status. Confidentiality means that results will not be disclosed to anyone not connected with the research where identification of the participant would be possible. One needs to guarantee that information about their health, for example, will not later be used against them, such as in employment situations. If you ensure anonymity and/or confidentiality in your informed consent form, then you must be certain you have the means to provide it.

## 11.2 ISSUES IN RESEARCH WITH NONHUMAN ANIMALS

Issues become murky when nonhuman animals – such as rats, pigeons, rabbits, dogs, or even simple multicelled organisms – are involved instead of people. Nonhuman animals cannot sign informed consent forms, for example. Most institutions vigorously attempt to ensure that animals are protected and that they have all they require in terms of food, shelter, and freedom from harm or discomfort. Furthermore, in recent years, the government has increasingly regulated scientific research and the appropriate treatment of animals. However, nonhuman animals sometimes are exposed to painful or even harmful procedures. In such cases, institutions attempt to weigh the potential benefits of the research to humans against the potential harm to the nonhuman animals.

Questions regarding how to guard animal rights are not easily answered. On the one hand, no scrupulous researcher actively wishes to cause harm to animals. On the other hand, some of the most important discoveries in both medicine and psychology have come from research in which laboratory animals were sacrificed to advance our knowledge about and our ability to help humans. Given the choice of testing new drugs that may be beneficial but whose side effects are unknown first on laboratory animals or first on people, society has opted for testing of laboratory animals. Those whose lives have been saved by such testing, or who have had relatives whose lives have been saved, understand at first hand why the testing has been accepted by much of society. Review boards and policymakers attempt to weigh the costs and benefits involved in all research, whether it employs human or laboratory-animal participants. Still, the controversy over use of laboratory-animal participants is far from over. Fortunately, there is much less controversy regarding another ethical issue, that of confidentiality.

## 11.3 FAKING OF DATA

Probably the single greatest research sin is faking of data: either making the data up entirely or collecting data but then inventing data that you did not actually collect. The faking of data is viewed as sufficiently grave that one can lose one's job or position as a student over it. Whereas some ethical issues can be gray – was a person's contribution of ideas great enough to merit coauthorship – faking is viewed as an absolute black-and-white issue. Don't ever even think about it. Those who have been caught doing it are disgraced, and there is not likely to be any redemption. It is not something that other scientists will forget, and they likely won't forgive it either.

## 11.4 INSTITUTIONAL REVIEW BOARD APPROVAL

Do not under any circumstances run a study without written approval from an Institutional Review Board (IRB), unless you have a written document stating that your research is exempt. Researchers can get into serious trouble if they run studies that are not approved. Sometimes, it is frustrating waiting for approval, and many researchers have complaints about the handling of their proposals to IRBs.

Nevertheless, you must make sure that you have written approval before you go ahead and collect data.

## 11.5 FINANCIAL MANAGEMENT AND MISMANAGEMENT

Rules regarding financial management are extremely strict. If you are given funds for a particular purpose, you must use those funds for that purpose. You cannot redirect them without permission. So if money is for payment of participants, it must be used to pay participants. If you want to redirect it to another use, you need permission to do so. You cannot use funds allocated for one research project to fund another project. Universities have been fined, sometimes millions of dollars, when funds were redirected from one project to another. These days, many and probably most grants and contracts are audited, sooner or later. So you need to keep a clear paper or digital trail of where money is going. Be extremely careful of how you manage funds because there is essentially no tolerance for diversion of funds from intended purposes.

## 11.6 WRITING ISSUES

In our experience, there are 12 areas in which ethics issues become salient when writing a paper: accuracy of reporting, inclusion/exclusion of data and data analyses, interpretation of data, authorship, origins of ideas, plagiarism, citations, permissions, reanalysis of data sets, piecemeal publication, simultaneous submission, and duplicate publication.

### 11.6.1 Accuracy of Reporting

Who among us can say he or she is never sloppy? Probably none of us. But writing a psychology paper is not the place to be sloppy. Sloppiness may not sound like an issue of ethics, but when your sloppiness results in people drawing wrong conclusions and possibly designing future research based on your inaccuracies, it becomes an ethical issue. Even worse would be treatments designed to help people based on inaccurately reported data, for which there would be a risk that the intervention designed to help people actually harms them.

There are many ways in which accuracy of reporting can be impugned in particular instances. Errors in reporting are especially possible because computers will analyze your data, even if you give them the wrong data to analyze. Are you sure you gave the computer the right data set? Are you sure that you distinguished clearly between values of "0" and missing values in each data cell? Are you sure that you have labeled the various data points correctly? Are you sure the columns and rows of tables are properly labeled? Are you sure that figures give an accurate rather than a misleading picture of the data? The basic point, then, is to be sure that your reporting is correct and as nearly complete as possible.

## 11.6.2 Inclusion and Exclusion of Data and Data Analyses

It is sometimes appropriate to exclude data from an analysis. For example, you may exclude outliers from data analysis, or data from participants who obviously did not take the task seriously (e.g., they responded randomly or failed to respond to many questions), or who did not understand the task. However, there is sometimes a fine line between concluding that someone did not understand the task or did not take the task seriously and concluding that someone just did poorly on the task because it was too hard or inadequately explained to him or her. You have a responsibility as a researcher not to bias your analyses or your reporting of the data.

For example, if you exclude participants from the data analyses, you have to say how many were excluded, why they were excluded, and if possible, how you knew that they fell into the category you claim they fell into. You also have an obligation to include data analyses that do not support your hypotheses or what you hoped to find, not only ones that support your views. It is tempting to include data analyses that support your idea and to exclude those that do not, but it is not ethical. You do not have to describe in detail every analysis you did that fails to reject the null hypothesis. But you have to indicate that you did these analyses and that no significant results turned up.

## 11.6.3 Interpretation of Data

Occasionally, data are self-evident and self-explanatory, but not often. Usually they can be interpreted in multiple ways. Because we are all susceptible to confirmation bias, our tendency is to interpret data in a way that best suits what we had hoped to find.

A problem is that reviewers often have a very different mind-set and look for alternative interpretations of the data. If authors are too one-sided, reviewers may come to believe that they are purposely biasing the interpretation of the data in a way that may even become unethical.

Recently, we have been involved both in seeking to sell a house and in trying to buy a house. We have been taken somewhat aback by the difference in perspectives. When you are trying to sell a house, you concentrate on all the really fine features of the house and tend to ignore or discount the negative features. When you are seeking to buy a house, you tend much more to notice all the flaws. It is the same with a journal article. When you write the article, you are the "seller" and your temptation is to ignore the weaknesses in your data and your article. To maximize your chances of success with reviewers and an editor, try your best to put yourself in the "buyer" state of mind. What weaknesses will the buyers see, especially those who tend to be critical of the particular kind of house you are selling? Editors often deliberately send papers out for review to scholars whose views are different from your own. So keep those reviewers in mind and write with the notion that they will likely be reviewing your work.

## 11.6.4 Authorship

Authorship is sometimes simple and other times remarkably complex. If the paper is sole authored and no one else has contributed scientifically to it, then your situation is perhaps simple. But often a number of people work on a project, and it becomes more of a challenge to decide who should be a coauthor and in what order coauthors should be listed.

We have found that, although there are no easy answers, seven general principles are worth keeping in mind.

1. If multiple individuals are involved, issues of coauthorship should be discussed before the study is even started. You may not know in advance in exactly what order coauthors will be listed, but to the extent possible, it is better to clarify issues before the research is conducted rather than after it is done.
2. Anyone who has contributed meaningfully to the scientific ideas in the paper should be a coauthor. Obviously, there is ambiguity in what constitutes a "meaningful" contribution. But that is the

nature of the enterprise. People who had ideas for the conceptualization, hypotheses, methods, data analysis, and interpretation are typically coauthors. We have had situations in which we talked to someone about the data and that person then demanded to be a coauthor. So you need to think carefully about what others will interpret as "meaningful scientific contribution," not just what you think about it.

3. Simply collecting data or preparing stimulus materials does not qualify a person for coauthorship. If all someone does is collect data or prepare materials, then that person is usually acknowledged in a footnote. But even here, things can get tricky. If the person not only prepared the stimulus materials but also designed them, then the designing of the materials may well qualify the person for coauthorship.

4. It is better to be over-inclusive rather than under-inclusive in inclusion of coauthors. You are much more likely to find yourself in conflict with people over exclusion than over inclusion. Recently, one of us worked on a paper for which it was ambiguous whether a particular person should be included. The person was invited to be a coauthor and declined but greatly appreciated the consideration of being asked.

5. The order of authorship generally reflects level of scientific contribution, except that the last position is often reserved for someone who has also contributed in a special way, such as through providing the funding through a grant or being integral in forming the team. However, simply providing grant money alone does not qualify individuals for coauthorship unless they have made a meaningful ideational contribution to the work.

6. If you find yourself in a dispute that is not resolving itself, rather than letting it get ugly, it is better to agree to a means for resolution of the conflict. For example, you might appeal collectively to the chair of a department or a dean. In general, administrators do not relish getting involved in such disputes, but they typically would rather get involved than see them turn ugly.

7. If you have greater seniority in the field (e.g., if you're a professor rather than a student), please remember what it was like when you were more junior. More junior people, in general, need credit to progress through the field. You may need the credit less. Sometimes, when people's promotions are on the line, their sense of ethics can be strained by the realization that if they do not have

sufficient professional credit, they may lose a promotion or even a job. But if one acts unethically in coauthorship matters, it not only speaks ill of one, but also gets around. Soon other people will not want to work with you because they believe you are a credit hog.

### 11.6.5 Origins of Ideas

Usually, when we think we have an idea, it is indeed our idea. But the origins of ideas can be complex. Sometimes we may have had a conversation with someone and an idea came out of that conversation. In such cases, the person with whom one had the conversation may (legitimately) expect to be involved in and to have coauthorship of subsequent research based on the conversation. The conversation may be in a professional office, but it also may be at a cocktail party. Sometimes, an idea may evolve in a research seminar with a number of people in it, and it will not be feasible for all of them to be involved in the study, although it may be appropriate to acknowledge them in a note. It behooves you to be careful in thinking about the origins of your ideas and to make sure that anyone who would have a legitimate claim to coauthorship is included.

### 11.6.6 Plagiarism

Plagiarism is basically a failure of attribution. There are few academic sins that are viewed more gravely than this one. Plagiarism takes two general forms: plagiarism of others' work and plagiarism of one's own work. We discuss both sequentially.

### 11.6.6.1 Plagiarism of Others' Work

Plagiarism of others' work occurs when you fail adequately to cite the work of others, or fail to cite it at all. Plagiarism applies both to ideas and to actual words used to express ideas. Never quote others without putting the material in quotation marks and giving a correct citation. Never use the words of others without citing them. If you paraphrase, that is fine, but then say you are paraphrasing and give the correct citation. Do not use material from tables or figures without citation and do not just copy tables or figures and use them as your own. When in doubt, cite!

Whereas once it was somewhat difficult to detect plagiarism, today there are electronic programs that can check a piece of work for plagiarism. These programs rely on enormous databases, and you should assume that whatever you are using as a source is in the databases. Moreover, even a simple search engine such as Google or Bing can be used to detect plagiarism. If you quote extensively, you may need to get permission, as discussed in Chapter 8.

### 11.6.6.2 Self-Plagiarism

Self-plagiarism occurs when you fail adequately to cite your own work. It is totally understandable that you may wish to cite or draw on past work you have done. But doing so becomes a problem when you fail to cite that past work. In extreme cases, someone might attempt to publish exactly the same paper twice without noting that the paper has been previously published. Be sure when you draw on previous work of your own that you accurately cite it.

### 11.6.7 Citations

On the one hand, when you write a paper you cannot possibly cite every past work that has been done on the topic you are discussing. On the other hand, if you do not cite work that reviewers see as directly relevant, you are likely to be called on it and criticized for not including it. In particular, you have an ethical obligation to cite not only work that supports your hypotheses but also work that runs contrary to them. Reviewers tend to get annoyed when you put together either a one-sided presentation or a presentation that seems to ignore everyone who has done relevant work except you and perhaps a handful of collaborators. So be sure to cite all work likely to be seen as directly relevant. In our experience, it also pays to cite, where possible and relevant, researchers who are likely to review your paper.

### 11.6.8 Permissions

If you use the work of others, you must get permission. Permissions can be for tables, figures, photographs, or long quotations. Failure to receive permission can hold up publication of your work or can even potentially put you in legal jeopardy if the work is published without needed permissions.

### 11.6.9 Reanalysis of Data Sets

If you reanalyze a data set that previously has been published, make sure you are clear that you are presenting a reanalysis of an existing dataset rather than an analysis of a new data set.

### 11.6.10 Piecemeal Publication

There is increasing pressure to publish fairly large quantities for hiring, tenure, and promotion. Such pressure creates a temptation toward piecemeal publication, which is the publication of one's work in small bits rather than as a more integrated whole. There are two other kinds of pressure that can lead to piecemeal publication. The first is that studies often are done sequentially, and one cannot always wait until all possible studies one might do are completed until one publishes. The other is that journals generally prefer shorter articles to longer ones because of scarce numbers of pages. In general, you should try to publish your work in meaningful wholes rather than bits, remembering at the same time that you do not want to wait too long to publish because, if you do, you risk the work's getting out of date or being scooped. You also risk its not being at least in press by the time you really need it to appear on your curriculum vitae as either in press or as published.

### 11.6.11 Simultaneous Submission

You are not permitted to submit the same article to more than one journal simultaneously. Hence, in making a submission, you need to take into account the journal's typical review time as well as your chances of acceptance, as you have to wait until the process is completed before resubmitting the piece.

If your article is rejected with resubmission allowed, you do not have to resubmit to the same journal. You can instead choose to submit it to another journal if you prefer.

You are generally permitted to submit a book proposal to more than one publisher simultaneously. If you do so, however, you should inform the publishers that you are multiply submitting the proposal.

### 11.6.12 Duplicate Publication

You are not permitted to publish the same work twice unless the second publication is clearly labeled as a reprint. You also may not publish a second work that is essentially the same as another without making clear to the editor of the second journal what you are doing, and then letting the editor decide if the piece is sufficiently newsworthy.

We cannot possibly include in this chapter every ethical issue that can arise in the life of researchers. In most cases, the best thing to do is to follow common sense and not rationalize unethical behavior. Nothing quite destroys a career the way unethical behavior does, so start and maintain your career the right way by scrupulously avoiding it!

# 12 Submitting a Paper to a Journal

If you write a paper that you believe makes a substantial contribution to psychological knowledge, you may want to consider submitting the paper for publication. This chapter will give you some information to help you decide on a journal. It also contains a list of the most important journals sorted according to subjects. We will give you an overview of what you need to do to submit your paper and what goes on behind the scenes in an editor's office.

## 12.1 DECIDING ON A JOURNAL

If you decide to submit a paper for publication, the first step you must take is to decide on a journal to which you want to submit the paper. Eight considerations should enter into your decision:

### 1. Quality

Journals vary widely in quality. Some journals publish papers that do little more than fill up journal space; other journals publish only outstanding contributions to the literature. Better journals generally have higher rejection rates for submitted papers, so the probability of a paper's being accepted in such journals is lower.

One way to evaluate quality is to look at the impact factor of the journal. In Point 8, we describe how you can determine the journal's impact factor, or the extent to which papers in the journal are cited by authors in the field.

## 2. Content

All journals limit by content the kinds of papers they accept. Journal editors use either or both of two criteria in deciding on the appropriateness of a paper's content. The first criterion is substantive focus. What is the topic of research? The journal may accept, for example, only developmental, or cognitive, or applied papers. The second criterion is methodological focus. How was the research done? The journal may accept, for example, only experimental or theoretical or review papers. The journal lists we provide later in this chapter describe the content restrictions of many psychological journals.

## 3. Readership

Journals vary in (a) who reads them and in (b) how many people read them. Readership depends in turn on the quality and content of each journal and, to a lesser extent, on the cost of the journal. Journals publish annual statements of their circulation, so the extent of the readership can be determined by looking through recent back issues of a journal for the annual statement. The composition of the readership can be inferred by assessing quality and content, and by examining the kinds of papers in which articles from the journal are cited.

## 4. Length Restrictions

Most journals have implicit restrictions on length of submitted papers, and some journals have explicit restrictions. If the journal's editorial statement (carried in every issue of most journals) does not make any statement about length, an examination of several recent issues of the journal will indicate the range in length acceptable to the journal editor.

## 5. Publication Lag

The length of time between acceptance of an article and publication of the article is the publication lag. Journals vary in publication lags from as little as 1 month to as much as 18 months or more. In submitting an article, authors should decide how long they are willing to wait for the article to be published, keeping in mind that there will be an additional lag from the time the paper is submitted to the time the paper is accepted or rejected.

## 6. Cost of Submission

Most journals do not charge authors for publication. Some journals do charge, however, so that publication of even a short article can cost an author several hundred dollars. The journal's editorial statement will indicate what costs, if any, are involved. Authors must decide before submitting an article to such a journal whether they are willing and able to meet the costs of publication.

## 7. Authorship Restrictions

A small number of journals restrict in some way their potential contributors. Submission may be by invitation only, or limited to individuals belonging to or sponsored by members of some organization. The journal's editorial statement will indicate whether any such restrictions apply.

## 8. Journal Citation Reports

A good way to compare and evaluate journals is to have a look at the Journal Citation Reports published by the ISI (formerly the Institute for Scientific Information). Of particular importance to social scientists is the Social Science Citation Index (SSCI), which contains statistics about hundreds of journals. You can access this information through your university library. To get to the SSCI, choose *ISI Web of Knowledge* as a database. You'll have to select a database again; choose *Journal Citation Reports* (JCR). Once you have chosen the database, you can select the Social Sciences Edition and view a list of all journals, get lists for groups of journals, or search for a specific journal. At the end of this section you can find a list that contains descriptions of journals along with their citation reports from the year 2007. The *JCR* will give you a variety of statistics about the journals. Here are some that might be of particular importance to you:

■ **Total cites**
This number indicates the total number of citations to a particular journal in a given year.

### ■ Impact factor

The impact factor is the average number of citations to articles of a given journal published during the two previous years. That means that the impact factor for the year 2008 of the *Journal for Psychology in the Vegetable Garden* gives you the average number of citations in 2008 to articles that were published in 2006 and 2007 in that journal. The impact factor is calculated by dividing the number of citations in the report year (in this case, 2008) by the total number of articles that were published in the preceding two years. Note that *all* citations count in journals that ISI monitors, including ones in different journals. However, ISI does not monitor all journals, so citations in some journals do not count simply because they are not included in the database.

### ■ 5-year journal impact factor

The 5-year impact factor does essentially the same thing as the impact factor; however, it indicates the average number of times in the particular *JCR* year that articles published by the journal in the last 5 years were cited.

### ■ Immediacy index

The immediacy index indicates how often an article is cited in the year it is published. The index is computed by dividing the number of citations to articles published in one year by the total number of articles published in that year. Note that articles published earlier in the year will have an advantage in the immediacy index, as they will have had more opportunity to be cited. Also, articles from journals that publish more frequently during the year will have an advantage, as there is more opportunity for articles in frequently publishing journals to appear earlier in the year.

### ■ Number of articles

The number of articles refers to the total number of articles that were published in a given year by the journal.

When you look at the Journal Citation Reports for different journals, remember that prestigious, high-impact journals are not always the best choice for your article. The previous seven points made above, about content and readership, play a role as well. A journal that is highly rated in *JCR* but that does not publish on the topic of your study will, in all likelihood, not publish your article. You should also consider that the more prestigious a journal, the higher are the rejection rates. Some journals have rejection rates of 90% or more, so you may end up wasting valuable time trying to get your paper published before it becomes out of date.

In general, then, you need to weigh many factors in deciding to what journal to submit an article. The decision is important but can be extremely difficult. For example, if you are trying to get a job or receive tenure, articles will count little on your curriculum vita (CV) if they are not at least in press. Articles "in preparation" or "in progress" or "under editorial consideration" often count little, if at all. If you aim too high in submitting an article to a journal, you may find that it does not have a publisher when you need it to count on your CV. If you aim too low, you may find that the article has an acceptance or even is published, but it is weighed less because it has not been published in a first-rate journal. Thus, an important part of the process in writing is targeting a journal at the right level – aiming neither too high nor too low. You might want to seek advice from people with more experience in the field as to what they believe is a reasonable journal to which to submit your article.

The journal descriptions are citations from the journal's web site unless otherwise noted by a*.

Foreign language publications that do not at least partially publish in English have been excluded from this list.

## General Psychology

### Annual Review of Psychology
www.annualreviews.org

**Publisher:** Annual Reviews
**Total Cites:** 5425
**Impact Factor:** 13.4
**5-Year Impact Factor:** 17.263
**Immediacy Index:** 3.583
**Articles:** 24

The *Annual Review* publishes reviews of areas of contemporary interest in the field of psychology.*

### Behavioral and Brain Sciences
http://www.bbsonline.org/

**Publisher:** Cambridge Univ Press
**Total Cites:** 4721

**Impact Factor:** 17.462
**5-Year Impact Factor:** 16.391
**Immediacy Index:** 3.5
**Articles:** 2

*BBS* publishes important and controversial interdisciplinary articles in psychology, neuroscience, behavioral biology, cognitive science, artificial intelligence, linguistics and philosophy. Articles are rigorously refereed and, if accepted, are circulated to a large number of potential commentators around the world in the various specialties on which the article impinges. Their 1000-word commentaries are then co-published with the target article as well as the author's response to each. The commentaries consist of analyses, elaborations, complementary and supplementary data and theory, criticisms and cross-specialty syntheses.

### Psychological Bulletin

www.apa.org/journals/bul.html

**Publisher:** APA
**Total Cites:** 19678
**Impact Factor:** 10.905
**5-Year Impact Factor:** 15.23
**Immediacy Index:** 1.841
**Articles:** 44

*Psychological Bulletin* publishes evaluative and integrative research reviews and interpretations of issues in scientific psychology. Primary research is reported only for illustrative purposes. Manuscripts dealing with topics at the interface of psychological sciences and society are welcome, as are evaluations of applied psychological therapies, programs, and interventions.

### Psychological Review

http://www.apa.org/journals/rev/

**Publisher:** APA
**Total Cites:** 15541
**Impact Factor:** 7.803
**5-Year Impact Factor:** 10.607
**Immediacy Index:** 2.351
**Articles:** 37

*Psychological Review* publishes articles that make important theoretical contributions to any area of scientific psychology. Preference is given to papers that advance theory, but systematic evaluation of alternative theories in a given domain will also be considered for publication.

**Psychological Methods**
www.apa.org/journals/met

**Publisher:** APA
**Total Cites:** 2619
**Impact Factor:** 3.5
**5-Year Impact Factor:** 8.978
**Immediacy Index:** 0.75
**Articles:** 24

*Psychological Methods* is devoted to the development and dissemination of methods for collecting, analyzing, understanding, and interpreting psychological data. Its purpose is the dissemination of innovations in research design, measurement, methodology, and quantitative and qualitative analysis to the psychological community; its further purpose is to promote effective communication about related substantive and methodological issues.

**American Psychologist**
www.apa.org/journals/amp.html

**Publisher:** APA
**Total Cites:** 10941
**Impact Factor:** 6.967
**5-Year Impact Factor:** 8.338
**Immediacy Index:** 2.25
**Articles:** 48

*American Psychologist* is the official journal of the American Psychological Association. As such, the journal contains archival documents and articles covering current issues in psychology, the science and practice of psychology, and psychology's contribution to public policy.

**Journal of Experimental Psychology-General**
www.apa.org/journals/xge.html

**Publisher:** APA
**Total Cites:** 4758
**Impact Factor:** 5.594
**5-Year Impact Factor:** 6.987

Immediacy Index: 0.385
Articles: 39

The *Journal of Experimental Psychology: General* publishes articles describing empirical work that bridges the traditional interests of two or more communities of psychology.

### Psychological Science
http://www.wiley.com/bw/journal.asp?ref=0956-7976

Publisher: Blackwell Publishing
Total Cites: 7521
Impact Factor: 4.251
5-Year Impact Factor: 5.346
Immediacy Index: 0.435
Articles: 186

The flagship journal of The Association for Psychological Science (previously the American Psychological Society), the journal publishes authoritative articles of interest across all of psychological science, including brain and behavior, clinical science, cognition, learning and memory, social psychology, and developmental psychology. In addition to these full-length articles, *Psychological Science* also features summaries of new research developments and discussions of psychological issues in government and public affairs.

### Journal of Applied Psychology
www.apa.org/journals/apl/

Publisher: APA
Total Cites: 11182
Impact Factor: 3.047
5-Year Impact Factor: 5.146
Immediacy Index: 0.449
Articles: 136

The *Journal of Applied Psychology* publishes investigations that contribute new knowledge and understanding to fields of applied psychology (other than clinical and applied experimental or human factors, which are more appropriate for other American Psychological Association journals). The journal primarily considers empirical and theoretical investigations that enhance understanding of cognitive, motivational, affective, and behavioral psychological phenomena.

**Educational Psychologist**
http://www.tandf.co.uk/journals/titles/0046-1520.asp

**Publisher:** Lawrence Erlbaum Assoc. Inc.-Taylor & Francis
**Total Cites:** 1135
**Impact Factor:** 2.231
**5-Year Impact Factor:** 3.823
**Immediacy Index:** 0.882
**Articles:** 17

The scholarly essays, reviews, critiques, and theoretical and conceptual articles featured in this exceptional journal contribute to understanding issues, problems, and research concerning all aspects of educational psychology. From meta-analyses of studies probing the effectiveness of teaching methods to historical examinations of textbook standards, the journal provides insightful explorations of new educational concepts and accepted educational practices. The journal, however, does not publish articles whose primary purpose is to report the methods and results of an empirical study.

**Journal of Educational Psychology**
www.apa.org/journals/edu.html

**Publisher:** APA
**Total Cites:** 5601
**Impact Factor:** 2.353
**5-Year Impact Factor:** 3.662
**Immediacy Index:** 0.213
**Articles:** 61

The main purpose of the *Journal of Educational Psychology*® is to publish original, primary psychological research pertaining to education across all ages and educational levels. A secondary purpose of the Journal is the occasional publication of exceptionally important theoretical and review articles that are pertinent to educational psychology.

**Psychological Assessment**
www.apa.org/journals/pas.html

**Publisher:** APA
**Total Cites:** 3283
**Impact Factor:** 2.196
**5-Year Impact Factor:** 3.529

**Immediacy Index:** 0.489
**Articles:** 45

*Psychological Assessment*® is concerned mainly with empirical research on measurement and evaluation relevant to the broad field of clinical psychology. Submissions are welcome in the areas of assessment processes and methods.

**Journal of Health and Social Behavior**
http://www.asanet.org/cs/journals/jhsb

**Publisher:** American Sociological Association
**Total Cites:** 3691
**Impact Factor:** 2.098
**5 Year Impact Factor:** 3.507
**Immediacy Index:** 0.207
**Articles:** 29

The *Journal of Health and Social Behavior* is a medical sociology journal that publishes empirical and theoretical articles that apply sociological concepts and methods to the understanding of health and illness and the organization of medicine and health care.

**Current Directions in Psychological Science**
www.blackwellpublishing.com/cdir

**Publisher:** Blackwell Publishing
**Total Cites:** 1990
**Impact Factor:** 2.75
**5-Year Impact Factor:** 3.333
**Immediacy Index:** 0.329
**Articles:** 70

*Current Directions in Psychological Science* presents the latest advances in theory and research in psychology. This important and timely journal contains concise reviews spanning all of scientific psychology and its applications.

**Quarterly Journal of Experimental Psychology Section B-Comparative and Physiological Psychology**
http://www.informaworld.com/smpp/title~db=all~content=
t716100704~tab=summary

**Publisher:** Psychology Press
**Total Cites:** 670

**Impact Factor:** 4.667
**5-Year Impact Factor:** 3.193
**Immediacy Index:**
**Articles:** 0

The *Quarterly Journal of Experimental Psychology* is a leading international journal that publishes original articles on any topic within the field of experimental psychology. The journal publishes Short Articles (under 3,000 words) reporting novel techniques or ground-breaking results, as well as substantial experimental reports.

### Review of General Psychology
www.apa.org/journals/gpr.html

**Publisher:** Educational Publishing Foundation
**Total Cites:** 839
**Impact Factor:** 2.333
**5-Year Impact Factor:** 3.158
**Immediacy Index:** 0.318
**Articles:** 22

*Review of General Psychology* seeks to publish innovative theoretical, conceptual, or methodological articles that cross-cut the traditional subdisciplines of psychology. The journal contains articles that advance theory, evaluate and integrate research literatures, provide a new historical analysis, or discuss new methodological developments in psychology as a whole.

### Behavior Genetics
www.springerlink.com/link.asp?id=105485

**Publisher:** Springer
**Total Cites:** 2825
**Impact Factor:** 2.953
**5-Year Impact Factor:** 3.157
**Immediacy Index:** 0.508
**Articles:** 59

*Behavior Genetics* – the leading journal concerned with the genetic analysis of complex traits – is published in cooperation with the Behavior Genetics Association. This timely journal disseminates the most current original research on the inheritance and evolution of behavioral characteristics in humans and other species.

### Evolution and Human Behavior
http://www.hbes.com/HBES/journal2.htm

**Publisher:** Elsevier Science Inc.
**Total Cites:** 1060
**Impact Factor:** 2.529
**5-Year Impact Factor:** 3.141
**Immediacy Index:** 0.537
**Articles:** 54

*Evolution & Human Behavior* is an interdisciplinary journal, presenting research reports and theory in which evolutionary perspectives are brought to bear on the study of human behavior.

### Psychonomic Bulletin & Review
http://pbr.psychonomic-journals.org/

**Publisher:** Psychonomic Soc. Inc.
**Total Cites.** 3626
**Impact Factor:** 1.935
**5-Year Impact Factor:** 2.85
**Immediacy Index:** 0.207
**Articles:** 174

*Psychonomic Bulletin & Review* provides coverage across a broad spectrum of topics in all areas of experimental psychology and is intended for a general readership. The journal is primarily dedicated to the publication of theory and review articles and brief reports of outstanding experimental work. Areas of coverage include attention and perception, cognitive psychology, psycholinguistics, behavioral and cognitive neuroscience, memory, comparative psychology, social cognition, and cognitive development.

### Experimental Psychology
http://www.hogrefe.com/?mod=journals&action=1&id=16

**Publisher:** Hogrefe & Huber Publishers
**Total Cites:** 493
**Impact Factor:** 2.781
**5-Year Impact Factor:** 2.822
**Immediacy Index:** 0.235
**Articles:** 34

As its name implies, *Experimental Psychology* publishes innovative, original, high-quality experimental research in psychology – quickly! It aims to provide a particularly fast outlet for such research, relying heavily on electronic exchange of information which begins with the electronic submission of manuscripts, and continues throughout the entire review and production process.

### Journal of Adolescent Health
www.elsevier.com/locate/jadohea

**Publisher:** Elsevier Science Inc..
**Total Cites:** 4358
**Impact Factor:** 2.387
**5-Year Impact Factor:** 2.819
**Immediacy Index:** 0.698
**Articles:** 172

The *Journal of Adolescent Health* is a multidisciplinary scientific Journal, which seeks to publish new research findings in the field of Adolescent Medicine and Health ranging from the basic biological and behavioral sciences to public health and policy.

### Archives of Sexual Behavior
www.springer.com/psychology/sexual+behaviour/journal/10508

**Publisher:** Springer/Plenum Publishers
**Total Cites:** 1644
**Impact Factor:** 2.393
**5-Year Impact Factor:** 2.705
**Immediacy Index:** 0.723
**Articles:** 65

*Archives of Sexual Behavior*, the official publication of the International Academy of Sex Research, is dedicated to the dissemination of information in the field of sexual science, broadly defined. Contributions consist of empirical research (both quantitative and qualitative), theoretical reviews and essays, clinical case reports, letters to the editor, and book reviews.

### Journal of Developmental and Behavioral Pediatrics
http://journals.lww.com/jrnldbp/pages/default.aspx

**Publisher:** Lippincott, Williams & Wilkins
**Total Cites:** 1923

**Impact Factor:** 2.097
**5-Year Impact Factor:** 2.68
**Immediacy Index:** 0.294
**Articles:** 51

*Journal of Developmental & Behavioral Pediatrics* (*JDBP*) is a leading resource for clinicians, teachers, and researchers involved in pediatric healthcare.

**Journal of Experimental Psychology-Applied**
www.apa.org/journals/xap.html

**Publisher:** APA
**Total Cites:** 712
**Impact Factor:** 1.81
**5-Year Impact Factor:** 2.663
**Immediacy Index:** 1.85
**Articles:** 20

The mission of the *Journal of Experimental Psychology: Applied*® is to publish original empirical investigations in experimental psychology that bridge practically oriented problems and psychological theory. The journal also publishes research aimed at developing and testing of models of cognitive processing or behavior in applied situations, including laboratory and field settings.

**Journal of Sport & Exercise Psychology**
www.humankinetics.com/jsep/journalAbout.cfm

**Publisher:** Human Kinetics Publ. Inc.
**Total Cites:** 1543
**Impact Factor:** 1.719
**5-Year Impact Factor:** 2.649
**Immediacy Index:** 0.2
**Articles:** 40

The *Journal of Sport & Exercise Psychology (JSEP)* publishes research articles by leading world scholars that explore the interactions between psychology and exercise and sport performance, editorials about contemporary issues in the field, abstracts of current research on sport and exercise psychology, and book reviews. *JSEP* is an official publication of the North American Society for the Psychology of Sport and Physical Activity (NASPSPA).

**Leadership Quarterly**
www.elsevier.com/locate/leaqua

**Publisher:** Elsevier Science Inc.
**Total Cites:** 1059
**Impact Factor:** 1.763
**5-Year Impact Factor:** 2.646
**Immediacy Index:** 0.343
**Articles:** 35

This journal brings together a focus on leadership for scholars, consultants, practicing managers, executives and administrators, as well as those numerous university faculty members across the world who teach leadership as a college course. It provides timely publication of leadership research and applications and has a global reach.

**Quarterly Journal of Experimental Psychology Section A-Human Experimental Psychology**
http://www.tandf.co.uk/journals/pp/02724987.html

**Publisher:** Psychology Press
**Total Cites:** 2801
**Impact Factor:** 2.449
**5-Year Impact Factor:** 2.517
**Immediacy Index:**
**Articles:** 0

Previously published in two sections, *Human Experimental Psychology (Section A)* and *Comparative and Physiological Psychology (B)*, the *Quarterly Journal of Experimental Psychology* merged in 2006 to form a single journal. The *Quarterly Journal of Experimental Psychology* is a leading international journal that publishes original articles on any topic within the field of experimental psychology. The journal publishes Short Articles (under 3,000 words) reporting novel techniques or ground breaking results, as well as substantial experimental reports.

**Multivariate Behavioral Research**
http://www.tandf.co.uk/journals/titles/0027-3171

**Publisher:** Lawrence Erlbaum Assoc. Inc.-Taylor & Francis
**Total Cites:** 1656
**Impact Factor:** 1.619
**5-Year Impact Factor:** 2.486

**Immediacy Index:** 0.286
**Articles:** 28

*Multivariate Behavioral Research* publishes a variety of substantive, methodological, and theoretical articles in all areas of the social and behavioral sciences. Substantive articles report on applications of multi-variate research methods. Methodological articles present new developments in multivariate methods or address methodological issues in current research. Theoretical articles provide research syntheses by integrating the findings of different studies within a specific area.

### Journal of Family Psychology
http://www.apa.org/journals/fam/

**Publisher:** APA
**Total Cites:** 1708
**Impact Factor:** 1.728
**5-Year Impact Factor:** 2.465
**Immediacy Index:** 0.22
**Articles:** 82

*Journal of Family Psychology* offers cutting-edge, ground-breaking, state-of-the-art, and innovative empirical research with real-world applicability in the field of family psychology. This premiere family research journal is devoted to the study of the family system, broadly defined, from multiple perspectives and to the application of psychological methods to advance knowledge related to family research, patterns and processes, and assessment and intervention, as well as to policies relevant to advancing the quality of life for families.

### Work and Stress
www.tandf.co.uk/journals/tf/02678373.html

**Publisher:** Taylor & Francis Ltd.
**Total Cites:** 817
**Impact Factor:** 2.089
**5-Year Impact Factor:** 2.363
**Immediacy Index:** 0.25
**Articles:** 20

*Work & Stress* is an international, multidisciplinary quarterly presenting peer-reviewed papers concerned with the psychological, social and organizational aspects of occupational and environmental health, and stress and safety management. It is published in association with the European Academy of Occupational Health Psychology.

### Journal of Cross-Cultural Psychology
http://jcc.sagepub.com/

**Publisher:** Sage Publications Inc.
**Total Cites:** 1674
**Impact Factor:** 1.524
**5-Year Impact Factor:** 2.351
**Immediacy Index:** 0.227
**Articles:** 44

For over three decades the *Journal of Cross-Cultural Psychology* has served as a leading interdisciplinary forum for psychologists, sociologists and educators who study how cultural differences in developmental, social and educational experiences affect individual behavior.

### Journal of Experimental Psychology-Animal Behavior Processes
www.apa.org/journals/xan.html

**Publisher:** APA
**Total Cites:** 1892
**Impact Factor:** 2.075
**5-Year Impact Factor:** 2.298
**Immediacy Index:** 0.095
**Articles:** 42

The *Journal of Experimental Psychology: Animal Behavior Processes* publishes experimental and theoretical studies concerning all aspects of animal behavior processes. Studies of associative, nonassociative, cognitive, perceptual, and motivational processes are welcome.

### British Journal of Psychology
www.bpsjournals.co.uk/bjp

**Publisher:** British Psychological Soc.
**Total Cites:** 2280
**Impact Factor:** 1.538
**5-Year Impact Factor:** 2.286
**Immediacy Index:** 0.3
**Articles:** 40

Publishes original papers covering a whole range of general psychology topics, and features reports of empirical studies, critical reviews of the literature and theoretical contributions which aim to further our understanding of psychology.

### Criminal Justice and Behavior
http://cjb.sagepub.com/

**Publisher:** Sage Publications Inc.
**Total Cites:** 1052
**Impact Factor:** 1.672
**5-Year Impact Factor:** 2.223
**Immediacy Index:** 0.427
**Articles:** 96

*Criminal Justice and Behavior* is the official publication of the International Association for Correctional and Forensic Psychology (IACFP). Criminal Justice and Behavior promotes scholarly evaluations of assessment, classification, prevention, intervention, and treatment programs to help the correctional professional develop successful programs based on sound and informative theoretical and research foundations.

### Journal of Consumer Psychology
www.elsevier.com/locate/jcps

**Publisher:** Elsevier Science Inc.
**Total Cites:** 830
**Impact Factor:** 1.72
**5-Year Impact Factor:** 2.199
**Immediacy Index:** 3.172
**Articles:** 29

The *Journal of Consumer Psychology* is devoted to psychological perspectives on the study of the consumer. It publishes articles that contribute both theoretically and empirically to an understanding of psychological processes underlying consumers' thoughts, feelings, decisions, and behaviors.

### Acta Psychologica
www.elsevier.com/locate/actpsy

**Publisher:** Elsevier Science BV
**Total Cites:** 2401
**Impact Factor:** 1.783

5-Year Impact Factor: 2.192
Immediacy Index: 1.102
Articles: 59

*Acta Psychologica* publishes original articles and extended reviews on selected books in any area of experimental psychology. The focus of the Journal is on empirical studies and evaluative review articles that increase the theoretical understanding of human capabilities.

### Law and Human Behavior
www.springerlink.com/link.asp?id=104390

Publisher: Springer/Plenum Publishers
Total Cites: 1528
Impact Factor: 1.551
5-Year Impact Factor: 2.181
Immediacy Index: 0.289
Articles: 38

*Law and Human Behavior* is a multidisciplinary forum for the publication of articles and discussions of issues arising from the relationships between human behavior and the law, the legal system, and the legal process. The journal publishes original research, reviews of earlier research results, and theoretical studies.

### Journal of Nonverbal Behavior
www.springer.com/psychology/personality+&+social+psychology/journal/10919

Publisher: Springer
Total Cites: 576
Impact Factor: 1.333
5-Year Impact Factor: 2.177
Immediacy Index: 0.333
Articles: 15

The *Journal of Nonverbal Behavior* publishes peer-reviewed original theoretical and empirical research papers on all major areas of nonverbal behavior. The coverage extends to paralanguage, proxemics, facial expressions, eye contact, face-to-face interaction, and nonverbal emotional expression, as well as other relevant topics which contribute to the scientific understanding of nonverbal processes and behavior.

### Psychological Research-Psychologische Forschung
http://www.springerlink.com/content/101575/

**Publisher:** Springer Heidelberg
**Total Cites:** 1211
**Impact Factor:** 1.847
**5-Year Impact Factor:** 2.168
**Immediacy Index:** 0.262
**Articles:** 65

The journal *Psychological Research* publishes articles that contribute to a basic understanding of human perception, attention, memory and action. It is devoted to the dissemination of knowledge based on firm experimental ground, independent of any particular approach or school of thought.

### Journal of Sex Research
http://www.sexscience.org/publications/index.php?category_id=439

**Publisher:** Routledge Journals, Taylor & Francis Ltd.
**Total Cites:** 1274
**Impact Factor:** 1.246
**5-Year Impact Factor:** 2.077
**Immediacy Index:** 0.118
**Articles:** 34

The *Journal of Sex Research (JSR)* is a scholarly journal devoted to the publication of articles relevant to the variety of disciplines involved in the scientific study of sexuality. *JSR* is designed to stimulate research and to promote an interdisciplinary understanding of the diverse topics in contemporary sexual science.

### International Journal of Human-Computer Studies
www.elsevier.com/wps/find/journaldescription.cws_home/622846/description

**Publisher:** Academic Press Inc. Elsevier Science
**Total Cites:** 1448
**Impact Factor:** 1.364
**5-Year Impact Factor:** 2.052
**Immediacy Index:** 0.409
**Articles:** 66

The *International Journal of Human-Computer Studies* publishes original research over the whole spectrum of work relevant to the theory and practice of innovative interactive systems. The journal is inherently interdisciplinary, covering research in computing, artificial intelligence, psychology, linguistics, communication, design, engineering, and social organization, which is relevant to the design, analysis, evaluation and application of innovative interactive systems.

### Political Psychology
www.wiley.com/bw/journal.asp?ref=0162-895X

**Publisher:** Blackwell Publishing
**Total Cites:** 738
**Impact Factor:** 1.405
**5-Year Impact Factor:** 2.038
**Immediacy Index:** 0.138
**Articles:** 29

*Political Psychology*, the journal of the International Society of Political Psychology, is dedicated to the analysis of the interrelationships between psychological and political processes. International contributors draw on a diverse range of sources, including clinical and cognitive psychology, economics, history, international relations, philosophy, political science, political theory, sociology, personality and social psychology.

### Journal of Adolescence
www.elsevier.com/locate/adolescence

**Publisher:** Academic Press Inc. Elsevier Science
**Total Cites:** 1479
**Impact Factor:** 1.207
**5-Year Impact Factor:** 1.982
**Immediacy Index:** 0.113
**Articles:** 71

The *Journal of Adolescence* is an international, broad based, cross-disciplinary journal that addresses issues of professional and academic importance concerning development between puberty and the attainment of adult status within society. It provides a forum for all who are concerned with the nature of adolescence, whether involved in teaching, research, guidance, counseling, treatment, or other services.

Media Psychology
http://www.tandf.co.uk/journals/titles/15213269.asp

**Publisher:** Lawrence Erlbaum Assoc. Inc.-Taylor & Francis
**Total Cites:** 272
**Impact Factor:** 1.41
**5-Year Impact Factor:** 1.927
**Immediacy Index:** 0.17
**Articles:** 53

*Media Psychology* is an interdisciplinary journal devoted to publishing theoretically-oriented empirical research that is at the intersection of psychology and media communication. These topics include media uses, processes, and effects.

Human Movement Science
www.elsevier.com/locate/humov

**Publisher:** Elsevier Science BV
**Total Cites:** 1262
**Impact Factor:** 1.252
**5-Year Impact Factor:** 1.924
**Immediacy Index:** 0.222
**Articles:** 54

*Human Movement Science* provides a forum for presenting, and bringing together, psychological, neurophysiological and biomechanical/biophysical research on human movement.

Nebraska Symposium on Motivation
http://www.springer.com/series/7596

**Publisher:** Springer
**Total Cites:** 464
**Impact Factor:** 1.333
**5-Year Impact Factor:** 1.92
**Immediacy Index:**
**Articles:**

The *Nebraska Symposium on Motivation* has been sponsored by the Department of Psychology at the University of Nebraska-Lincoln since 1953. Each year the Symposium invites leading scholars from around the world on a topic of current interest in psychology for a conference at the University followed by publication of an edited volume.

**Journal of Applied Research in Intellectual Disabilities**
http://www.wiley.com/bw/journal.asp?ref=1360-2322

**Publisher:** Blackwell Publishing
**Total Cites:** 443
**Impact Factor:** 1.725
**5-Year Impact Factor:** 1.888
**Immediacy Index:** 0.131
**Articles:** 61

*JARID* is an international, peer-reviewed journal which draws together findings derived from original applied research in intellectual disabilities. The journal is an important forum for the dissemination of ideas to promote valued lifestyles for people with intellectual disabilities.

**Computers in Human Behavior**
www.elsevier.com/locate/issn/07475632

**Publisher:** Pergamon-Elsevier Science Ltd.
**Total Cites:** 1147
**Impact Factor:** 1.344
**5-Year Impact Factor:** 1.87
**Immediacy Index:** 0.38
**Articles:** 179

*Computers in Human Behavior* is a scholarly journal dedicated to examining the use of computers from a psychological perspective. Original theoretical works, research reports, literature reviews, software reviews, book reviews and announcements are published. The journal addresses both the use of computers in psychology, psychiatry and related disciplines as well as the psychological impact of computer use on individuals, groups and society.

**Journal of Comparative Psychology**
www.apa.org/journals/com.html

**Publisher:** APA
**Total Cites:** 1854
**Impact Factor:** 1.793
**5-Year Impact Factor:** 1.825
**Immediacy Index:** 0.104
**Articles:** 48

The *Journal of Comparative Psychology* publishes original empirical and theoretical research from a comparative perspective on the behavior, cognition, perception, and social relationships of diverse species.

## Assessment

http://www.sagepub.com/journalsProdDesc.nav?prodId= Journal201629

**Publisher:** Sage Publications Inc.
**Total Cites:** 727
**Impact Factor:** 1.59
**5-Year Impact Factor:** 1.822
**Immediacy Index:** 0.135
**Articles:** 37

The journal presents information of direct relevance to the use of assessment measures, including the practical applications of measurement methods, test development and interpretation practices, and advances in the description and prediction of human behavior.

## Journal of Applied Sport Psychology

http://www.tandf.co.uk/journals/titles/10413200.asp

**Publisher:** Taylor & Francis Ltd.
**Total Cites:** 501
**Impact Factor:** 1.25
**5-Year Impact Factor:** 1.815
**Immediacy Index:** 0.161
**Articles:** 31

The *Journal of Applied Sport Psychology* is a refereed journal designed to advance thought, theory, and research on applied aspects of sport and exercise psychology. Submissions such as position papers, reviews, theoretical developments specific to sport and/or exercise and applied research conducted in these settings or having significant applied implications to sport and exercise are appropriate content for the JASP.

## Psychology, Public Policy, and Law

www.apa.org/journals/law.html

**Publisher:** APA
**Total Cites:** 518
**Impact Factor:** 2.4

**5-Year Impact Factor:** 1.791
**Immediacy Index:** 0.167
**Articles:** 6

*Psychology, Public Policy, and Law* focuses on the links between psychology as a science and public policy and law.

### Cyberpsychology & Behavior
http://www.liebertpub.com/products/product.aspx?pid=10

**Publisher:** Mary Ann Liebert Inc.
**Total Cites:** 912
**Impact Factor:** 1.368
**5-Year Impact Factor:** 1.787
**Immediacy Index:** 0.048
**Articles:** 125

This bimonthly peer-reviewed journal explores the impact of the Internet, multi-media and virtual reality on behavior and society.

### Journal of Motor Behavior
http://www.heldref.org/pubs/jmb/about.html

**Publisher:** Heldref Publications
**Total Cites:** 1392
**Impact Factor:** 1.318
**5-Year Impact Factor:** 1.772
**Immediacy Index:** 0.14
**Articles:** 43

The *Journal of Motor Behavior*, a multidisciplinary journal of movement neuroscience, is devoted to the further understanding of the basic processes underlying motor control and learning. The journal publishes articles from such diverse disciplines as neuroscience, biomechanics, neurophysiology, electrophysiology, psychology, bioengineering, and rehabilitation.

### Psychology of Women Quarterly
www.blackwellpublishing.com/0361-6843

**Publisher:** Blackwell Publishing
**Total Cites:** 1403
**Impact Factor:** 1.253
**5-Year Impact Factor:** 1.73
**Immediacy Index:** 0.167
**Articles:** 36

*Psychology of Women Quarterly (PWQ)* is a feminist journal that publishes primarily qualitative and quantitative research with substantive and theoretical merit, along with critical reviews, theoretical articles, and invited book reviews related to the psychology of women and gender. Topics include career choice and training; management and performance variables; education; lifespan role development and change; physical and mental health and well-being; physical, sexual, and psychological abuse; violence and harassment; prejudice and discrimination; psychobiological factors; sex-related comparisons; sexuality, sexual orientation, and heterosexism; social and cognitive processes; and therapeutic processes.

### Applied Psychology-An International Review-Psychologie Appliquee-Revue Internationale

http://www.wiley.com/bw/journal.asp?ref=0269-994X

**Publisher:** Blackwell Publishing
**Total Cites:** 667
**Impact Factor:** 1.317
**5-Year Impact Factor:** 1.626
**Immediacy Index:** 0.656
**Articles:** 32

*Applied Psychology: An International Review* is the official journal of the International Association of Applied Psychology (IAAP), the oldest worldwide association of scholars and practitioners of the discipline of psychology (founded in 1920). Particularly invited are articles that advance understanding of psychological processes across a range of applied phenomena and studies that examine the effects of different national and cultural contexts. Review papers that stimulate debate and discussion are also encouraged.

### Behavioural Processes

www.elsevier.com/locate/behavproc

**Publisher:** Elsevier Science BV
**Total Cites:** 1602
**Impact Factor:** 1.684
**5-Year Impact Factor:** 1.579
**Immediacy Index:** 0.86
**Articles:** 86

*Behavioural Processes* is dedicated to the publication of high-quality original research on animal behaviour from any theoretical perspective.

It welcomes contributions that consider animal behaviour, from behavioural analytic, cognitive, ethological, ecological and evolutionary points of view.

### Journal of Adolescent Research
http://jar.sagepub.com/

**Publisher:** Sage Publications Inc.
**Total Cites:** 909
**Impact Factor:** 1.24
**5-Year Impact Factor:** 1.481
**Immediacy Index:** 0.115
**Articles:** 26

In the *Journal of Adolescent Research*, "articles are emphasized that combine both quantitative and qualitative methods, use a systematic qualitative or ethnographic approach, break new theoretical ground, or use a new methodological approach."

### Journal of Mathematical Psychology
www.elsevier.com/locate/jmp

**Publisher:** Academic Press Inc. Elsevier Science
**Total Cites:** 928
**Impact Factor:** 1.282
**5-Year Impact Factor:** 1.156
**Immediacy Index:** 0.125
**Articles:** 24

The *Journal of Mathematical Psychology* includes articles, monographs and reviews, notes and commentaries, and book reviews in all areas of mathematical psychology. Empirical and theoretical contributions are equally welcome.

### Integrative Psychological and Behavioral Science
http://www.springer.com/psychology/journal/12124

**Publisher:** Springer
**Total Cites:** 256
**Impact Factor:** 2.429
**5-Year Impact Factor:**
**Immediacy Index:** 1.281
**Articles:** 32

This journal explores the cultural nature of human conduct and its evolutionary history, anthropology, ethology, communication processes between people and within – as well as between – societies. It integrates perspectives of the social and biological sciences through theoretical models of epigenesis.

## 12.2 SUBMITTING THE PAPER

Once you have decided on a journal, you should make certain that your paper meets the editorial requirements of the journal. In most cases, this means that the paper conforms to the APA guidelines outlined in Chapter 8. If your paper conforms to these (or other) guidelines, you are ready to send it out. Most (but certainly not all) journals nowadays have an electronic submission portal where you can submit your manuscript. If you submit a paper version, you will generally be required to submit several copies of the paper, with the exact number depending on the journal.

You may not submit what is essentially the same paper to two different journals, even if the papers differ in minor respects. You should therefore send the paper initially to your first-choice journal, keeping in mind a second and possibly a third choice in case your paper is rejected.

When you send the manuscript, include a cover letter indicating

- your intention to submit the manuscript;
- the title of the manuscript;
- the length of the manuscript and the number of tables and figures in the manuscript;
- requests for masked review (i.e., review that does not identify you to reviewers), if you wish it and the journal offers this option;
- information regarding any previous presentations of the data (such as in scientific talks);
- information regarding any closely related manuscripts, such as ones that report portions of the data;
- suggestions for potential reviewers or persons who should not review the manuscript (optional);
- notice of any possible conflicts of interest;
- verification that human or animal subjects have been treated in accordance with APA guidelines; and

- any permissions that may be needed for reproduction of copyrighted material.

Be sure to indicate in the notes to the paper sources of financial support you received for the research described in the article and for preparation of the article.

Here is a sample of a cover letter to your editor:

---

Dear Dr. Knowitall,

Attached please find my submission entitled "Do I Like It or Do I Not: The Impact of Personal Preferences on Personal Preferences." The manuscript is 27 pages long and includes 1 table.

I wish to request masked review, and I have deleted all references in the manuscript that contain my name.

Parts of the data in this paper have been previously presented at the Annual Convention of Preferential Psychology in Adversity, OH, in May 2010.

When conducting the research, I followed informed consent procedures as well as APA ethical standards. The article is original and not submitted elsewhere

Thank you very much in advance for considering my paper.

Sincerely,
Like A. Roni

Department of Psychology
University of Likeridge
144 Chooseitall Way
Favortown, MN 11222
222-333-4444 (voice)
222-333-5555 (fax)

LikeARoni@likeridge.edu

---

## 12.3 A LOOK BEHIND THE SCENES: IN THE EDITOR'S OFFICE

### 12.3.1 What Happens After Submission to the Editor

Once you submit your manuscript to the editor, it will be assigned a manuscript number. With the help of this number, your manuscript can be tracked throughout the whole process until it is published or rejected. You will receive a confirmation e-mail or snail-mail letter that your manuscript has been received that also contains your manuscript number.

Next, the editor chooses external reviewers – typically two or three – who will be sent your manuscript for review. Some journals have a policy of "blind reviewing." All identifying information is removed from the manuscript, and reviewers are not informed of authors' identities. Almost all journals keep the identity of the reviewer(s) a secret from the author. Some reviewers choose to reveal their identities, and it is then the editor's decision whether to reveal the identity to authors.

External reviewers do their work on a voluntary basis and in their free time. Therefore, it is not uncommon for it to take several weeks or, more likely, several months for the editor to receive all requested reviews. The speed of the review process also depends on the journal. Some journals pride themselves for having a speedy publication process. This fact may influence your decision to submit to a particular journal. Once a journal gets a reputation for a slow review process, some authors are reluctant to submit to the journal because they do not want inordinately to delay publication of their paper.

If you would like to learn more about the review process, you may be interested in the book *Reviewing Scientific Works in Psychology* (Sternberg, 2006), which discusses how to review literature reviews, experimental papers, and book chapters, as well as book and grant proposals.

## 12.3.2 The Editorial Decision

Once journal editors have received reviews, they typically make any one of five decisions:

**1.** Acceptance without revision

The article is accepted as is and is immediately placed into the publication queue. Such acceptances are relatively rare.

**2.** Acceptance with revision

The article is accepted contingent on revisions, usually minor ones. The editor sends back the article and review(s), informing the author of the changes that need to be made. Typically, the article is not sent out for re-review.

### 3. Rejection with suggestions for revisions

The article is rejected, but the editor suggests ways in which the article might be made suitable for publication in the journal. Because the article is rejected, however, the editor does not commit to publication of the article, even if the author makes the specified changes. This decision is sometimes called "rejection without prejudice." In this case, the article is typically sent out for re-review.

### 4. Rejection

The article is rejected outright. The editor makes clear in a letter to the author that the paper is not suitable for the journal.

### 5. No decision

The editor decides not to decide on the article. The editor indicates to the author that a decision is being withheld pending either additional information or the incorporation of suggestions for revision.

Although most articles that are rejected are rejected after external review, this is not always the case. Sometimes an editor or associate editor may read an article and decide that it is not appropriate for the journal. In this case, the article may be rejected without being sent to external referees.

What are the major reasons that editors reject articles? We asked this question of Professor Allan Wagner, former editor of the *Journal of Experimental Psychology: Animal Behavior Processes*. He indicated that, by far, the most common reason papers are rejected is lack of substance: The paper represents too little work; the findings do not present a sufficient advance over what is already known; or the findings are insufficient to establish a real, reproducible phenomenon. Other reasons for rejection include omission of necessary experimental procedures and controls, inappropriate or inadequate data analyses, shoddy scholarship, and a failure to place the work in a proper perspective. But Wagner indicated that the primary consideration in his decisions is the substance of the work. If the work represents a genuine contribution, then he (and other editors) would often bend over backward to help the author make the paper acceptable for publication.

### 12.3.3 The Aftermath

If an article is rejected, the author can either give up on the article or restart the editorial process by submitting the article elsewhere. If the article is accepted, the article goes into press. The author may be asked to sign over the copyright to the publisher of the journal. The author may also be sent back a copyedited version of the article. This version includes instructions to the printer and may include queries to the author. The copy editor may want to know, for example, whether a certain symbol is meant to be a particular Greek letter or whether an editorial revision is acceptable to the author. Authors almost always receive page proofs of their articles. Proofs are the printed version of the article as it will appear in the journal. The author checks the proofs for typographical and other errors. If an author makes what the publisher deems to be excessive changes in the article at this point, the author may be charged for a portion of the cost of the changes to the printer. Finally, the article is published. Most journals are willing to supply reprints to the author. Some journals charge for any reprints the author orders; others supply a certain number of free reprints, and charge for additional ones. Increasingly, reprints are handled electronically rather than by mail: The author is sent by e-mail a PDF of the article, which lets the author keep a copy of the article as it was published.

When an article is rejected, you can either submit to another journal or give up on it. If you choose to submit to another journal, it is a good idea first to read the reviews carefully and to make revisions to the new journal before resubmission so you do not receive from the new journal the same comments you got from the old journal. If your article is rejected several times, you may wish either to give up on it, or, as we do, put it away for a while and then look at it again a few months later in the hope of being able to evaluate its chances for publication more objectively.

The senior author once wrote an article. He submitted it to three journals and all of them rejected it. He put it away in a file drawer and pretty much forgot about it. Ten years later, he was cleaning out the file drawer and discovered the article. He brazenly submitted it to another journal, not changing a thing. The journal was comparable in quality to those that rejected the article. He got back reviews that were glowing except for one point: They noted that the references appeared to be ten years out of date. He updated the references and the article was published. So sometimes you just have to put an article aside and wait, and then maybe reconsider at a later time!

# 13 How to Make Your Paper Even Better: Proofreading, Revising, and Editing

## 13.1 BEFORE SUBMISSION: PROOFREADING AND REVISING

It is a common misperception that once you have written your first draft, you are done. Good writers do not submit their first draft. Indeed, a good part of the work on your manuscript starts only once the first draft has been written. Don't get into the bad habit of thinking that the draft is the final version. Advisers, editors, reviewers, and others are likely to make you do at least one and probably more revisions before your paper ever sees the light of day.

Here are some general tips for successful proofreading and revising:

- Get some distance.
- Rethink.

- Don't fix what you think is good.
- Revisit the checklists in this book and use them for proofreading.
- Make structural changes first.
- Check for typos and orthographic errors.

- Write for your likely referees and readers.
- Try to think of your work in terms of explaining it to a layperson.
- Check for fit to journal guidelines and subject matter.
- Read your paper at least once while imagining yourself to be a critical reviewer, or even better, ask a colleague to do the same.
- Cite likely referees (who conceivably merit citation).
- Make sure all cited works are in your references.

Part of the material in this chapter was previously published in Sternberg, R. J. (1992). How to win acceptances by psychology journals: Twenty-one tips for better writing. *APS Observer, 5,* 12–13; and in Sternberg, R. J. (2001). Writing for your referees. In R. J. Sternberg (Ed.), *Guide to publishing in psychology journals* (pp. 161–168). New York: Cambridge University Press. Reprinted with permission of the American Psychological Society and Cambridge University Press, respectively.

■ **Get some distance.**

When you have worked on your paper for a long time, you become so involved in it that it is hardly possible to see it in an objective way. You don't read sentences carefully anymore because you have read them so many times that you feel like you know already what comes next. You might even be bored when you read your paper for the tenth time. Just put it away for a while. Ideally, let it rest for a few days or weeks, or if you are in a rush, try not to look at it for at least a day or so. A fresh perspective will be very helpful in revising your chapter by aiding you in finding incongruities and passages that are difficult to comprehend and in seeing other shortcomings that might have eluded you.

■ **Rethink.**

When you look at a paragraph, think about its intention. And then try to think about what you are saying in a different way. Are there other ways to put it? Are there parts of the picture that have been left out so far, or have you taken sides without being justified? Once you have reconsidered what you have written, you are ready to reformulate problematic sentences or paragraphs and to add or delete information that you have reevaluated.

■ **Don't fix what you think is good.**

In the heat of the battle, it is easy to keep revising and making changes until your paper looks very different from your first draft. Be cautious and selective in revision. Don't revise things just for the sake of revising them – have a reason for changing them.

■ **Revisit the checklists in this book and use them for proofreading.**

This book contains several checklists you can use to assess and evaluate your manuscript. Go back to these checklists and use them to revise the content, style, and language of your manuscript.

■ **Make structural changes first.**

Before you start working on the details, reconsider the big picture. What is the message of your paper? Does it come across clearly? Does your paper contain a lot of redundancy that you could eliminate? Does the organization of your paper follow logical principles? Evaluate these aspects of your paper first, and make those changes before concentrating on details.

■ **Check for typos and orthographic errors.**

As the editor of the journal *Psychological Bulletin*, the first author found that the single most annoying flaw in a submitted article is a slew of typographical errors. Why? Because they're the easiest thing for the author to correct. It's neither the editor's nor the reviewers' job to do your proofreading for you. Always proofread. It's the one thing you most easily can do to improve the impression you make. If you don't proofread, some reviewers and editors will simply tell you to do it. But others won't be so congenial, and you may have problems changing that first impression. (No matter hwat, you loose.) Spell-check features associated with word processors help, but they are no substitute for proofreading, as shown in the preceding sentence. A spell checker would pick up the first spelling error (*hwat*) because it is not an English word, but it would not detect the other spelling error (*loose*), which is an English word.

■ **Write for your likely referees and readers.**

Expert article writers do not just write articles. They write for an audience. They decide on likely journals before they put pen to paper (or fingers to computer keys).

You can get a good idea of the types of articles a given journal publishes simply by reading the journal's mission statement (usually near the front or back of the journal and often on the Web) and by looking at recent past issues. But there is a more informal kind of knowledge you need to acquire either through you own experience or by profiting from the experience of others.

Many characteristics of journals go beyond mission statements. Some journals seem to emphasize methodological rigor above all else. One reads them and has the feeling that the study could be infinitely trivial but nevertheless published as long as it was methodologically sound. Other journals seem to emphasize articles that are interesting but lacking in substance or rigorous methodology: The ideas are provocative but the evidence for them is slim. Still other journals seem more concerned about length than about anything else. Such journals will not publish relatively longer articles, no matter how good those articles may be. One journal to which we have submitted seems to care more about the article's being in standard APA journal-article format than about what is said in this or any other format. These kinds of characteristics tend to come and go as the editorships of journals change, but oftentimes, the culture of a given journal endures beyond any single editorial board.

It thus behooves you to find out as much as you can about the kinds of issues that are important to the editor and referees of a given journal. You can save yourself a lot of lost time by seeking out journals that publish the kind of article you have written and by avoiding journals that do not publish that kind of article.

■ **Try to think of your work in terms of explaining it to a layperson.**

If you feel stuck with the organization and formulation of your paper, try to think about ways to convey your message to a layperson. This rethinking will help you reflect on your subject in a different way. It will facilitate finding simpler words and ways to explain what you are talking about.

■ **Check for fit to journal guidelines and subject matter.**

One of the single most common causes of outright rejection is the submission of articles that even a casual review would reveal to be inappropriate for that journal. For example, many authors sent the senior author of this book, as editor, empirical studies of substantive psychological phenomena, despite the fact that *Psychological Bulletin* never accepts articles of this type. Those authors wasted their own time and the editor's. The editor also returned articles that departed substantially from APA writing guidelines (e.g., were single spaced or used notes in place of references). You can save yourself and others major headaches by checking the submission guidelines, usually printed in each issue of the journal, to make sure that your article fits its intended home. (You've probably guessed by now that this very article was rejected from *Physical Sciences Ideas of the Century*.)

■ **Read your paper at least once while imagining yourself to be a critical reviewer, or even better, ask a colleague to do the same.**

We tend to be enamored of our own work. We often don't see the flaws that would be obvious if the same paper had someone else's name on it. So try reading your paper with the same devastating analytical acuity you would use if you wished to demolish the work of your most loathsome enemy. Ask a colleague to do the same. In this way, you will be able to anticipate and perhaps eliminate some reviewer criticisms – use of faulty logic, for example. If your logic is faulty, your paper suffers; of course, that also means that if your logic is perfect, so is your paper.

■ **Cite likely referees (who conceivably merit citation).**
Suppose the junior author considers herself one of the world's greatest experts on the effects of high-fat, sugary foods on amorous behavior. (She doesn't, really!) And suppose she views herself as one of the few people who really knows what happens subsequently when romantically involved couples go out on a date and share a large piece of cheesecake. She gets an article to review on the topic and looks forward to reading it. First, of course, she checks the references to see which of her superlative articles on this topic have been cited. She discovers that none of them are cited. She cannot believe it. How could anyone write about this topic without citing her work? She now starts reading the article, but she already knows it is a pretty poor piece with awful scholarship. All she needs to do is find some reason to reject it, and she most likely will.

It is impossible to anticipate everyone who might referee an article. Nor can one cite every potential reviewer. But it is important to cite likely referees who have made a serious contribution to work in the field that the article covers. And if the editor has sent the article to a particular reviewer, the editor, at least, considers that individual to be one of the more active contributors to the field the article covers. Thus, this suggestion is not a cynical one: The likely referees are the same people who are likely to be the major contributors to the field.

■ **Make sure all cited works are in your references.**
Always ensure that the works and sources you are citing in your paper are listed in the reference list.

## 13.2 AFTER SUBMISSION: MAKING THE BEST OF REVIEWS

Some time after you submit your article, you can expect to receive several reviews of your work. Here are some tips on how to deal with reviews and how to benefit most from them.

■ **Don't take reviewers' comments personally.**
Reviewers criticize work, not people (unless they do their job incorrectly). We have written fairly strong critiques of the work of some of our closest friends in the field, and they have done the same of our work. We know better than to take professional differences personally. If you do so, you will find yourself holding grudges against an awful lot of people. (Send us a self-addressed stamped envelope with

$10 worth of postage if you'd like a copy of our own 300-page list of personal enemies!)

■ **Take journal reviews seriously, but remember that reviewers are not gods (a fact that has escaped some reviewers).**
Many but not all criticisms by reviewers are credible. Sometimes, individual comments are downright asinine. But points gain force when they are repeated across reviews or by editors in their letter to you. You don't have to make every change suggested in every review. But should you be given the opportunity to revise, you are expected to write a letter accompanying your revision. This letter should explain to the editor how you dealt with each point of criticism or why you did not respond to selected points. You should realize that, although you usually don't have to address every point in every review, the editor's comments should not be ignored. Reviewers and editors do not expect perfection; they do expect, however, to be taken seriously. They put the time and effort into reviewing the article and want to see something for it.

One final note about reviewers: People often whine and moan about how nasty reviewers are. Some of them are. But remember: We have met the enemy, and we are it. Reviewers are drawn roughly from the same pool of people as those who write articles. If we all do our part, there will be fewer nasty reviews. (And if you don't agree with us, you must be stupid and utterly worthless!)

■ **Perseverance pays, to a point.**
While the senior author was editor of *Psychological Bulletin*, no article submitted to that journal was accepted outright with no changes. In other journals, the rate of outright acceptance may be slightly higher, but not by much. It can easily take two, three, or even more revisions before an article receives final acceptance. Journal editors differ in terms of how many rounds are typical. Moreover, even if one journal flatly rejects your article, another may love it. We're not alone in having been brutally rejected by one journal only to be welcomed with open arms by another. But if your article is being rejected across the board, you need at least to consider the possibility that you don't need to go to the supermarket for your next turkey.

Finally, remember that the journal reviewing process and science as a whole are basically conservative. Articles are often rejected because they're just not very good, but we believe that some of the best work in psychology and in other sciences is rejected because people are not yet ready to hear the message (see Sternberg & Lubart, 1992). We're not personally impressed by people who tell us they've never had an article turned down.

To do creative work, you must take risks, and to take risks, you must occasionally fail. Much more important than whether you fail (and everyone does sometimes) is how you handle the failure and learn from your mistakes. Should you ever reach the point at which you never fail to get your articles accepted and no one ever disagrees with you, beware: You are probably not doing your best and most creative work. And if you really want to avoid rejections, then don't take chances. Never submit. You'll be completely safe from criticism and from making a scientific contribution, as well.

## 13.3 AFTER ACCEPTANCE: EDITING FOR PUBLICATION

Once your manuscript has been accepted for publication, you most likely receive proofs at some point from the publisher that need to be proofread before they go to press. Proofs are very time sensitive, so you are well advised to look at them in time. Although nowadays, with the use of computers, errors are less common in preparing the typesetting, they still do occur. Look over your proofs carefully, and make sure there are no typos and that the numbers are all correct.

Generally, editing is done electronically these days. There are some publishers, however, that still work with paper-based page proofs. If this is the case with your publisher, you may want to familiarize yourself with the standard proofreader's marks that indicate unambiguously what changes you want to be made. You can find lists of proofreader's marks online, such as at http://www.merriam-webster.com/mw/table/proofrea.htm or at http://webster.commnet.edu/writing/symbols.htm.

# 14 Writing a Grant or Contract Proposal

The senior author's first grant proposal was a horror story: It was long, verbose, and poorly organized. Fortunately for him, in 1975, one could write a grant proposal that had all of these flaws and more and still get funded. He did. But in 2010, he probably wouldn't have had a prayer and would have had to rewrite the whole thing. In 1975, the competition for grants was stiff; in the 2000s, it is close to ridiculous. Only the very best proposals even have a chance of success, and many that meet all of the scientific criteria for funding are not funded, simply because of a lack of money. Therefore, it is important to know how to write a grant proposal to maximize your chances of getting funded. In this chapter, we describe some basics of proposals, some keys to writing good proposals, and some things that agencies look for in making funding decisions.

Different funding organizations have different guidelines for writing proposals. There would be no sense to consume space in this book describing the requirements of various organizations; there are too many organizations and requirements, and the requirements are constantly changing. Rather, we here describe 18 keys to writing a good proposal. Paying attention to these keys does not ensure that you will be funded, but they will surely help!

## 14.1 SOME BASIC CONCEPTS ABOUT GRANTS AND CONTRACTS

Before describing the keys, we briefly summarize some basic concepts, beginning with a proposal. A proposal is a description of what you will carry out – usually research – if you receive funding. The proposal may request money for salaries, equipment, supplies, travel, reproduction, communication costs, experimental subjects, or whatever. Some proposals request funding for educational programs rather than for research. Typically, a proposal contains a statement of what is being requested, a description of why the research or program is important, a review of relevant literature, pilot data showing that your hypotheses are plausible, a description of just what will be done with the money, a budget, human-subjects approval from the review board of your institution (if necessary), and the proposer's curriculum vitae. A proposal can be for a grant or a contract.

When you receive a grant, you receive support to accomplish some end, usually research and almost always research that you have described in the grant proposal. Although grants can be given for other things, we concentrate in this chapter on research grants. The agencies that give out grants almost always do some monitoring of how their money is spent, but the monitoring is generally flexible. If you want to add some experiments that were not in the original proposal or modify ones that were in the proposal to capitalize on what you have already discovered, doing so usually is not a problem if your money was given to you in the form of a grant and if you get permission for the change. Major changes in the research or budget almost always require approval, however. In other words, if you request funds for paying personnel, and you want to switch some of those funds to travel, you probably have to ask permission of the granting organization for the switch. However, if you want to switch funds from one category of personnel to another category of personnel (e.g., graduate to postdoctoral students), you are less likely to need to request permission for the switch. Organizations differ widely in their flexibility with respect to reallocation of funds. If you are not sure about a switch, always ask permission.

Contracts generally allow less flexibility than grants. All but the most minor deviations from the original plan generally require permission. Moreover, with contracts, usually you must generate specific producibles at agreed-on times. These producibles can take various forms, such as progress reports, budget statements, technical reports, products, and the like. With a contract, you are generally held fairly strictly to the deadlines that are given for the producibles. The fundamental difference between a contract and a grant is that, with a contract, you are being contracted to produce specific pieces of work, whereas with a grant, you receive money to do more or less what you described in your proposal. Some funding organizations give only grants, others give only contracts, and still others give both. Should you be awarded a grant or a contract, it is essential that you be clear on the reporting requirements before you begin, as failure to render required financial or progress reports could result in termination of the funding.

Should you receive funding, it is also imperative that you make sure that you or a financial officer of your institution keeps careful track of spending and how money is allocated. Virtually all organizations require regular and fairly detailed reports of expenses. These reports are carefully scrutinized. If you are not keeping careful records, you may find yourself in some very hot water.

A warning: Never spend money from one project on another grant-receiving project. It is illegal to do so. If and when you are audited, switching money between grants can cause great hardship both for you and for your institution. Funds awarded for a grant can support research only for that grant.

You should also realize that unless the grant is made directly to you personally – an unusual arrangement – the institution for which you work will most likely take out overhead on most or all expenses, as well as benefits on personnel expenses. *Overhead* refers to an amount charged by your institution for administering a grant. It goes to pay for the people who keep records, the space you use for doing the research, library facilities, custodial services, heating, air-conditioning, and all other expenses the institution believes might conceivably be charged against your funding. Overhead rates are negotiated between your institution and the source of funding. Overhead ranges from zero (some foundations do not allow any overhead to be taken out of the grants they give) to roughly 70% in some private universities. In non-university organizations, the overhead may be even higher. The percentage refers to the amount of money the institution takes out for every $1 you spend on research. For example, if you spend $1 on research at No Name University, the university may take out from the grant or contract another $0.64 as overhead. You can see that the charging of overhead results in your not having available to you for research all of the money that the granting institution provides. Different funding organizations have different arrangements both for requesting and for paying out overhead. In general, private universities charge more in overhead than do public ones, although there are many exceptions to this generalization.

*Benefits* refers to amounts of money taken out by the institution to pay for extra expenses that are associated with the hiring and maintenance of personnel. For example, if a research assistant is hired on a grant, the university generally contributes some percentage of the assistant's salary toward retirement pension, health benefits, insurance benefits, Social Security, and the like. These charges are figured into benefits costs. Benefits have generally been going up and can reach as high as 40% of personnel costs or even more. In other words, for every $1 you pay an employee on a grant, the university may take out as much as $0.40 for benefits that the employee receives. When you combine overhead and benefits, you begin to realize just how limited is the amount of a grant that you will be able to use for research or other intended purposes.

There is one general exception to the taking out of overhead, and that is a grant received directly from a university or other institution for which you work. In other words, if you receive a direct grant from your university or other institution to do research, it will almost certainly not take out overhead on the money that it directly provides you. Rather, those costs will have already been figured in by the organization providing the money.

It is hard to overestimate the value of having a grant or contract. Most institutions have little or no money available for research, and almost all institutions smile on their faculty and students who receive outside support. If you are a faculty member, having a grant almost inevitably helps you when it comes to promotion or tenure time and enables you to do the research that will get you that promotion or tenure. Moreover, even if you are able to do research without a grant, you will often find that you are better able to do the research you really want to do with more funds available. You can use the grant to pay for summer salary, among other things. Summer salary is money that you pay yourself over the summer to work on research related to the grant. You can pay yourself summer salary off a grant only if the salary your institution pays you is for fewer than 12 months. Many institutions pay on a 9-, 10-, or 11-month schedule, and so summer salary is an issue. Typically you can pay yourself for no more than 12 months, and some institutions have rules that enable you to pay yourself only up to 11 or fewer months. In typical situations, grantees receive 9 months of salary from the institution and pay themselves 2 months of summer support off a grant if money in the grant is available to pay for it. Remember that overhead and benefits will be taken out of your own salary, just as they would be taken out of salary paid to others.

In general, you need to be careful about payments to yourself or to anyone else, as it is common these days for grants to be audited at some time during their duration. Questionable expenses may be disallowed, and auditors who see any such expenses are likely to start digging further. Therefore, it is to your advantage to make sure that you spend money carefully and that you monitor your expenses.

## 14.2 EIGHTEEN TIPS FOR WRITING PROPOSALS

Having reviewed the major concepts behind proposals, we now consider 18 tips for writing proposals.

1. Clearly state the big question you hope to address.

2. Show why the big question is important.

3. State how your work both builds on and departs from work that has been done before.

4. State your theory and how it relates to the theories of others.

5. Show why your theory is better than its competitors.

6. Present pilot data.

7. Make sure that the research you propose fits the amount of time for which you are requesting funding.

8. Clearly state the proposed research and leave no holes.

9. Be concise.

10. Be very organized.

11. If your proposal involves empirical research, make sure that you clearly describe how you will analyze the data.

12. State clearly what the producibles of the work will be, especially for contracts.

13. Make clear what kinds of results you expect, and why they will be interesting.

14. State your qualifications for doing the proposed research.

15. Request all the funds you need to do the proposed work, but not more.

16. Show that you have the facilities you need to do the research.

17. Write a clear and compelling abstract.

18. Make sure that you have observed all formal requirements in writing the proposal.

1. **Clearly state the big question you hope to address.**

   You should state right up front what the big question is that you hope to address in your grant proposal. Do not leave it as a puzzle for readers to figure out. If you are not sure about what the big question is, do not expect that your readers somehow to be able will fill in what you are unable to supply.

   Evaluators generally prefer proposals that address some larger question and that address it in a fairly deep way. They look less favorably on proposals that are scattered and that seem to address a lot of smaller questions superficially, none of them very well. Therefore, you should be able to describe in a sentence or two the issue that you are dealing with and how you hope to address it.

2. **Show why the big question is important.**

   After stating clearly what the big question is that you hope to address, you need to say why it is important and for whom. Again, do not assume that just because you think the question is important, others will as well. You need to build a case for why the granting or contracting agency should fund research on this question over research on other questions that other investigators might address. Even if the competition is restricted to proposals that all address the same issue, you need to say how you are framing the issue and why it makes sense to frame it that way. For example, all proposals in a given competition may be on memory, but why is your approach to memory a significant one? In sum, justify up front why the work you propose is important.

3. **State how your work both builds on and departs from work that has been done before.**

   Virtually all grant proposals contain some amount of literature review. The amount will depend in part on the requirements of the agency that is providing the funds and in part on how much relevant past work there is. In your review, concentrate on past work that is clearly relevant; do not try to show that you know all literature that is remotely related to what you are going to study. But be sure that you cite work that is directly relevant. Outside reviewers see many proposals, and they tend not to be favorably impressed if their own work is not cited. Reviewers are likely to perceive their own work as highly relevant, even if you do not. It is therefore important in the literature review to show both how your work builds on what others have done and how it is different from past work. If you do not show how your work builds on that of others, you are likely to be perceived as grandiose – as someone who does not appreciate the value to your own endeavors of what others have done. But if you do not make clear how your work goes beyond past work, you may be perceived as uncreative and as not having anything new to propose.

### 4. State your theory and how it relates to the theories of others.

Funding agencies tend to look more favorably on work that has some motivating theory. The theory does not necessarily have to be your own. The important thing is that there is a set of ideas that motivates the work you propose. Merely proposing experiments or reviewing literature, or producing a product without any rationale or framework for what you are going to do, is usually considered unsatisfactory. Of course, agencies differ greatly in what counts as theory. The important thing is that you show both that a coherent set of ideas motivates the work you propose and your awareness of how the set of ideas is similar to and different from that of others.

### 5. Show why your theory is better than its competitors.

Show why you chose or formulated the theory you did and why you chose it in comparison with other competing theories. Usually, there are a number of different accounts of the same phenomena. For example, there are a number of different theories of perceptual, learning, or attribution phenomena. In choosing one theoretical framework, you automatically exclude others. Justify your choice.

### 6. Present pilot data.

With funds so tight these days, agencies have become more and more concerned that the work they fund has a good chance of being successful. Probably the single best way to convince an agency that the work is likely to be successful is to present pilot (preliminary) or informal data showing that the paradigms you suggest or the results you expect are plausible. In other words, build the case for the new research by showing that there exists at least a preliminary demonstration of the phenomenon you hope to uncover. In some cases, investigators have already done more than they let on. It is unethical to request funding for work already completed. But it is not only ethical but also sensible to request funds for work that you have shown to a first approximation is likely to be successful. The pilot data need not have tremendous numbers of cases or even necessarily have been published. But they should be relevant to the phenomena you wish to study and useful in showing the likely success of your approach to these phenomena.

### 7. Make sure that the research you propose fits the amount of time for which you are requesting funding.

Grants may be funded for anywhere from one year (or even less) to five years. Funding for more than five years is unusual. With most agencies, typical funding is for three years. Agencies and reviewers check to make sure that the work you are proposing is reasonable, given the time frame you are suggesting. If you propose only one year of work, an agency is not likely to want to fund you for three years. But conversely, it will wonder about your sense of reality if you propose five years of work to be done in three years. The work should match the time frame.

### 8. Clearly state the proposed research and leave no holes.

Reviewers are overburdened, and agencies have many more proposals than they can handle. Reviewers do not have time to figure out what you meant to say or what you might have said had you remembered to say it. You need to write very clearly so that the reader can easily grasp your points and so that there are no holes in the descriptions. Do not expect readers to fill in what you have not provided, because they will probably assume that what is missing you do not know.

### 9. Be concise.

Many agencies have a page limit. Such page limits are strictly enforced. Some agencies will even return proposals that exceed the specified page limit. Therefore, it is to your advantage to write not only clearly but also concisely. Often, to cut out excess words, you can go through a proposal after you have written it and have someone else do so, too. Remember, also, that readers of grants often volunteer their time, so they want to read the maximum possible in as little time as possible. Therefore, reviewers and the agencies themselves appreciate concisely written proposals.

## 10. Be very organized.

Good organization is always important in writing, but there are times when it matters more and other times when it matters less. In grant proposals, it matters more. Often, agencies specify the organization for the proposal, and you are expected to use their guidelines. But even if they do so specify, organization within the sections of the proposal is important. You want to make the proposal as easy to read and as logical as possible. Readers almost never appreciate having to figure out where they are or where they are going in the proposal. Therefore, you should give some kind of advance organizer in the front of the proposal and in each section. This advance organizer specifies what will come when. A sentence or two of summary at the end of each section also helps. It is often useful to construct an outline before you write the proposal to make sure that you are maintaining a tight and logical organization. If you have not done an outline in advance, consider doing one at the end to check whether the proposal is tightly organized. Again, with such a premium on funds, every little edge you can get will help you in the competition, and a well-organized proposal is a definite edge.

## 11. If your proposal involves empirical research, make sure that you clearly describe how you will analyze the data.

In addition to describing clearly the proposed research, you are expected to show that you know how you will analyze the data. When data analysis is fairly straightforward, as with a simple two-way analysis of variance or even a set of $t$ tests, the description of data analysis may be a short paragraph. If more complex forms of data analysis are involved, however, make sure you specify clearly what you are going to do and why. If the form of analysis is nonstandard (e.g., some nonparametric statistical tests), it is in your best interest to specify a reference that justifies your use of the chosen technique. Make sure that you are explicit in your description and that the form of analysis does fit the form of data you will collect.

## 12. State clearly what the producibles of the work will be, especially for contracts.

What will come out of the proposed research? Grant and contract monitors want to know. Do you expect to write articles, books, or particular chapters? Will there be any curriculum or other kind of product? Be as clear as possible in stating what you intend to produce. Also, you should clarify in advance whose property the producibles will be. Such clarification is especially important for contracts, with which typically the producibles become the property of the funding agency. You also want to know what credit (e.g., authorship, acknowledgment), if any, you will receive in the case of such producibles and whether your name will even be identified with them.

## 13. Make clear what kinds of results you might expect and why they will be interesting.

Funding agencies are generally not interested in proposals that look like fishing expeditions. They want you to show that you know what the plausible alternative outcomes might be and, especially, what these outcomes might mean. It helps to show that the results will be interesting almost without regard to how they come out. Agencies know as well as you do that many experiments do not come out in the way experimenters intend, and hence they would like to see that even if the results do not come out in the intended way, the funding will still produce something of interest. The more clearly you can specify the alternative outcomes, their meanings, and their value, the more confidence a funder will have that it is getting something for the money you want it to provide.

## 14. State your qualifications for doing the proposed research.

When you submit a grant proposal, you nearly always submit along with it a curriculum vitae, which contains the record of your accomplishments. The curriculum vitae, at minimum, includes

(a) your name;
(b) your address;
(c) your phone number;
(d) your government identification (e.g., Social Security) number;

(e) your educational history (degrees, starting with a college degree, or institutions attended);

(f) your employment history (including all jobs, full-time or part-time, that are potentially relevant to the grant, but not those that have no relevance, such as being a waiter during the summer or a camp counselor);

(g) your special honors and achievements (such as Phi Beta Kappa, cum laude, honors, or any prizes you may have received);

(h) your publications, if any;

(i) past and current grant support;

(j) committee service, offices held, or special assignments;

(k) any consulting or other work you have done that might be potentially relevant to the grant; and

(l) anything else you can think of that helps build a case for your receiving the grant.

Granting agencies also typically ask if you are submitting the same proposal to any other agencies and for the percentage of your time that you plan to spend on the proposed grant. You may also include a brief statement outlining your main credentials in prose format. Again, the important thing is to emphasize that you have the needed background to do the proposed work successfully.

Obviously, a new investigator will have a thinner curriculum vitae than will a more established investigator, but granting agencies take this fact into account. Often, they give a slight edge to younger investigators, realizing how difficult it is for them to get started. Whether or not an agency does so depends on the particular agency. Although you should be sure to include all relevant qualifications, avoid including things that are obviously irrelevant and may make a statement about you. Including irrelevant things (e.g., your summer experience as a waiter) makes it look as though you are padding the curriculum vitae and that you have so few worthwhile things to say that you have been forced to say things that are irrelevant to the grant.

## 15. Request all the funds you need to do the proposed work, but not more.

Think very carefully about how much money you need to do the proposed work. It is usually very difficult to obtain supplementary funds later. At the same time, agencies have "mental radar" for detecting padded budgets. If you ask for considerably more money than you need, your budget request is likely to be cut, and you may even be turned down because the research is deemed not worthy of the funds being requested.

### 16. Show that you have the facilities that you need to do the research.

It does not make sense to propose to do research that requires a supercomputer if you do not have such a computer available, or that requires you to have extensive knowledge of French if you do not know French. Therefore, you should state the facilities that you have available to get the research done. If there are facilities you will need that you do not have (such as microcomputers or work stations), you can request these facilities in the budget line for equipment. Remember, though, that equipment funds tend to be rather modest in most agencies, and you might even want to talk with someone in the agency in advance to determine whether your equipment request will be considered reasonable. You can also request funds for consultants, if they are a "human facility" you will need to get the work done (e.g., translators in cross-cultural work).

### 17. Write a clear and compelling abstract.

Although the abstract appears at the beginning of the grant proposal, people almost always write their abstract after they write the proposal. It is much easier to state the main points of your proposal after you have written it than before. The abstract should state the big question, name and briefly describe the theory, summarize the proposed research, and summarize the kinds of conclusions you hope to draw (though not, necessarily, the specific results, which you do not yet know). Some reviewers of grant proposals decide from the abstract how interesting the proposal is likely to be, so it is to your advantage to take care in writing the abstract – and remember that there may be a length requirement that you may not exceed.

### 18. Make sure that you have observed all formal requirements in writing the proposal.

As we noted earlier, agencies sometimes return proposals that do not strictly adhere to their guidelines. Government bureaucracies such as the National Institutes of Health have people whose job it is to check that proposals conform to guidelines. To you and us, this job may seem like the most boring one in the world; but to others, it is a living. And they want to justify their living. So be scrupulous in checking adherence to length, margins, type size, format, and all other requirements. Such detail might seem like a Mickey Mouse exercise, and for you, perhaps it is. But formal requirements are taken seriously.

## 14.3  WHAT DO AGENCIES LOOK FOR?

Different agencies look for different things in grant proposals. Foundations and some government agencies pay very close attention to whether the proposed research fits into their list of priorities. Therefore, you want to make sure that the proposal matches the priorities of the funding organization. If it does not, it may be turned down, no matter how good the proposed research is. Funders also look for whether the proposal deals with important questions, whether the work has the potential to make a real contribution to science or society, whether the work is interesting, and whether the investigator will be able to accomplish the proposed work. The experience of the researchers – their qualifications and expertise – will also be taken into account. Evaluators also consider the affordability of the proposed research and possibly the likelihood that the outcomes of the research can be used in practice at some point. Proposal readers also evaluate whether the experiments fit the theory that is supposed to underlie them, whether there are any errors in experimental designs or other aspects of methodology, whether the data analyses are correct and fit the proposed form of data to be collected, and whether the resources are there to do the proposed work. Having been on a granting panel for several years ourselves, we think that the most important single criterion is the potential contribution of the work to science. Methodological errors can be remedied, budgets can be pared down, and mistaken judgments about details (e.g., the number of subjects that will be required) can all be corrected. But work without the potential to make a contribution is viewed as not fundable. Therefore, more than anything else, you want to show that the work is worthwhile. If you can do that, the agency is more likely to be forgiving of other defects of the proposal.

Remember that a grant or contract proposal is not just expository writing; it is persuasive writing. You need to persuade an agency that your proposed work is so valuable that the agency simply must fund it. Ideas generally don't sell themselves. You need to sell them.

Getting funded these days requires a measure of good luck. Although you can never guarantee good luck, you can help make your own good luck by following the keys to writing proposals that are outlined in this chapter.

## CHECKLIST FOR GRANT AND CONTRACT PROPOSALS

- ☐ Have you stated up front the big question you hope to address?
- ☐ Have you shown why your research is important?
- ☐ Have you said how your approach builds on and departs from previous ones?
- ☐ Have you stated your theory and how it relates to other theories?
- ☐ Have you shown why your theory is better than competitors' theories?
- ☐ Have you presented pilot data?
- ☐ Can you complete your research in the time frame for which you request funding?
- ☐ Is your writing clear and concise?
- ☐ Does your proposal have a logical organization and advance organizers?
- ☐ Have you clearly described the data analyses to be done?
- ☐ Have you stated the producibles?
- ☐ Have you specified the expected and alternative outcomes, as well as why they are interesting?
- ☐ Have you stated your qualifications?
- ☐ Do you have the facilities needed for the research?
- ☐ Is your abstract convincing?
- ☐ Have you observed all formal requirements?

# 15 How to Find a Book Publisher

Although good books differ from one another in a multitude of ways, good book proposals are surprisingly similar. All of them have a set of standard features. In this chapter, we will describe what these features are.

## 15.1 CHOOSING A PUBLISHER

One thing you should realize right away is that, whereas a scientific article generally may be submitted to only one scientific journal at a time, a book proposal typically may be submitted to several publishers simultaneously. It is to your advantage to submit the proposal to multiple publishers, because what greatly interests one publisher may be of limited or no interest to another. Each publisher has its own set of priorities and standards for judging proposals. Before sending a book proposal to a given publisher, look at some of that publisher's recent books to determine whether your book would be a good match. Or you may even want to write the publisher a letter of inquiry, briefly describing what you would like to do and asking whether the publisher would be interested in seeing a full-length proposal. In this way, you can save yourself and the publisher the bother of a submission if the proposal does not fit into its publishing program. Publishers vary in the level of prestige, the quality of the books they produce, the amount of royalties they pay, and many other respects. You may therefore want to talk to publishers' representatives (called acquisitions editors) as well as to other people who have worked with various publishers to get advice as to which houses are worth pursuing. Looking at a publishing house's publication list, however, is usually the best way of evaluating both the range and quality of the books it produces.

In our careers, we have worked with a large number of different publishers and have found that they vary greatly in almost every respect imaginable. Some are completely honest, and others less so. Some always pay royalties on time; others get around to it sooner or later, but often later. Some spare no expense to produce the finest-quality books; others produce books that start to come loose from the binding as soon as they are opened. Working with a publisher is like forming a close relationship. It is to your advantage to make sure that you carefully investigate the publisher with which you will enter into a relationship.

Three fundamental kinds of proposals are frequently found in psychology. Two of these are relatively infrequent, and we do not discuss them here: textbook proposals and trade-book proposals. Textbook proposals are, as their name implies, for texts, and they require certain special techniques that are beyond the scope of this book. Trade-book proposals are for books that will sell primarily in general bookstores. These proposals are even more specialized and difficult to write, and they often are submitted to publishers through literary agents. Again, they are beyond the scope of this book. In this chapter, we will concentrate on the features of scholarly book proposals, the kind that psychologists most often write.

## 15.2 THE PROPOSAL

A book proposal contains several different parts. In the following, we describe those parts.

### 15.2.1 Opening

A book proposal opens with the title "Book Prospectus" or "Book Proposal" at the top and the proposed title and author or authors of the book below that.

### 15.2.2 Description of the Book

You start the main body of the proposal by describing what the book is about. What story do you want to tell? Why is it a story that bears telling, and what makes it interesting? Book publishers have to sell books, and so no matter what the scholarly value of the contribution, they have to care about whether you have interesting things to say. If you do not, they would likely lose money if they published the book. Even university presses, which are willing to take more risks on scholarly work that has scholarly value even if it does not have great sales potential, still need their books to sell to remain financially solvent.

### 15.2.3 Audience of the Book

Next, you need to specify the intended audience or audiences for your book. What kinds of people are likely to read it? Will it be written in a language that can be understood only by people in the field, or by graduate students, or by undergraduates, or even by educated people in other fields? Publishers are interested not only in the level of the book but also in the breadth of audience to which it will appeal. Is your book written only for developmental psychologists, or will it be of interest to a broader range of psychologists? The broader the range of people who may be interested in the book, the better the potential sales are, and therefore the greater the potential interest of the publisher. However, if the appeal is very broad, then the publisher will check to make sure that the book makes a real contribution and is not written at such a general level that it has nothing new or interesting to say. Audiences can range across as well as within fields. For example, you might write your book to appeal to people in education as well as to those in psychology or to people in sociology or anthropology as well as psychology. Perhaps certain computer scientists or philosophers would also have an interest. Specify as thoroughly as you can who might be interested and why.

### 15.2.4 Outline of the Book

After specifying what the book is about, why it is important, and who the potential audience is, provide a general outline of the book. This outline should cover the chapters of the book and, if there are parts into which the chapters are organized, a description of what they will be. It should give the chapter names and a summary of what will go into each chapter. The book should show a logical organization and a sensible progression of ideas from beginning to end. Try to make the summaries as readable as possible, illustrating abstract points with concrete examples whenever such examples will help clarify the points you want to make. You need not cover every detail in every chapter, but you need to convey a sense of the flavor of the book. You also need to show in the sequencing how you developed the main idea of the book that you stated at the beginning. Even scholarly books must tell a story, and you cannot expect readers to figure out what the story is. The proposal should make clear what the story will be.

Occasionally, people submit proposals for edited books. Such books consist of a sequence of chapters by different authors, all revolving around some general theme. In the case of edited books, it is particularly important to show how the chapters tie together. There are any number of edited books that seem to be a motley collection of unrelated essays, and such books generally do not sell well. With edited books, it is especially important to have an introductory chapter that sets the framework for the chapters to follow, and a concluding chapter that integrates the various contributions of the authors.

### 15.2.5 The Competition of the Book

After describing the main contents of the book, you need to describe the competition. This section is particularly important, because book publishers want to know what they are up against. When there are potential competitors for a new volume, the potential audience for that new volume is reduced, so it is particularly important that you assure the publisher that your book will make some kind of unique contribution that other books do not make. Therefore, it is important to state not only what the competition is but also why your book is better, or more nearly complete, or more up to date, or broader, or more representative of the field, or whatever. The same principle holds for both written and edited books. Pay a lot of attention to this section, because unless it is well done, your book may be rejected not because it is perceived as inadequate but because the competition is perceived as insurmountable.

### 15.2.6 Details

Typically, the next thing you will specify is nitty-gritty detail. What is the proposed length of your book in double-spaced, single-sided manuscript pages? How many tables, roughly, do you expect there to be? How many figures? Generally, you are expected to provide figures, but not tables, in camera-ready form, which means that the figures can be photographically reproduced and used as is. If you need special kinds of reproduction, such as that required for color plates, you need to specify as much. Most important, you need to specify the expected completion date for the book. It is generally better to pick a date that is somewhat later but more realistic than one that is somewhat earlier but that you cannot meet. Publishers of scholarly books are usually willing to give reasonable extensions on due dates if it appears that you cannot meet the deadline that you set for yourself. (Publishers of textbooks and trade books tend to be less forgiving because such books often involve substantial advances, and the publisher loses money each day that the advance on royalties is not recovered. Moreover, the publisher may have made specific sales commitments for such books – commitments it will be unable to meet if books are delivered late.)

### 15.2.7 Your Qualifications

You need also to specify your qualifications for writing the book. It is common to include a curriculum vitae and possibly a written summary of accomplishments. Publishers want to make sure that you are qualified to write the book. Moreover, with books, as with practically anything else, name recognition counts. It is generally easier for a well-established author to get a book proposal accepted than for a new author. However, publishers are always looking for new, potentially successful authors, and so if you can convince them that you have a product of quality that will sell, they may be quite interested in your book, even if you are new to the field or have not previously published widely or at all.

### 15.2.8 Sample Chapter(s)

Some publishers require that you submit a sample chapter or several sample chapters of the book, especially if you are not a well-known author. Practices differ widely among publishers, and some publishers may agree to publish the book only if they have the complete item in front of them to evaluate. If you can write one or more sample chapters, it is to your advantage to send them, because publishers will then have a better idea of what the book will actually consist of. If you do send a sample chapter or chapters, it is important to make sure that the chapters represent the best effort you can make.

### 15.2.9 Summary

At the end of the proposal, you will want to summarize the main points of your proposal. Here, and possibly at the beginning, it does not hurt to pay attention to special features. What sets your book apart? What particular features does the book have that would make it particularly salable? For example, do you take a new approach to a problem that you think is bound to catch the eye of the reader? Do you have access to special information that no one else has reviewed? Do you have recent data that are likely to shed a new perspective on the field? Publishers are always interested in knowing special angles that may increase sales.

## 15.3 CONTRACT OFFERS

Up to now, we have discussed what you need to do to convince a house that it should contract your book. But if several publishers are interested, you will then be in a position of asking them what it is that makes them special. Why should you publish with one publisher as opposed to another that is interested in your book? There are a number of different things to look for in choosing among alternative publishers, or even deciding whether you should pursue more alternatives.

### 15.3.1 Royalties

Royalties are sums of money, based on a percentage of sales, paid to the author. Royalties can be paid either on gross receipts or on net receipts. These two quantities are quite different, and it is important to know on which quantity the publisher bases its royalties. Relatively few book contracts grant royalties paid on gross receipts. "Gross receipts" refer to the selling price of the book. For example, if your book costs $40, and your royalty rate is 10% of gross, you will receive $4 per book sold.

By far the more common way of writing contracts is in terms of net receipts. Net receipts are the publisher's actual receipts for the books it sells. For example, suppose that the publisher sells to a bookstore. Although the book may sell for $40, the publisher will receive considerably less than $40 from the bookstore, because bookstores receive a discount in buying books from a publisher so that they can make a profit when they sell the books to their customers. Your royalty would be based on the amount the publisher received from the bookstore (perhaps $30), rather than on the ultimate selling price of the book. If there are sales to book clubs, net receipts may be proportionately even less than they are for bookstores. Publishers frequently give away sample copies for promotional purposes, and no royalties are paid on sample copies. Moreover, royalties tend to be lower on foreign sales and on paperback sales (if there is a paperback version). Royalties are usually lower in foreign sales because of the added costs entailed in such sales, especially when they are done through a distributor or intermediary, who takes a portion of the receipts. Paperback books receive lower royalties because they generally have to be priced lower than hardcovers, and so publishers receive less profit per book.

In comparing royalties among publishers, make sure that you compare apples with apples. In other words, make sure that the royalties are on the same basis (e.g., net receipts) and involve the same exclusions (e.g., for sample copies that are given away free by publishers for promotional purposes).

It is sometimes possible to work out a sliding-royalty arrangement with a publisher. Such an arrangement more fairly shares risk between author and publisher. Publishers are often reluctant to give higher royalties because they want to make sure that they recover their own costs of producing and marketing the book. A sliding-scale arrangement results in a greater proportion of royalties being paid as more books are sold. For example, you might receive a royalty of 10% of net on the first 2,500 copies sold, 12% of net on the next 2,500 sold, and 15% of net on all copies sold thereafter. Sliding-scale royalties are usually negotiable (both in terms of thresholds for increases in royalties and for amounts of increase), especially if competing publishers are in the picture. However, not all publishers are willing to offer a sliding-scale arrangement. What level of royalties can you expect on a scholarly book? Typically, it seems to the authors, surprisingly little. Commonly, royalties are between 10% and 12% of net receipts. A high royalty rate is 15%, and rates greater than that are relatively rare. Although this level might not seem like much to you, you need to remember that the publishing house bears most of the expenses and is eager not only to recover those expenses but to make a profit as well. The more competitive offers you have, and the stronger they are, the greater the royalty rate you may be able to negotiate for yourself.

### 15.3.2 Advance on Royalties

An advance is money that a publisher pays up front in anticipation of future royalties. Once the book is published and begins selling, royalty payments to the author will be withheld until the publisher has recouped the advance. In the event that the book does not sell enough copies to earn back the advance given to the author, the publisher forfeits the money – the author does not have to pay back the advance. Usually, the only circumstances under which authors must pay back an unearned advance are those in which they don't finish the book or if they complete it but the publisher deems the manuscript unacceptable and declines to publish it. These eventualities are usually spelled out in the contract.

Some publishers are willing to give small advances on royalties, although advances for scholarly books are relatively rare and, when they are given, relatively small. At most, they will be a few thousand dollars, and even that is high for scholarly books. In general, unless you are a well-known author or have multiple competitive offers, you should not expect an advance on royalties.

### 15.3.3 Payment of Royalties

Check when royalties are paid. Most publishers pay once a year. However, it is to your advantage if the royalties are paid twice a year, because you receive them more quickly after books are sold. The month or months in which royalties are paid varies, although a typical schedule would be that royalties are paid once a year in May for sales of the preceding calendar year. Publishers are generally not flexible on royalty payment schedules, as they tend to do all their accounting for all their books at the same time.

### 15.3.4 Publication Lag

Publication lag is the time between the submission of the final draft of your book and the publication of that book. Publishers vary widely in how long it takes them to produce a book. Typically, the publication lag should be no longer than 1 year. We have worked with a publisher that has taken close to 2 years to publish a book, and for certain this will be the last time we work with that publisher. You can ask the publisher to write into the contract a "reasonable" amount of time, although the publisher will usually write the language to exclude delays due to unforeseen causes. Remember, to minimize publication lag, you should submit the book in a form that maximizes efficiency for the publisher. For example, having camera-ready figures that can be readily reproduced helps cut the time to publication. Submitting manuscripts electronically also can help.

## 15.3.5 Marketing and Promotional Efforts

Publishers will rarely write into a contract the specific marketing and promotions efforts that they will do for your book, but you may be able to get them to write a separate letter. Such a letter generally has no legal force, and thus it represents a moral rather than a legal commitment. In publishing, as in most endeavors, oral agreements mean little, if anything: If you do not have it in writing, you do not have it. You should get a clear sense of what the publisher plans to do to promote the book. Will the book appear at professional conventions? Will it be advertised in journals? Will there be direct-mail promotions? If so, to whom will the mail be sent? Books do not sell themselves. They need efforts not only on your part in writing but also on the publisher's part in marketing, and you should find out as much about the intended marketing as possible.

## 15.3.6 Physical Appearance of the Book

As we mentioned earlier, publishers differ widely in how attractive the books they produce are. Publishers also differ widely in the quality of their books' materials. The best indication of the quality of the production of your book is the quality of production of other books published by the same house. Therefore, review copies of other books that the publisher has produced and check the quality of the binding, the paper, the printing, and the like. Are the publisher's books attractive? A book should last for many years, and so it pays for you to know how well produced the book will be.

### 15.3.7 Out-of-Print Policy

Some publishers keep almost all of their books in print for many, many years; others put them out of print if the book stops selling some minimum number of copies. For some publishers, this minimum may be quite high. Therefore, it is to your advantage to inquire of the publisher as to its out-of-print policy, because it can have a major effect on the life of your book. And it is something that authors often forget to consider in choosing a publisher. Some houses will put a book out of print after only a couple of years, and you will want to know in advance if that is a possibility for your book. If it is, make sure that your book contract states that the rights to the book will revert to you in case the book does go out of print.

### 15.3.8 In-House Assistance

You need to make clear in negotiating a contract exactly who is going to do what. Sometimes publishers compile indexes; other times they expect authors to do them. Many scholarly books separate author indexes from subject indexes, and some publishers will do one (e.g., the author index) but not the other. Usually, authors are expected to obtain permissions for long quotations or figures taken from other volumes, but some publishers take on this responsibility. Some publishers have in-house copy editors; others send their manuscripts to freelance copy editors. Moreover, publishers differ in the care with which they copy edit the manuscripts they receive. Copyediting is important because it involves the correction of various errors, as well as the clarification of the text. Therefore, having a good copy editor is important.

### 15.3.9 Communication

We have found that the quality and quantity of communication with publishers differ widely across publishers, and they depend on more than just how chatty we happen to feel about a particular book. Some publishers' representatives (acquisitions editors) seem to disappear the moment you sign the contract; others are there to support you throughout the entire book-writing process. Obviously, it is to your advantage to work with the kind of editor who is willing to communicate more rather than less. Having a good editor to work with can make the entire publishing process remarkably smooth, whereas having no one to work with or having someone who is unhelpful or unpleasant can turn a simple process into a nightmare. Therefore, know in advance with whom you are going to work and convince yourself that it is someone with whom you are going to enjoy working and from whom you will be able to profit.

## 15.3.10 Hidden Aspects of the Contract

Although we do not take our contracts for scholarly books to a contracts lawyer, we do take those for textbooks and trade books to such a lawyer. And it probably is not a bad idea to show even a contract for a scholarly book to a lawyer. There are often hidden features of the contract that you will not be able to see, but that a lawyer will see. Every contract that we have brought to a lawyer has contained passages that are unduly unfavorable to the author that we never would have recognized as such. Therefore, you should read the contract carefully; do not just assume that the contract will be written in a way that is favorable to you. On the contrary, it is generally written to be maximally favorable to the publisher. Business being business, publishers look out for themselves. Therefore, check your contract very carefully, and if you have any doubts about it, take it to a lawyer. We recommend that you consult a lawyer who specializes in contracts, because such attorneys, in our experience, are much more knowledgeable than general practice lawyers, who may have handled very few publishing contracts.

## 15.3.11 Reputation of the Publisher

The most important consideration of all we have saved for last, and that is the reputation of the publisher. Publishers, like organizations of any kind, differ widely in quality. Some of them are completely reputable, and others less so. Some of them are world renowned, and others are fly-by-night organizations that may disappear before your book is ever published. Investigate the reputation of the publisher with which you are considering signing by checking with others who have published there and by asking for a catalog of published titles. One of the best signs of a good publisher is the stable of authors who have published with it and who continue to do so. If possible, speak with authors who have worked with the press. Do not assume that a publisher must be good because you have heard of it or because it writes on impressive stationery or has fancy headquarters.

We especially warn readers about so-called subsidy publishers or vanity presses. These "publishers" require that you pay a large amount of money up front to have your book published. They will publish almost anything, provided that you are willing to pay the publication costs. Their royalties are much higher than those of other houses, but don't be seduced by this fact; such publishers can afford to pay higher royalties because they take essentially no risk. In our opinion, such publishers are houses of last resort, because authors rarely receive back in royalties what they have paid to have the books published. Moreover, vanity presses know this fact and may even state it in their literature. Such presses make little effort to promote the books because their real receipts are in the payments made by authors to get their books published. Even worse, publishing with such a press probably will not enhance your professional credentials. Psychologists and others know who these publishers are and may devalue rather than value a book published by one of these houses.

Let us make one last observation in closing. Between us, we have written or edited more than 100 books, and the writing and editing of books has been one of the most enjoyable experiences we have had as psychologists. Our experiences with publishers have ranged from excellent to poor, but we have learned from our mistakes, as will you. Going through the steps of publishing a book can be one of the most rewarding experiences of a career as a psychologist, and after all is said and done, many of the greatest contributions that have been made in psychology have been made through books. Therefore, although you may experience anxieties, enjoy yourself. If you write a book, you are in for an experience that is always challenging, often rewarding, and many times, great fun.

## CHECKLIST FOR BOOK PROPOSALS

**Content**
- ☐ Have you stated what makes your book interesting and why it is important for your message to be published?
- ☐ Are your chapters supported empirically and theoretically?
- ☐ Are the facts in your proposal accurate?
- ☐ Did you define basic terms?

☐ Have you reviewed the relevant literature?
☐ Does your proposed book have the best possible organization?
☐ Do you have an outline of all the chapters with chapter names and summaries?

### Market

☐ Have you shown that there is a need for the book?
☐ Have you shown that there is a market for the book?
☐ Have you shown that your book makes a unique contribution to the market?

### Audience

☐ Have you described the target audience of your book?
☐ Have you specified at which level the book will be written?

### Details

☐ Have you specified the suggested length of your manuscript, as well as the number of tables and figures you intend to use?
☐ Have you specified the expected completion date?
☐ Does your summary once more point out the special features of your book?

### Credentials

☐ Have you presented your qualifications as an author?

# 16 | Writing a Lecture

Lecturing is one of the most important parts of being a psychologist. All of us have attended countless lectures and know what a difference it makes to listen to someone exciting versus someone dull. Sometimes you may not have any choice in terms of the material you present. But there are 15 keys that everyone can follow to write better lectures:

1. Do not read your lecture from a script.

2. Start off on an exciting note.

3. Organize and emphasize.

4. Say what you are going to say, say it, and say what you have said.

5. Use concrete examples.

6. Do not cram.

7. Be enthusiastic.

8. Make it relevant.

9. Know your audience.

10. Vary your pace and the kinds of content you present during the course of the lecture.

11. Pace yourself.

12. Do not be condescending.

13. Do not be defensive.

14. Do not wing it.

15. Be confident.

## 1. DO NOT READ YOUR LECTURE FROM A SCRIPT.

Listening to a lecture that is read directly from text is one of the more boring experiences known to humankind. Written language does not sound like oral language. If you ever read the transcript of a good talk, you will find it hard to comprehend. It should be! People just do not talk the way they read. When you hear a talk that is read word for word, the talk sounds unnatural. It is also boring to hear. Therefore, when you write a lecture, you are best off doing it in outline form or in some other form that will enable you to talk the lecture rather than read it.

## 2. START OFF ON AN EXCITING NOTE.

Listeners often decide in the first minute or two whether they will continue to listen to a lecture or tune out. Starting with an exciting opening can make the difference between capturing an audience and losing them from the start. Try to start off with an anecdote, a joke that is relevant to the lecture, a concrete example of something you'll be talking about, or some other topic that will catch the interest of listeners. Jokes can be good in an opening, but only if they are related to the rest of the talk. In fact, many people find it annoying to hear a joke that is obviously canned and that is used by either the same person or others as an opening for almost any speech they give. A creative opening can make the difference, but you have to be willing to put in the effort to make sure that it is creative.

## 3. ORGANIZE AND EMPHASIZE.

A person who is knowledgeable about a field may be able to follow a poorly organized lecture, but someone who is new to a field is much less likely to be able to do so. Therefore, organize your lecture clearly and tightly. A logical sequence of points will help listeners understand. Moreover, organize hierarchically. Emphasize main points and deemphasize subordinate ones. Listeners who are new to an area cannot be expected to know what your main points are. You need to tell them, and to give them a sense of what is more important to remember and what is less so.

## 4. SAY WHAT YOU ARE GOING TO SAY, SAY IT, AND SAY WHAT YOU HAVE SAID.

In giving a lecture, even more than in writing, it is important to start by foreshadowing your main points in the organization of your talk, then to give the main body of the talk, and finally to summarize the main points of what you have said. Such an organization helps listeners both to be prepared for the main body of the lecture and to understand what they have learned after the lecture is done. This organization may seem redundant, but some redundancy helps listeners better understand the content. Obviously, you do not want to say the same things again and again, but you do want to emphasize and reemphasize your main points to be sure that your listeners understand them.

## 5. USE CONCRETE EXAMPLES

In speaking, as in writing, concrete examples help listeners understand fairly abstract points or points that may be slightly beyond their initial comprehension. A talk that never leaves the abstract plane is likely to be incomprehensible to many listeners. Whether or not people are willing to admit it, they learn best from general points that are illustrated by examples. Do not expect members of the audience to be able to fill in their own examples – you provide them.

## 6. DO NOT CRAM.

Don't you just hate it when someone tries to give 2 hours of material in 40 minutes? So do the people who are going to listen to you. Some lecturers try to show how erudite they are or how quickly they can think by cramming in too much material for the time that they are given to lecture. Most people in the audience will be unimpressed and, to the contrary, will come to the conclusion that you do not know how to lecture. The idea is not to present as much material as possible but to make the material you present as clear and as comprehensible as possible. Therefore, make sure that the amount of material fits the time you have to present it. It is better to present less and clearly convey main points than it is to overpresent and have your audience understand next to nothing.

### 7. BE ENTHUSIASTIC.

Do not expect your audience to be enthusiastic if you are not. If you are enthusiastic, you may or may not transmit your enthusiasm to your audience. But if you are unenthusiastic, you certainly will not transmit any enthusiasm at all. Enthusiasm is contagious, and by showing yours, you may win converts to your way of seeing things that you otherwise would not win. You have likely always hated to hear people who are bored with what they present; so will your audience.

### 8. MAKE IT RELEVANT.

One of the best things you can do to increase comprehension of a lecture is to make the lecture relevant to the people to whom you present it. The more you can adjust your lecture to the interests and prior knowledge of your audience, and the more you can make it relevant to their own concerns, the more likely the audience will be to listen and comprehend. You probably find that you listen more if you feel that you are learning something useful in a class. Your audience will do the same. Moreover, even if you cannot make the lecture completely relevant to your audience, show why it may be interesting anyway. Do not expect them to know. The more you can show why your audience should find something interesting, the more likely they are to respond to what you have to say.

### 9. KNOW YOUR AUDIENCE.

A corollary of making your talk relevant to your audience is knowing who your audience is in the first place. When we give a talk or a lecture, we always try to find out as much as we can about the people to whom we are talking. How much knowledge do they have about the topic? What are their interests? What are they looking for in our talk? The more you know your audience, and the more you can adjust your remarks to fit your audience, the better you will likely be received.

## 10. VARY YOUR PACE AND THE KINDS OF CONTENT YOU PRESENT DURING THE COURSE OF THE LECTURE.

Varying pace and kinds of content helps maintain audience interest. Too much of anything can become too much of a good thing. Therefore, it helps to vary level of abstractions with concrete examples, generalities with specifics, and lighter topics with heavier ones. Variety is the spice of life, and it is also the spice of a good talk.

## 11. PACE YOURSELF.

Many people have a tendency to talk too fast. For listeners, the result is often that they are lost before they even begin to understand what the lecture is about. Therefore, you do not want to talk too fast, or labor so slowly over your words that people lose track of where they are. The best procedure is to vary your pace somewhat but to stay within a range of speed that enables you to remain comprehensible.

## 12. DO NOT BE CONDESCENDING.

No one likes to hear a condescending lecturer or one who obviously has no respect for the audience. If people are turned off to you, they are likely to be turned off to your material as well. Being condescending or arrogant, or treating people as though they lacked even the most basic mental abilities, is a great way to turn people off completely to everything you have to say. It is generally better to err on the side of modesty than on the side of being a know-it-all, if only because your talk should speak for itself. If you give a good talk, people will respect you for doing it, without your acting as if you are the world's greatest expert on the topic of your talk.

## 13. DO NOT BE DEFENSIVE.

Accept questions, comments, and even criticisms openly. If you want people to learn, then it helps to give them a chance to interact with you. If you react defensively to what they say, the chances are that they will not want to say anything. Therefore, belittling the contributions of your audience or immediately defending yourself against anything you perceive as an attack hurts the audience's ability to learn from you and your ability to learn from the audience. Accept comments openly and profit from them.

## 14.  DO NOT WING IT.

People quickly recognize if you have come into a lecture unprepared. You have always recognized it in others, and people recognize it in you. Therefore, be prepared.

## 15.  BE CONFIDENT.

Perhaps most important, be confident and self-assured. No one is expected to be perfect, and no one is expected to know everything. If you have prepared for your lecture and have a reasonable command of your material, give it your best shot and have the confidence in yourself to do well. And then go and enjoy yourself. If you do, your audience probably will as well.

### CHECKLIST FOR LECTURES

- ☐ Are you starting off in an exciting way?
- ☐ Is your lecture organized?
- ☐ Are you emphasizing your main points?
- ☐ Are you using concrete examples?
- ☐ Is your lecture relevant to your audience?
- ☐ Have you adapted your lecture to your audience?

# 17 Article Writing 101

This final chapter summarizes 50 tips from experts on writing articles. We're first presenting the tips to you in list format so you can gain a quick overview. We then elaborate on each of the tips.

1. Ask yourself whether your ideas are interesting to you, and why they would be interesting to other people.

2. Realize that new ideas are often difficult to get accepted.

3. Write the article that emerges from your research rather than the article you planned to write.

4. Explore the data to find out what they have to say and not just what you expected them to say.

5. A good article tells a story.

6. Write the story the data tell rather than the story of your discovery of the data's story.

7. Write at a level students will understand.

8. Make clear what is new in your article.

9. Write with your reviewers in mind.

10. Write in the manner of an hourglass: Start broadly, become more specific, and then end broadly.

11. Make clear how your study tests your hypotheses.

12. Polish and proofread.

This chapter is adapted from R. J. Sternberg (2000). Article Writing 101: A crib sheet of 50 tips for the final exam. In R. J. Sternberg (Ed.), *Guide to publishing in psychology journals* (pp. 199–206). New York: Cambridge University Press. Reprinted with permission.

13. Do not use synonyms, especially for technical terms, just to avoid redundancy.

14. Make length proportional to contribution.

15. Use a title that clearly expresses what the article is about and that also, if possible, captures attention.

16. Write an abstract that contains the information readers would want to know most.

17. Accept feedback non-defensively but critically.

18. A good literature review (whether as a general article or as part of an article) defines and clarifies a problem; summarizes previous research to inform readers of existing research; identifies relations, contradictions, gaps, and inconsistencies; and suggests next steps.

19. Good authors write with their readers in mind.

20. A good article has a take-home message.

21. Write for a class of journals.

22. Choose carefully the journal to which you submit your article.

23. Do not take reviews personally.

24. When you resubmit an article, be clear as to how you handled each of the points made in the reviews.

25. Relate what you are writing about to people's everyday experiences.

26. Use interesting rhetorical questions.

27. Say clearly why what you are studying should matter to your readers.

28. Review relevant literature in a way that relates it to the argument you want to make.

29. Use direct quotes only when necessary.

30. State your research question(s) clearly.

31. Treat differences of opinion with respect.

32. Keep in perspective the importance of your own work.

33. Be generous in your citations of others.

34. Be current in your citations of others.

35. Avoid secondary sources.

36. Actively solicit feedback.

37. Make sure your article includes a description of the main elements of your design.

38. Make clear why the design you chose is appropriate to the problem you have studied.

39. Make clear the strengths and limitations of your design.

40. Provide a top-down structure.

41. Let the story of your data rather than an arbitrary order based on statistical tests guide your explanation of the results.

42. Justify your choices of statistical tests.

43. Be thorough in your reporting of results without being overwhelming.

44. If you cleaned up your data, be clear as to how you did it.

45. Be sure your conclusions follow from your data.

46. The "Discussion" should make clear what you have contributed, how your study helped resolve the original problem, and what conclusions and theoretical implications can be drawn from your study.

47. The "Discussion" should be viewed as argumentation, not just as explanation

48. Decide what is worth emphasizing in your "Discussion" and what is not.

49. Use the "Discussion" to make clear the limitations of your work.

50. Never end an article with an expression like "Further research is needed."

**1. Ask yourself whether your ideas are interesting to you, and why they would be interesting to other people (Tesser, 2000).**
All of us read articles that leave us gasping for breath: How could anyone find the work interesting other than the author? You are more likely to avoid the embarrassment of proposing boring ideas if you ask yourself why others and not just you should be interested in the ideas you have to offer.

**2. Realize that new ideas are often difficult to get accepted (Sternberg, 2000; Tesser, 2000).**
The more your ideas depart from mainstream ways of thinking, the harder it probably will be to get your ideas accepted. Thus, the more the ideas depart from the mainstream, the more effort you have to devote in your article to convincing people that what you have to say is worth listening to.

**3. Write the article that emerges from your research rather than the article you planned to write (Bem, 2000).**

It is rare that the research you do leads you to the particular outcomes you expected. Write up the article that best takes into account what you found rather than the one that takes into account what you had hoped to find but never did.

**4. Explore the data to find out what they have to say and not just what you expected them to say (Bem, 2000; Grigorenko, 2000).**
Data often are perverse: They come out a way you did not expect or perhaps never even considered. You should analyze your data to find out what they really tell you rather than only analyzing them for what you thought they might tell you.

**5. A good article tells a story (Eisenberg, 2000; Salovey, 2000).**
You may view story writing as different from professional writing in psychology. In fact, in many ways they are the same. A good psychological article has a story to tell and develops that story from the beginning to the end, or at least the end as the author knows it.

**6. Write the story the data tell rather than the story of your discovery of the data's story (Bem, 2000).**
Readers do not want an autobiographical account of how you got to where you are. They just want to know where you are and why.

**7. Write at a level students will understand (Bem, 2000).**
Many writers grossly overestimate the background knowledge of their readers. Write an article that any bright introductory-psychology student could understand. Be accurate, clear, well organized, and direct. Write linearly. Stick to material that elaborates on your main story and avoid subplots. Avoid jargon where possible, but if you need it, be sure to define it.

**8. Make clear what is new in your article (Sternberg, 2000).**
It often is not clear what is new in an article. Make sure you state it directly rather than hoping readers will see it.

**9. Write with your reviewers in mind (Sternberg, 2000).**
Think of the people who are likely to review your article and the kinds of objections they are likely to raise. They represent many other readers who may see things differently from you and who need to be convinced of the validity of what you say.

**10. Write in the manner of an hourglass: Start broadly, become more specific, and then end broadly (Bem, 2000).**
Start your article dealing with the broad questions you will address. Then get specific in terms of what you did. Finally, you should discuss broadly the implications of your work.

**11. Make clear how your study tests your hypotheses (Kendall et al., 2000).**
Sometimes authors present a set of hypotheses and research, but it is not at all obvious how the research actually tests the hypotheses. Make clear how it does.

**12. Polish and proofread (Bem, 2000; Eisenberg, 2000; Sternberg, 2000).**
Do not expect referees or editors to do your rewriting for you or to tolerate loose, sloppy, or error-laden writing. Polishing and proof-reading are your responsibilities.

**13. Do not use synonyms, especially for technical terms, just to avoid redundancy (Bem, 2000).**
Readers may believe you are varying the words you use because you are referring to different concepts.

**14. Make length proportional to contribution (Kendall et al., 2000).**
Journals have limited space. Longer articles therefore consume valuable resources. Hence you need to be confident that the longer your article, the greater its contribution.

**15. Use a title that clearly expresses what the article is about and that also, if possible, captures attention (Sternberg, 2000).**
An irrelevant title tricks people into scanning (but rarely reading) something they do not want to read. A boring title may lead them to avoid reading the article altogether.

**16. Write an abstract that contains the information a reader would want to know most (Sternberg, 2000).**
Some people never will see anything more than the abstract. The better the abstract captures the key ideas and findings of your article, the better disseminated your work will be.

**17. Accept feedback non-defensively but critically (Wagner, 2000; Warren, 2000).**

Most of the comments you get from referees will help you produce a better article. Some will not. In revising an article, make the changes that will improve the article. Consider making the changes that, at least, will not hurt the article. But do not make the changes that will hurt it. In your letter to the editor, you can explain why you did not make certain changes. Editors, of course, are free to accept or not accept your explanation, as they wish.

**18. A good literature review (whether as a general article or as part of an article) defines and clarifies a problem; summarizes previous research to inform readers of existing research; identifies relations, contradictions, gaps, and inconsistencies; and suggests next steps (Eisenberg, 2000).**

The literature review thus informs readers of where things have been, where they are, and where they need to go.

**19. Good authors write with their readers in mind (Eisenberg, 2000; Reis, 2000).**

Write with your readers in mind. Ask yourself how well they will be able to understand what you write. For example, readers often become confused by pronouns without clear antecedents and imprecise language.

**20. A good article has a take-home message (Eisenberg, 2000).**

Often, readers finish an article without any clear idea of what the main point of the article was supposed to be. A good article has a clear take-home message so that readers briefly can summarize what the article was about.

**21. Write for a class of journals (Eisenberg, 2000).**

You should have a journal or class of journals in mind when you write an article. You can then target the article to the readership and requirements of that journal or class of journals.

**22. Choose carefully the journal to which you submit your article (Warren, 2000).**

You can save yourself a lot of time by choosing a journal that is appropriate in terms of what it publishes and that is likely to accept an article of the quality of yours.

**23. Do not take reviews personally (Warren, 2000).**

Reviews are of work, not of you. Some reviewers get personal. Ignore such remarks. Read the reviews in the spirit of using them to improve your article.

**24. When you resubmit an article, be clear as to how you handled each of the points made in the reviews.**

Reviewers and editors get annoyed when they are ignored. You should follow most of their suggestions and indicate how you did so in a resubmission letter. Those suggestions you cannot accept should be highlighted in the letter, and you should explain why you did not follow them.

**25. Relate what you are writing about to people's everyday experiences (Kendall et al., 2000).**

You capture people's attention and interest when you draw them in by relating what you are studying to experiences they have faced or expect to face in their lives.

**26. Use interesting rhetorical questions (Kendall et al., 2000).**

People often find themselves wanting to answer rhetorical questions, thus drawing themselves into the article they are reading.

**27. Say clearly why what you are studying should matter to your readers (Kendall et al., 2000).**

Do not expect readers to see on their own the importance of your work. Make clear why the work should matter to them.

**28. Review relevant literature in a way that relates it to the argument you want to make (Kendall et al., 2000).**

No one likes to read an unfocused, rambling literature review. Organize your literature review around the ideas that you wish to communicate in your article.

**29. Use direct quotes only when necessary (Kendall et al., 2000).**

Use direct quotes only if they are needed to convey the flavor or exact message of an original text. Otherwise, they just clutter up and often obscure your message.

**30. State your research question(s) clearly (Kendall et al., 2000; Sternberg, 2000).**

You need to be very clear just what questions will be addressed in your article. Often, you also need to make clear what questions readers may expect to be addressed that are not, in fact, addressed.

**31. Treat differences of opinion with respect (Kendall et al., 2000).**
Treat others the way you would want them to treat you – with respect – even if you disagree with what they say and are convinced that anyone in his or her right mind would see things as you do.

**32. Keep in perspective the importance of your own work (Kendall et al., 2000).**
Readers tend to be turned off by authors who glorify the importance of their own work beyond reasonable bounds or who fail to make clear the ways in which their own work builds on the work of others.

**33. Be generous in your citations of others (Smith, 2000; Sternberg, 2000; Tesser, 2000; Wagner, 2000).**
No one likes to be ignored, especially referees of articles. It therefore is important to cite relevant past work, especially if someone is likely to be a referee of your article. It further is important to cite work that is not consistent with your point of view in addition to the work that is consistent.

**34. Be current in your citations of others (Smith, 2000).**
No one likes to read an article whose author obviously stopped keeping up with the field a decade ago. Make sure your citations are current.

**35. Avoid secondary sources (Smith, 2000).**
Extensive use of secondary sources suggests laziness on the part of author. Cite primary sources. In this way, you not only show better scholarship skills but also greatly increase the likelihood that what you say people said will correspond to what they actually did say.

**36. Actively solicit feedback (Sternberg, 2000; Wagner, 2000; Warren, 2000).**
You can avoid a lot of headaches and heartaches if you anticipate the comments referees are likely to make before they get a chance to make them. Ask colleagues to read your work and comment on it before you submit the work to a journal.

**37. Make sure your article includes a description of the main elements of your design (Reis, 2000).**
The main elements of design are type of design, how participants were assigned to groups, independent variables, and dependent variables.

**38. Make clear why the design you chose is appropriate to the problem you have studied (Reis, 2000).**
Do not expect readers to figure out why you designed your study as you did.

**39. Make clear the strengths and limitations of your design (Grigorenko, 2000; Reis, 2000).**
Claim only what you can on the basis of the design you used, and show readers that you know what appropriate claims are.

**40. Provide top-down structure (Salovey, 2000).**
It often is difficult for readers to follow the line of argument in an article. By providing top-down structure and making transparent how you will organize, you facilitate your readers' understanding of what you have to say.

**41. Let the story of your data rather than an arbitrary order based on statistical tests guide your explanation of the results (Salovey, 2000).**
Do not write your "Results" section merely to conform to the order of output in a bundle of computer outputs. Write in the order that best conveys the message you wish to convey.

**42. Justify your choices of statistical tests (Grigorenko, 2000; Salovey, 2000).**
Do not assume that readers will know why you did the tests you did. Explain why you did them.

**43. Be thorough in your reporting of results without being overwhelming (Grigorenko, 2000; Salovey, 2000; Sternberg, 2000).**
Often, referees will ask for just those data analyses you chose to omit, so include the full set of data analyses you need to tell your story completely. But omit analyses that are irrelevant to the story you have to tell.

**44. If you cleaned up your data, be clear as to how you did it (Grigorenko, 2000).**
Say how you handled missing data, outliers, or any other peculiarities in the data, such as non-normality.

**45. Be sure your conclusions follow from your data (Grigorenko, 2000; Sternberg, 2000).**
It is often tempting for authors to go beyond the data in establishing conclusions, saying what they want to conclude rather than what the

data allow them to conclude. Draw only the proper conclusions, and properly label anything else as speculation.

## 46. The "Discussion" should make clear what you have contributed, how your study helped resolve the original problem, and what conclusions and theoretical implications can be drawn from your study (Calfee, 2000).

A good "Discussion" goes well beyond summarizing the results: It relates your results back to why you originally did the study and makes clear the meaning of what you found out.

## 47. The "Discussion" should be viewed as argumentation, not just as explanation (Calfee, 2000).

Good writing in articles is not merely expository, but also persuasive. You are trying to convince readers of the validity of your position and, often, of the lack of validity of alternative positions. However, be realistic in terms of what alternative positions you can rule out.

## 48. Decide what is worth emphasizing in your "Discussion" and what is not (Calfee, 2000).

Good writing is hierarchical: It clearly distinguishes between the important points and the supporting points.

## 49. Use the "Discussion" to make clear the limitations of your work (Sternberg, 2000).

Reviewers will notice them. You take some of the wind out of their sails when you anticipate what they are likely to say in objection to your work.

## 50. Never end an article with an expression like "Further research is needed" (Sternberg, 2000).

What a bore! Of course further research is needed.

You now are ready to write better articles. The tools are right in this book. You need only use them. Good luck in your endeavors!

# References

Alexander, J. E., & Tate, M. A. (1999). *Web wisdom: How to evaluate and create information quality on the web*. Mahwah, NJ: Erlbaum.

American Psychological Association (2009). *Publication manual of the American Psychological Association* (6th ed.). Washington, DC: American Psychological Association.

Aron, A., Aron, E. N., & Coups, E. (2007). *Statistics for the behavioral and social sciences*. Upper Saddle River, NJ: Prentice-Hall.

Beebe-Center, J. G., Rogers, M. S., & O'Connell, D. N. (1955). Transmission of information about sucrose and saline solutions through the sense of taste. *Journal of Psychology, 39*, 157–160.

Bem, D. J. (1967). Self-perception: An alternative interpretation of cognitive dissonance phenomena. *Psychological Review, 74*, 183–200.

Bem, D. J. (2000). Writing an empirical article. In R. J. Sternberg (Ed.), *Guide to publishing in psychology journals* (pp. 3–16). New York: Cambridge University Press.

Calfee, R. (2000). What does it all mean: The discussion. In R. J. Sternberg (Ed.), *Guide to publishing in psychology journals* (pp. 133–145). New York: Cambridge University Press.

Clark, H. H. (1969). Linguistic processes in deductive reasoning. *Psychological Review, 76*, 387–404.

Clark, H. H. (1974). Semantics and comprehension. In T. A. Sebeok (Ed.), *Current trends in linguistics: Vol. 12. Linguistics and adjacent arts and sciences* (pp. 1291–1428). The Hague: Mouton.

Clark, H. H., & Chase, W. (1972). On the process of comparing sentences against pictures. *Cognitive Psychology, 3*, 472–517.

Cleveland, W. S. (1994). *The elements of graphing data*. Summit, NJ: Hobart Press.

Dietz-Uhler, B. (2002). *The effectiveness of an exercise to critically examine information on the World Wide Web*. Unpublished manuscript, Miami University.

Dowling, D. (2008). *The wrong word dictionary*. Victoria, BC, Canada: Castle Books.

Dymond, R. (1949). A scale for the measurement of empathic ability. *Journal of Consulting Psychology, 13*, 127–133.

Dymond, R. (1950). Personality and empathy. *Journal of Consulting Psychology, 14*, 343–350.

Ehrenberg, A. S. C. (1978). *Data reduction: Analyzing and interpreting statistical data*. New York: Wiley.

Ehrenberg, A. S. C. (1982). *A primer in data reduction: An introductory statistics textbook*. New York: Wiley.

Eisenberg, N. (2000). Writing a literature review. In R. J. Sternberg (Ed.), *Guide to publishing psychology journals* (pp. 17–34). New York: Cambridge University Press.

Federal Bureau of Investigation (2005). Crime in the United States [Electronic Version] from http://www.fbi.gov/ucr/05cius/data/table_05.html.

Federal Bureau of Investigation (2006). Crime in the United States [Electronic Version] from http://www.fbi.gov/ucr/cius2006/data/table_05.html.

Federal Bureau of Investigation (2007). Crime in the United States [Electronic Version] from http://www.fbi.gov/ucr/cius2007/data/table_05.html.

Festinger, L. (1957). *A theory of cognitive dissonance*. Evanston, IL: Row, Peterson.

Festinger, L., & Carlsmith, J. M. (1959). Cognitive consequences of forced compliance. *Journal of Abnormal and Social Psychology, 58*, 203–211.

Garner, B. A. (2003). *Garner's modern American usage*. New York: Oxford University Press.

Garner, W. R. (1953). An informational analysis of absolute judgments of loudness. *Journal of Experimental Psychology, 46*, 373–380.

Gravetter, F. J., & Wallnau, L. B. (2008). *Statistics for the behavioral sciences*. Belmont, CA: Wadsworth.

Grigorenko, E. L. (2000). Doing data analyses and writing up their results: Selected tricks and artifices. In R. J. Sternberg (Ed.), *Guide to publishing in psychology journals* (pp. 98–120). New York: Cambridge University Press.

Hair, J. F., Black, W. C., Babin, B. J., & Anderson, R. E. (2009). *Multivariate data analysis*. Upper Saddle River, NJ: Prentice-Hall.

Hake, H. W., & Garner, W. R. (1951). The effect of presenting various numbers of discrete steps on scale reading accuracy. *Journal of Experimental Psychology, 42*, 358–366.

Harris, J. S., & Blake, R. H. (1976). *Technical writing for social scientists*. Chicago: Nelson-Hall.

Janis, I. L., & King, B. T. (1954). The influence of role-playing on opinion change. *Journal of Abnormal and Social Psychology, 49*, 211–218.

Kahneman, D., & Tversky, A. (1971). Subjective probability: A judgment of representativeness. *Cognitive Psychology*, *3*, 430–454.

Kahneman, D., & Tversky, A. (1979). Intuitive prediction: Biases and corrective procedures. *Management Science*, *12*, 313–327.

Kaufman, E. L., Lord, M. W., Reese, R. W., & Volkmann, J. (1949). The discrimination of visual number. *American Journal of Psychology*, *62*, 498–525.

Kendall, P. C., Silk, J. S., & Chu, B. C. (2000). Introducing your research report: Writing the introduction. In R. J. Sternberg (Ed.), *Guide to publishing in psychology journals* (pp. 41–57). New York: Cambridge University Press.

Krantz, J. H., & Dalal, R. (2000). Validity of Web-based psychological research. In M. H. Birnbaum (Ed.), *Psychological experiments on the Internet* (pp. 35 60). San Diego, CA: Academic Press.

Lubart, T. I., & Sternberg, R. J. (1995). An investment approach to creativity: Theory and data. In S. M. Smith, T. B. Ward, & R. A. Finke (Eds.), *The creative cognition approach* (pp. 269–302). Cambridge, MA: MIT Press.

McGuire, W. J. (1997). Creative hypothesis generating in psychology. *Annual Review of Psychology*, *48*, 1–30.

*Merriam-Webster's collegiate dictionary*. (2005). (11th ed.). Springfield, MA: Merriam-Webster.

Milgram, S. (1974). *Obedience to authority: An experimental view*. New York: Harper & Row.

Miller, G. A. (1956). The magical number seven, plus or minus two: Some limits on our capacity for processing information. *Psychological Review*, *63*, 81–97.

Piaget, J. (1952). *The origins of intelligence in children* (M. Cook, Trans.). New York: International Universities Press.

Pollack, I. (1952). The information of elementary auditory displays. *Journal of the Acoustical Society of America*, *24*, 745–749.

Poulton, E. C. (1985). Geometric illusions in reading graphs. *Perception and Psychophysics*, *37*, 543–548.

Reips, U.-D. (2000). The Web experiment method: Advantages, disadvantages, and solutions. In M. H. Birnbaum (Ed.), *Psychological experiments on the Internet* (pp. 89–120). San Diego, CA: Academic Press.

Reis, H. T. (2000). Writing effectively about design. In R. J. Sternberg (Ed.), *Guide to publishing in psychology journals* (pp. 81–97). New York: Cambridge University Press.

Salovey, P. (2000). Results that get results: Telling a good story. In R. J. Sternberg (Ed.), *Guide to publishing in psychology journals* (pp. 121–132). New York: Cambridge University Press.

Smith, R. A. (2000). Documenting your scholarship: Citations and references. In R. J. Sternberg (Ed.), *Guide to publishing in psychology journals* (pp. 146–160). New York: Cambridge University Press.

Sternberg, R. J. (1980). Representation and process in linear syllogistic reasoning. *Journal of Experimental Psychology: General, 109*, 119–159.

Sternberg, R. J. (1988a). Mental self-government: A theory of intellectual styles and their development. *Human Development, 31*(4), 197–224.

Sternberg, R. J. (1988b). *The psychologist's companion* (2nd ed.). New York: Cambridge University Press.

Sternberg, R. J. (1997a). *Successful intelligence*. New York: Plume.

Sternberg, R. J. (1997b). *Thinking styles*. New York: Cambridge University Press.

Sternberg, R. J. (1998a). A balance theory of wisdom. *Review of General Psychology, 2*, 347–365.

Sternberg, R. J. (1998b). *Love is a story*. New York: Oxford University Press.

Sternberg, R. J. (Ed.). (2000). *Guide to publishing in psychology journals*. New York: Cambridge University Press.

Sternberg, R. J. (2001). Why schools should teach for wisdom: The balance theory of wisdom in educational settings. *Educational Psychologist, 36*(4), 227–245.

Sternberg, R. J. (2002a). Smart people are not stupid, but they sure can be foolish: The imbalance theory of foolishness. In R. J. Sternberg (Ed.), *Why smart people can be so stupid* (pp. 232–242). New Haven, CT: Yale University Press.

Sternberg, R. J. (Ed.). (2002b). *The anatomy of impact*. Washington, DC: American Psychological Association.

Sternberg, R. J. (Ed.). (2002c). *Psychologists defying the crowd*. Washington, DC: American Psychological Association.

Sternberg, R. J. (2003). A duplex theory of hate: Development and application to terrorism, massacres, and genocide. *Review of General Psychology, 7*(3), 299–328.

Sternberg, R. J. (2004). Why smart people can be so foolish. *European Psychologist, 9(3)*, 145–150.

Sternberg, R. J. (2005a). Foolishness. In R. J. Sternberg & J. Jordan (Eds.), *Handbook of wisdom: Psychological perspectives* (pp. 331–352). New York: Cambridge University Press.

Sternberg, R. J. (2005b). The theory of successful intelligence. *Interamerican Journal of Psychology, 39*(2), 189–202.

Sternberg, R. J. (Ed.). (2006). *Reviewing scientific works in psychology*. Washington, DC: American Psychological Association.

Sternberg, R. J. (2007). A systems model of leadership: WICS. *American Psychologist, 62(1)*, 34–42.

Sternberg, R. J. (2008). The WICS approach to leadership: Stories of leadership and the structures and processes that support them. *Leadership Quarterly, 19*(3), 360–371.

Sternberg, R. J., & Bower, G. H. (1974). Transfer in part–whole and whole–part free recall: A comparative evaluation of theories. *Journal of Verbal Learning and Verbal Behavior, 13*, 1–26.

Sternberg, R. J., & Dobson, D. M. (1987). Resolving interpersonal conflicts: An analysis of stylistic consistency. *Journal of Personality and Social Psychology, 52*, 794–812.

Sternberg, R. J., Hojjat, M., & Barnes, M. L. (2001). Empirical aspects of a theory of love as a story. *European Journal of Personality, 15*(3), 199–218.

Sternberg, R. J., & Lubart, T. I. (1992). Buy low and sell high: An investment approach to creativity. *Current Directions in Psychological Science, 1*(1), 1–5.

Sternberg, R. J., & Lubart, T. I. (1995). *Defying the crowd: Cultivating creativity in a culture of conformity.* New York: Free Press.

Sternberg, R. J., & the Rainbow Project Collaborators. (2006). The Rainbow Project: Enhancing the SAT through assessments of analytical, practical and creative skills. *Intelligence, 34*(4), 321–350.

Sternberg, R. J., & Soriano, L. J. (1984). Styles of conflict resolution. *Journal of Personality and Social Psychology, 47*, 115–126.

Sternberg, R. J., & Sternberg, K. (2008). *The nature of hate.* New York: Cambridge University Press.

Sternberg, R. J., & Tulving, E. (1977). The measurement of subjective organization in free recall. *Psychological Bulletin, 84*, 538–556.

Sternberg, R. J., & Weil, E. M. (1980). An aptitude–strategy interaction in linear syllogistic reasoning. *Journal of Educational Psychology, 72*, 226–234.

Strunk, W., & White, E. B. (2008). *The elements of style–50th anniversary edition.* New York: Longman.

Tabachnik, G. B., & Fidell, L. S. (2006). *Using multivariate statistics.* Boston: Allyn & Bacon.

Tesser, A. (2000). Theories and hypotheses. In R. J. Sternberg (Ed.), *Guide to publishing in psychology journals* (pp. 58–80). New York: Cambridge University Press.

Tufte, E. R. (1983). *The visual display of quantitative information.* Cheshire, CT: Graphics Press.

Tufte, E. R. (2001). *The visual display of quantitative information.* Cheshire, CT: Graphics Press.

Tukey, J. W. (1977). *Exploratory data analysis.* Reading, MA: Addison-Wesley.

Tulving, E. (1966). Subjective organization and effects of repetition in multi-trial free-recall learning. *Journal of Verbal Learning and Verbal Behavior, 5*, 193–197.

Tulving, E., & Madigan, S. A. (1970). Memory and verbal learning. In P. H. Mussen & M. R. Rosenzweig (Eds.), *Annual review of psychology* (Vol. 21, pp. 437–484). Palo Alto, CA: Annual Reviews.

Wagner, R. K. (2000). Rewriting the psychology paper. In R. J. Sternberg (Ed.), *Guide to publishing in psychology journals* (pp. 187–198). New York: Cambridge University Press.

Wainer, H. (1984). How to display data badly. *American Statistician, 38,* 137–147.

Warren, M. G. (2000). Reading reviews, suffering rejection, and advocating for your paper. In R. J. Sternberg (Ed.), *Guide to publishing in psychology journals* (pp. 169–186). New York: Cambridge University Press.

*Webster's third new international dictionary, unabridged.* (2002). Springfield, MA: Merriam-Webster.

# Appendix: Sample Psychology Paper

This appendix contains a sample student psychology paper. The paper was written a number of years ago by an undergraduate majoring in psychology: the senior author. The data presented in the paper are real but previously unpublished. The paper is presented (with minor modifications to conform to the 2009 APA style) as it was actually typed, rather than as it would appear in a journal. The purpose of including the paper in this volume is to illustrate the proper format for a paper typed according to APA guidelines. Remember, though, that your paper should be double-spaced throughout, rather than single-spaced, as here.

The Effects of Time-Limit Cues upon Test Means, Variances, and
Reliabilities

Robert J. Sternberg
Yale University

Author Note

Robert J. Sternberg is now at the Office of the Provost and Senior Vice President, Oklahoma State University, Stillwater, OK.

An earlier version of this paper was submitted to Professor Leonard Doob in partial fulfillment of the 1969 requirements for Psychology 36a, Yale University. I am grateful to Dr. Doob for his comments on the paper. A version of this paper was presented at the 1972 annual meeting of the National Council on Measurement in Education, Chicago, Illinois.

If this paper appeared in a journal, correspondence would be sent to Robert J. Sternberg, office of the Provost and Senior Vice President, Oklahoma State University, Stillwater, OK 74078. Email: Robert.sternberg@okstate.edu

## Abstract

Two 3-min, 40-item multiple-choice synonyms tests were administered consecutively to 411 juniors in a suburban high school. Students were divided into three groups, labeled Groups 1, 2, and 3. Each group received successively more information about time limits. Directions for a given group were identical before each test. Under the naive condition (first test), the test mean and variance were significantly higher for Group 3 than for Group 1. Under the sophisticated condition (second test), no significant differences were observed. Alternate-form reliability was significantly higher for Group 3 than for either Group 1 or Group 2. The results are discussed in terms of psychometric properties of tests and fairness of test instructions to students.

*Keywords*: time-limit cues, test means, variance, reliabilities

### The Effects of Time-Limit Cues upon Test Means, Variances, and Reliabilities

Mental ability test directions have long followed a variety of procedures regarding time limits. Directions for some tests, such as those for the Ohio State University Psychological Test (Toops, 1941), impose no time limit at all. Most test directions, however, do impose a time limit.

Directions for tests that impose time limits differ in the amount of information they convey to subjects about time limits. Some sets of directions, such as those for Level 5 of the Lorge–Thorndike Intelligence Tests (Lorge & Thorndike, 1957) and for the Terman–McNemar Test of Mental Ability (Terman & McNemar, 1941), inform subjects that they will be timed, but do not specify to them just how much time they will have. Other sets of directions, such as those for grades 9–12 of the Henmon–Nelson Tests of Mental Ability (Lamke & Nelson, 1957) and for the Beta Test of the Otis Quick-Scoring Mental Ability Tests (Otis, 1954), inform subjects both of the existence of a time limit and of what the time limit is. The Otis directions further provide for subjects to be visually reminded of how much time they have left to work. Examiners are instructed to write on a blackboard the time that the test began, and they are urged to write below it the time that the test will end.

In all four of these speeded tests, subjects are informed that they will be timed. The amounts of information they are given about time limits differ, however. There seem to exist in these tests, and in others like them, two basic procedures and a variation in one of them regarding how much information subjects are given about time limits. For convenience, the two procedures and variation will be referred to as Procedures 1, 2, and 3, and subjects taking tests under these procedures will be referred to as subjects in Group 1, Group 2, and Group 3, respectively. Under Procedure 1, subjects are not told how much time they will have to work and are also reminded during the test of how much time they have left to work.

This experiment was designed to investigate the effects of subjects' differential exposure to time-limit cues upon means, variances, and reliabilities of tests administered under two conditions. The first (naive) condition was the administration of a first test under a particular procedure. The second (sophisticated) condition was the administration of a second form of that test under the same procedure immediately following the administration of the first test.

The motivation underlying this experiment is that supplying subjects with more information about time limits results in a test that is both fairer to subjects and psychometrically more sound. Subjects not given full information about time limits will not know how quickly they are expected to work, and hence will not be able to pace themselves to finish as many test items as they can. Subjects who might do quite well if they knew how much time they had may do quite poorly simply because they do not realize how quickly they need to work. These considerations led to five hypotheses regarding experimental outcomes:

1. The mean of a first test administered under Procedure 1 will be lower than that of the test administered under Procedure 2, and

this mean in turn will be lower than that of the test administered under Procedure 3.

Subjects taking a first test under each of the successive procedures should be increasingly better able to employ what Millman, Bishop, and Ebel (1965) call time-using strategies. Such strategies are employed by test-wise examinees in order to obtain high scores. Millman et al. (1965) note that a "rule of thumb is to determine how far one should be when a specific proportion of the testing period has elapsed" (p. 714). Periodic checks on rate of progress facilitate the maintenance of proper speed (Cook, 1957; Millman et al., 1965).

2. The means of an alternate form of the first test, when the alternate form is administered to each group immediately after and under the same procedure as the first test, will not differ significantly from each other.

The signal to stop work on the first form of the test can itself serve as a time-limit cue. The less information subjects have when they take the first test, the more information this implicit cue can be expected to impart. Thus, subjects in each successive group will profit increasingly less from the cue, and test means will tend to converge.

3. The variance of a first test administered under Procedure 1 will be lower than that of the test administered under Procedure 2, and this variance in turn will be lower than that of the test administered under Procedure 3.

Subjects may differ greatly in the speeds at which they can solve test items, but the extent of the difference will be masked if subjects work at their typical rates rather than their maximum rates. Greater amounts of time-limit information enable potentially rapid test takers to show how rapidly they can work.

4. The variances of an alternate form of the first test, when the alternate form is administered to each group immediately after and under the same procedure as the first test, will not differ significantly from each other.

Because the signal to stop work on the first form of the test serves as a time limit cue telling subjects the tests are strictly timed, subjects in each group realize they must work at their maximum rate on the second test. Hence, the variances in the different groups should tend to converge.

5. If two alternate forms of a test are administered under the same procedure, one immediately following the other, the alternate form reliability of the test will be lower under Procedure 1 than under Procedure 2, and lower under Procedure 2 than under Procedure 3.

As an implicit time-limit cue, the signal to stop work on the first test imparts new time limit information to subjects. The greater the amount of new information transmitted, the greater will be the potential for new variance to enter into scores on the second test. The greater the amount of new variance that enters into scores on the second test, the lower will be the correlation (alternate form reliability) between forms of the test. In other words, increasing the amount of time-limit information explicitly given to subjects increases the extent to which two successive forms of the test measure the same thing.

# Method

## Subjects

Subjects were 411 juniors in a suburban New Jersey public high school. There were 140 students in Group 1, 148 students in Group 2, and 123 students in Group 3.

## Materials

The stimulus materials were alternate forms of a 40-item multiple-choice synonyms test. Test items were ordered and forms equated according to the frequency of occurrence of the test words in the English language as reported by Thorndike and Lorge (1944).

## Design

Dependent variables were the number of items correctly answered on each form of the synonyms test minus one-fourth the number of items incorrectly answered. Omissions were not counted as incorrect. Independent variables were time-limit instructional procedure (1, 2, or 3) and test form (1 and 2). Each subject was assigned to only one instructional procedure, but all subjects received both test forms under that procedure. Homerooms (where testing took place) were randomly assigned to groups. In the high school, students are assigned to homerooms at random.

## Procedure

Students were tested by their homeroom teachers preceding their daily classes. The students were given no advance notice of the tests. Instructions for each of the three groups were identical except for time-limit and group-coding information. Students were instructed to answer as many items as they could, but to guess on items only if they had some idea of what the correct answer was, because a percentage of the number of wrong (but not omitted) answers would be subtracted from the number of correct answers.

Students in Group 1 were told that they would be timed, but they were not told how much time they would have. Students in Group 2 were told before the beginning of each of the two tests that they would have 3 min in which to work on the particular test. Students in Group 3 were also given this information, and were further informed that they would be told when they had 2 min, 1 min, and 30 s left to work.

After the initial instructions were completed, students in all groups received Form 1 of the synonyms test. After the test, the instructions were repeated, and then students received Form 2 of the synonyms test. Following administration of Form 2, the homeroom teacher collected the test booklets, ending the experimental session.

## Results

Test means, variances, and alternate form reliabilities are presented in Table 1.

### Test 1 Means

The first hypothesis was partially confirmed by the results. The three group means for the first test fell into the rank order predicted, although only the difference between the first and third means was significant, $t(261) = 1.85, p < .05$.

### Test 2 Means

The Test 2 means were consistent with the second hypothesis. None of the means differed significantly from each other.

### Test 1 Variances

The experimental data provided a partial confirmation of the third hypothesis. Test 1 variances fell into the rank order predicted, although again, only the difference between the Group 1 and Group 3 variances was significant, $F(122,139) = 1.67, p < .01$.

### Test 2 Variances

The Test 2 variances were consistent with the fourth hypothesis. None of the variances differed significantly from each other.

### Alternate-form Reliabilities

The rank order of the alternate-form reliabilities was that predicted by the fifth hypothesis. The difference between Groups 1 and 3 was significant, $z = 3.40, p < .01$, as was the difference between Groups 2 and 3, $z = 2.47, p < .01$.

## Discussion

The data presented above suggest that authors of mental ability tests may have been too cavalier in determining how much time-limit information should be imparted to examinees. Reduced time-limit information has been shown in this experiment to result in lower test means and variances for an initial test, and to result in lower alternate form reliability. This last finding is of particular importance, because it suggests that withholding time-limit information from subjects may result in a psychometrically poorer test. Telling subjects the time limit of a test and reminding them during testing of how much time is left is fairer to the subjects, because it enables them to budget their time, and fairer to the tester, because it gives a better, more consistent view of each subject's maximal performance. Given the choice, subjects opt for the additional information.[1]

It would be worthwhile to determine whether differences in test means, variances, and reliabilities hold up across different types of test content, and to determine whether differences extend to other test statistics, particularly predictive validity. An experiment investigating the generalizability of these findings is presently being prepared (Sternberg, 1971). If the findings are generalizable, then test authors should provide an explicit rationale for the type of time-limit instructions they select.

## References

Cook, D. L. (1957). A comparison of reading comprehension scores obtained before and after a time announcement. *Journal of Educational Psychology*, 48, 440–446.

Lamke, T. M., & Nelson, M. J. (1957). *The Henmon–Nelson Tests of Mental Ability, Grades 9–12*. Boston: Houghton Miffiin.

Lorge, I., & Thorndike, R. L. (1957). *The Lorge–Thorndike Intelligence Tests, Level 5*. Boston: Houghton Miffiin.

Millman, J., Bishop, H., & Ebel, R. (1965). An analysis of test-wiseness. *Educational and Psychological Measurement*, 25, 707–726.

Otis, A. S. (1954). *Otis Quick-Scoring Mental Ability Tests, Beta Test*. New York: Harcourt, Brace, & World.

Sternberg, R. J. (1971). *Effects of time-limit cues upon validity of verbal and mathematical ability test scores*. Manuscript in preparation.

Terman, L. M., & McNemar, Q. (1941). *Terman–McNemar Test of Mental Ability*. Yonkers, NY: World Book Company.

Thorndike, E. L., & Lorge, I. (1944). *The teacher's word book of 30,000 words*. New York: Teachers College, Columbia University.

Toops, H. A. (1941). *The Ohio State University Psychological Test*. Chicago: Science Research Associates.

## Footnote

[1] An informal poll of 15 students who had participated in the experiment revealed unanimous agreement that providing greater amounts of time-limit information is better for students because it enables them to budget their time more efficiently.

Table 1

*Means, Variances, and Alternate-Form Reliabilities*

| | Means | | Variances | | Reliabilities[a] |
|---|---|---|---|---|---|
| Group | Test 1 | Test 2 | Test 1 | Test 2 | |
| 1 | 7.43 | 12.35 | 32.49 | 43.82 | .74 |
| 2 | 8.10 | 11.64 | 41.47 | 59.75 | .79 |
| 3 | 8.95 | 12.89 | 54.17 | 56.25 | .88 |

[a] Reliabilities are of the alternate-form type.

# Index